# The Winemaker's Hand

ARTS AND TRADITIONS OF THE TABLE: PERSPECTIVES ON CULINARY HISTORY

ARTS AND TRADITIONS OF THE TABLE: PERSPECTIVES ON CULINARY HISTORY
*Albert Sonnenfeld, Series Editor*

*Salt: Grain of Life*, Pierre Laszlo, translated by Mary Beth Mader

*Culture of the Fork*, Giovanni Rebora, translated by Albert Sonnenfeld

*French Gastronomy: The History and Geography of a Passion*, Jean-Robert Pitte, translated by Jody Gladding

*Pasta: The Story of a Universal Food*, Silvano Serventi and Françoise Sabban, translated by Antony Shugar

*Slow Food: The Case for Taste*, Carlo Petrini, translated by William McCuaig

*Italian Cuisine: A Cultural History*, Alberto Capatti and Massimo Montanari, translated by Áine O'Healy

*British Food: An Extraordinary Thousand Years of History*, Colin Spencer

*A Revolution in Eating: How the Quest for Food Shaped America*, James E. McWilliams

*Sacred Cow, Mad Cow: A History of Food Fears*, Madeleine Ferrières, translated by Jody Gladding

*Molecular Gastronomy: Exploring the Science of Flavor*, Hervé This, translated by M. B. DeBevoise

*Food Is Culture*, Massimo Montanari, translated by Albert Sonnenfeld

*Kitchen Mysteries: Revealing the Science of Cooking*, Hervé This, translated by Jody Gladding

*Hog and Hominy: Soul Food from Africa to America*, Frederick Douglass Opie

*Gastropolis: Food and New York City*, edited by Annie Hauck-Lawson and Jonathan Deutsch

*Building a Meal: From Molecular Gastronomy to Culinary Constructivism*, Hervé This, translated by M. B. DeBevoise

*Eating History: Thirty Turning Points in the Making of American Cuisine*, Andrew F. Smith

*The Science of the Oven*, Hervé This, translated by Jody Gladding

*Pomodoro! A History of the Tomato in Italy*, David Gentilcore

*Cheese, Pears, and History in a Proverb*, Massimo Montanari, translated by Beth Archer Brombert

*Food and Faith in Christian Culture*, edited by Ken Albala and Trudy Eden

*The Kitchen as Laboratory: Reflections on the Science of Food and Cooking*, edited by César Vega, Job Ubbink, and Erik van der Linden

*Creamy and Crunchy: An Informal History of Peanut Butter, the All-American Food*, Jon Krampner

*Let the Meatballs Rest: And Other Stories About Food and Culture*, Massimo Montanari, translated by Beth Archer Brombert

*The Secret Financial Life of Food: From Commodities Markets to Supermarkets*, Kara Newman

*Drinking History: Fifteen Turning Points in the Making of American Beverages*, Andrew Smith

*Italian Identity in the Kitchen, or Food and the Nation*, Massimo Montanari, translated by Beth Archer Brombert

*Fashioning Appetite: Restaurants and the Making of Modern Identity*, Joanne Finkelstein

*The Land of the Five Flavors: A Cultural History of Chinese Cuisine*, Thomas O. Höllmann, translated by Karen Margolis

*The Insect Cookbook*, Arnold van Huis, Henk van Gurp, and Marcel Dicke, translated by Françoise Takken-Kaminker and Diane Blumenfeld-Schaap

*Religion, Food, and Eating in North America*, edited by Benjamin E. Zeller, Marie W. Dallam, Reid L. Neilson, and Nora L. Rubel

# The Winemaker's Hand

*Conversations on Talent, Technique, and Terroir*

## NATALIE BERKOWITZ

COLUMBIA UNIVERSITY PRESS    NEW YORK

Columbia University Press
*Publishers Since 1893*
New York   Chichester, West Sussex
cup.columbia.edu

Library of Congress Cataloging-in-Publication Data

Berkowitz, Natalie.
The winemaker's hand: conversations on talent, technique, and terroir / Natalie Berkowitz.
pages cm.—(Arts and traditions of the table)
Includes bibliographical references.
ISBN 978-0-231-16756-7 (cloth : alk. paper) — ISBN 978-0-231-53737-7 (ebook)
1. Vintners—Interviews.   2. Vintners—Bibliography.   3. Wine and wine making.
I. Title.   II. Series: Arts and traditions of the table.
TP547.A1B47 2014.
663'.2—dc23

2013039524

Columbia University Press books are printed on permanent and durable acid-free paper.
This book is printed on paper with recycled content.
Printed in the United States of America

c 10 9 8 7 6 5 4 3 2 1

COVER IMAGE: © FOTOLIA
COVER DESIGN: CATHERINE CASALINO

References to Web sites (URLs) were accurate at the time of writing. Neither the
author nor Columbia University Press is responsible for URLs that may have
expired or changed since the manuscript was prepared.

The wine urges me on, the bewitching wine,

which sets even a wise man to singing and laughing gently. . . .

HOMER

# CONTENTS

CONTENTS

CONTENTS

xi

# PREFACE

Remembering a first wine experience is as potent as the memory of a first kiss. I had my first experience with wine on a student trip to Europe. My companions charged me with the responsibility of ordering wine in a café under the shadows of the cathedral in Cologne, Germany. How could I, at twenty and an American without a wine heritage, whose experience with wine was limited to holidays when thick, sugary reds accompanied dinners, be brave enough to order from an undecipherable German wine list? I might as well have thrown a dart at the carte des vins. The affordable, poetically titled bottle of Lacrima Christi, or Tears of Christ, seemed an attractive choice. I was clueless as to the wine's color, or if it was sweet or dry. I half-expected it to have a touch of real tears.

From that romantic moment I was hooked on the idea that a glass of wine, even ordinary plonk, was coupled with sophistication. I subsequently realized wine is more varied, more seductive, more entertaining, whether it stands alone as an aperitif or as food's enticing partner. Sharing Two Buck Chuck or a stratospherically priced Bordeaux adds conviviality to social occasions.

A visit to a potato chip factory when I was a teenager provoked an early interest in deciphering the mystery of how raw materials convert into consumable products. Seeing a large bin of potatoes washed, peeled, sliced, fried, salted, and bagged in the blink of an eye was a Wow! experience. Today most Americans are far removed from understanding how the basic components of food and beverages arrive on store shelves and onto their tables. In a roundabout way, the potato chip experience led to questions that ultimately helped unravel the complexities of wine.

I am by nature a sharer of information. It is addicting to see someone's eyes light up when they comprehend new information. After my career as a high school history and art teacher, I wrote a wide variety of lifestyle articles that began to center primarily on wine and wine travel for major newspapers and magazines, including *The Wine Enthusiast, The Wine Spectator, The New York Times, Vogue, Harper's Bazaar,* and *Town & Country.* My husband Phil and I became partners in *The International Wine Review* and my articles focused on wine. Around the same time, I served as a director of the International Wine and Food Society. I organized fund-raising wine dinners in the United States and Europe. Yet my most pleasurable and important mission was to introduce seniors at Barnard College (my alma mater) and Columbia University, where I was awarded a master's degree, to the joys and intricacies of wine. The course's quick acceptance reflected the exponential growth of wine's popularity among young students.

At each session, students compared a single varietal, took notes, and referred to the Aroma Wheel. My goal was to get each student to understand the importance of personal judgment. The students' confidence in their own perceptions grew, especially after each in the class sensed an array of aroma and taste profiles in the wines. I hope that the young men and women developed a personal approach to a lifestyle that went beyond wine. It is a better idea than reliance on a critic's judgments and numerical ratings in magazines.

Phil and I traveled to every continent where grapes grow and wineries proliferate. We tramped through many vineyards and sampled a small portion of the world's immense diversity of wines in wineries. We absorbed each winemaker's commitment to take the best of nature's bounty and limitations to make wine.

# INTRODUCTION

Over years of teaching wine courses to wine virgins and wine veterans, I discovered each wine has its own voice, as does every winemaker. Wines speak if you listen closely, but vintners rarely have a platform to give voice to their visions. *The Winemaker's Hand* is an opportunity for a few articulate vintners to open a window into the intricacies of their work.

André Tchelistcheff, the visionary winemaker who touched the lives of many fellow vintners, said in 1985 that the first prerequisite of a good winemaker is practical and theoretical knowledge. "Outside of that . . . the winemaker . . . must understand the wine, to really know how to listen. I believe every wine has its own voice." Like an artist working with a canvas and paints, or a conductor working with a score and an orchestra, winemakers work with a palette of grapes, arranging hundreds of discreet choices as they seek to achieve their own personal visions. The skilled touch of the winemaker's hand is the illusive X factor that makes a good wine great.

The vintners speak in many voices to personalize the process and bring their struggles, zeal, and goals into sharp focus. They acknowledge hazards of the farming life, the financial costs, and the strains of marketing. For many their words flowed as easily as wine from an uncorked bottle. For others it took some coaxing. Like their wines, vintners are complicated. The way they express their vision for their wines goes beyond their words into their bottles.

They go by many names: winemakers, vintners, or enologists. In France they are called *vignerons*. Some are newcomers who leap into an untried venture, enchanted by the cachet of a difficult business that encompasses both art and craft. Winemakers are bold modern-day Magellans in search of new advances and technologies to transmogrify grapes into wine. They take pleasure in a job with few dull moments. They look forward to every new season and relish a year-round commitment to overcome nature's vagaries. Each vintner competes for a share of the market, but all are bound together by an obsession to transform grape juice into wine.

Inside every winemaker beats the heart of a farmer who struggles to bring a crop to harvest and to complete the winemaking cycle. Most farmers sell their crops at the end of the season, but vintners begin long weeks of intense work after harvest. A winemaker's happiness begins with a great crop of well-behaved grapes that maintain their potential from vine to bottle. "Beach chair" vintages occur when all the positive elements combine to produce sugars, acids, and tannins in the right proportions and quantities in grapes. A perfect combination of events is a rare event, something devoutly to be wished for. Too often, challenges of wayward vines and negative aspects of terroir disrupt their best plans.

*Terroir* is a catch-all term for the special characteristics of geography, geology, and microclimate that create distinctions between vineyard sites or regions. Terroir comprises variables of climate, rainfall, hours of sunshine, frosts, wind, temperature, and maritime influences. It includes stable characteristics of soils such as clay, loam, gravel, sand, or shale. Each terroir brings to bear special challenges as a vintner's loyal or capricious friend. There are those who argue terroir is the single absolute factor in wine, but a winemaker's skill controls nature in pursuit of an elusive task. It is the author's contention that a winemaker's personal perspective and skills are the most powerful forces to harness nature's unpredictable behavior and to manage all other factors of terroir that influence each season's crop. A symbiotic relationship exists among vines, grapes, nature, and winemakers, but the human hand takes ultimate control with step-by-step negotiations with hundreds of careful decisions to metamorphose grapes into wine. After all, grapes don't jump into a bottle by themselves.

Wines run the gamut from insipid plonk to sublime offerings. Conversations with vintners in *The Winemaker's Hand* explain why wines present complex variations, flavors, and aromas, even from the same varietal. The discussions offer insights into the commonalities and differences between vintners and how these individual characteristics affect their wines. One winemaker in the book says that even though it doesn't take rocket science to make good wine, an untalented vintner can wreck a harvest of good grapes, and even the most skilled winemaker can't convert a bad harvest into fine wine. The best of all possible worlds happens when nature and talent align to produce a great harvest of grapes and a vintner who can caress, massage, and convert those grapes into a fine wine.

Each vintage in all terroirs challenges winemakers, who are part farmer, part artisan. They are always committed to producing what they hope will be the best wine wrested from a vineyard. Some winemakers are traditionalists committed to age-old techniques, whereas others incorporate new methods. Most mix the two. Read their stories and gain a new perspective about why wines differ from year to year, sometimes dramatically, often subtly, even when made from the same grape from the same vineyard. Understand how two vintners working in the same vineyard with the same grape varietal produce different wines. Learn how an individual's personality, passion, and skill impact on every vintage. As distinct as their voices are, they all share a passion to produce the best wines their vines, terroir, and nature afford them.

Thousands of winemakers around the world have stories to tell about their connection to the vine, grape, and wine. Most wine lovers rarely have an opportunity to meet them and hear their personal challenges to convert grapes into wine. *The Winemaker's Hand* offers wine novices and enophiles an opportunity to look inside the winemaking world as vintners explain their pivotal roles in the creation of a complex alcoholic beverage made from simple grape juice. The firsthand accounts give voice to the difficulties of how and why each vintage is unique.

I like to think that wine is the voice of its maker and that, in the end, a duet between winemaker and nature makes the wine sing.

# The Winemaker's Hand

# TRACING THE HISTORIC WINE TRAIL

T HE RICH HISTORY of viticulture and vinification parallels the journey of prehistoric man to the ancient world to the twenty-first century. No one knows who was the first brave soul to taste fermented grapes, but the historical, undocumented moment probably occurred wherever wild grapes grew. Our curious, very observant ancestors who counted the stars and traveled to new habitats were obsessive observers of the natural world. Visualize early man picking a strange fruit from a vine and popping a grape tentatively into his mouth. Picture him relishing its fruity flavor. Then imagine how the pleasure doubled after he tasted a grape that ripened and fermented naturally, adding a frisson of alcoholic pleasure to his experience. A sip of an alcoholic libation must have been considered a gift from the gods, something to share quickly with others. Titillated by the new experience, it became a challenge to reproduce the intoxicating sensation of fermented juice.

Evidence supports the early connection between man and wine. Archeologists prove beverages fermented from grapes, rice, and figs were a regular feature in the life of Neolithic man. For centuries, stomping was probably the most efficient way to release juice from grapes. A place to store the fermented juice came next. Innovations in pottery containers used to store food and liquids went hand in hand with developments in bread, wine, and beer. The discovery of an Iranian drinking cup with traces of wine residue revised earlier estimates of the original date of 5000 B.C. as an early date of wine consumption.

Stories and myths confirm the importance of wine in early civilizations. The Sumerian Epic of Gilgamesh and Egyptian hieroglyphics depict winemaking and drinking. Greek frescoes and pottery decorations depict grape harvests and the role wine played in celebrations. Greek and Roman writers, including Homer and Virgil, described the pleasures of the vine and winemaking techniques. The pursuit of fermented grape juice continued, with each generation building on the experience of the past. Winemakers slowly developed skills over millennia that allowed them to gain control over the magical process of making wine. More time elapsed before wine production became an industry and moved out from its beginnings in ancient Egypt and the Shiraz region to Mesopotamia to slowly move west into across the European continent. One hundred and forty references to wine are found in the Old Testament and the Talmud. The book of Deuteronomy describes the arrival of Moses in the land of Canaan and how he sent twelve scouts representing the twelve tribes of Israel in every direction to explore the fertility of the region. All came back with discouraging reports except for Caleb and Joshua, who returned bearing a staff laden with grapes, figs, and pomegranates that proved the land's fertility. The New Testament often mentions the functions of wine used for religious practices and pleasure. Writers and philosophers throughout time have lauded its healing powers.

But it was the Romans who exerted the biggest influence on viticulture as they expanded their empire. They planted grapes to satisfy the thirst of their legions. Perhaps wine was safer and more enjoyable to drink than local water. Wine was so revered by the Romans that it had its own god—Bacchus. The actual taste of Roman wine will forever remain a mystery, but it may have been sweet and thick, reportedly diluted with water and flavored with lemon peels, fermented fish oil, or pepper. Roman conquerors accepted wine as payment for tribute and taxes, and their love affair with it ensured the development of grape production and winemaking across the empire.

Alcoholic beverages were prohibited when Islam rose to power in Europe and the Middle East. Viticulture declined, except where Moslems permitted Christians to make wine for religious purposes. As Christianity spread across Europe in the Dark and Middle Ages, monks at powerful Benedictine and Cistercian monasteries pushed the boundaries of viticulture to Northern Europe's cooler regions.

Explorers had a hand in the spread of winemaking. Norsemen sailing west from Greenland in the eleventh century may have been the first to discover wild vines in Greenland and North America. During the Age of Exploration at the end of the fifteenth century, the crews on ships like the *Nina,* the *Pinta,* and the *Santa Maria* included a cooper who made barrels to hold provisions for the voyage. Water became undrinkable on long voyages, so barrels filled with wine or rum slaked a sailor's thirst, a custom that continued well into the nineteenth century. Gold and the Fountain of Youth eluded avaricious explorers sailing along the eastern coast of North America, but a wealth of wild grapes was a serendipitous find. European settlers migrated across the United States with their rootstocks and winemaking skills, creating new varietals by crossing their European Vinifera Vines with native grapes.

Viticulture moved with immigration to new lands. The last century saw consumers making a gradual shift from European wines to those produced in North and South America and South Africa. Competition provoked countries with long traditions of winemaking to develop new markets and state-of-the-art techniques. Vintners from the Old and New World wine regions continue to perfect their mastery over nature and to elevate winemaking by combining science, art, and a labor of love.

Nations with a limited heritage in viticulture, like India and China, are racing to be contenders in the wine market. Marco Polo took note of wine production in Cathay during his historical journey, so it's not a surprise to find the Chinese—with their long tradition of turning rice, fruit, and grapes into wine—aggressively engaged in wine production. By 1892, European grape varieties were introduced into China and a Western-style winery was built. A French friar in 1910 converted a church graveyard near Beijing into a wine cave and hired a French enologist to produce both red and white wines. In recent years, joint-venture partnerships with foreign winemakers are helping the Chinese adopt Western viticultural and winemaking techniques.

Entrepreneurial farmers with small plots of land around the Great Wall and elsewhere in the country are experimenting with a host of imported grape varietals to see which are best suited for China's immense range of terroirs. The wine trail continues to trace its way around the world.

# CONVERSATIONS
# WITH THE WINEMAKERS

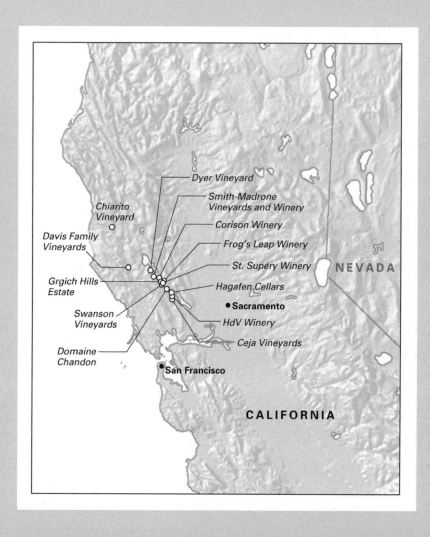

Dyer Vineyard

Smith-Madrone
Vineyards and Winery

Chiarito
Vineyard

Corison Winery

Davis Family
Vineyards

Frog's Leap Winery

St. Supéry Winery

Grgich Hills
Estate

Hagafen Cellars

Swanson
Vineyards

●Sacramento

HdV Winery

Domaine
Chandon

Ceja Vineyards

●San Francisco

NEVADA

CALIFORNIA

# THE UNITED STATES

## California

AFTER THE AGE OF EXPLORATION in the fifteenth century, the Spanish claimed mammoth acreage along the Pacific Coast. In 1769, Franciscan missionaries, led by Father Juniper Serra, built missions with the ultimate goal of converting Native Americans to Christianity, and planted grapes for sacramental wine. Jump past California's statehood, the Gold Rush, and the huge population expansion to the state that began in the late nineteenth century. An emerging wine industry took hold in northern California's Sonoma and Napa counties. Disaster struck the nascent industry when a phylloxera epidemic destroyed many vineyards and many wineries. Undiscouraged, Californian winemakers took control with grafted American rootstock resistant to the disease. It was a fortuitous opportunity to expand plantings of new grape varieties. Prohibition caused vineyards to be uprooted. Wineries closed, although some persisted, producing table grapes, grape juice, and sacramental wine. It took until the 1960's for the Californian wine industry to recover from this setback. A wave of enterprising young winemakers ushered in new winemaking technologies with an emphasis on quality. By the mid-twentieth century, California's wine lagged behind those of the prestigious European countries, particularly France and other well-regarded winemaking countries. America became a contender on the international stage when California winemakers took the French to the mat in both red and white wine categories at the 1976 Judgment of Paris wine competition.

The quick growth of America's wine production led to the establishment of the American Viticultural Area (AVA). The Bureau of Alcohol, Tobacco, and Firearms is responsible for designating AVA's. The system identifies compatible terroirs, soils, and other descriptive information that creates distinct wine regions. Large AVA's like Napa are often subdivided into smaller districts. Labeling regulations require 85 percent of grapes to come from the specific AVA. The number of appellations continues to emerge in wine-growing regions in the United States and across the world. The designations represent a boon and a source of confusion for wine buyers.

It's often said that if California were a separate country, it would be the world's fourth-largest wine producer. Four hundred thousand acres of vines benefit from its celebrated sunshine, microclimates, and terroirs of mountains and valleys. California winemakers lead the way in experimentation with growing and blending different varietals to create distinctive wine styles. Primary grape varieties are Cabernet Sauvignon, Chardonnay, Merlot, Pinot noir, Sauvignon blanc, Syrah, and Zinfandel. Some are bottled as single varietals and others are blended with compatible partners in tune with winemakers' aspirations. Boutique wineries compete with giant corporations with big advertising budgets and recognizable labels.

## Napa Valley

Napa Valley is renowned for producing some of the world's finest wines in highly diverse soils and terroirs. Almost four and a half million people visit Napa Valley each year, coming for its scenic beauty and lifestyle. They are drawn to the wineries situated on the valley floor and on two mountain ranges. Many consumers think of Napa Valley as one entity, but it is a region, county, city, and AVA. As a winemaking region, Napa Valley as a whole has sixteen AVA's, with more clamoring to be recognized for their individual characteristics. Every winemaker declares its appellation a star, producing superior wines that represent a sense of place, a community of spirit, and a common terroir. Winemakers praise their particular microclimates and soils for excellent wines. Some of California's most prized vineyards are found in Napa's AVA's.

# JOEL BURT
## DOMAINE CHANDON

Chandon is hailed for its notable sparkling wines based on the classic combination of Chardonnay, Pinot noir, and Pinot Meunier. It seemed sensible to think about bottling the grapes as still wines as well as sparkling. The facility embarked on a still wine program under the leadership of Joel Burt, assistant winemaker for still wines since 2009. The winery's 900-acre Carneros property grows dedicated blocks of Burgundian clones. "I'm married to the three varietals that are the historic backbone of Champagne and sparkling wine. My still wines come from the same estate fruit as our sparkling wines. Cabernet Sauvignon requires one mindset, whereas the two Pinots and Chardonnay require infinite patience."

Burt understands that his process for still wines is quite different from that of sparkling wine.

*I work with a viticulturist to get the fruit I want. Factors like the number of shoots, irrigation, and stress on the vines are decisions that affect the amount and consistent quality of fruit. The vines are exposed to a lot of sunshine to achieve thick skins and higher tannins than more delicate sparkling wine needs. For still wine we start in the vineyard, looking for low yields of small berry clusters that grow from one or two shoots per vine. Carneros soil is heavy clay with small amounts of topsoil pockmarked with golf-ball- and softball-sized stones above hardpan that limit the vines' vigor. Morning fogs roll in until the sun appears from ten until two in the afternoon. Then the winds come in and shut down the vines. Daily ripening time that is limited to four to six hours each day challenges Pinot noir from consistent ripening. Canopies are trained to produce color and tannins. It's* a long season that keeps acid in the fruit and develops thicker skins, generous tannins, and more flavors, in contrast to grapes for sparkling wine that require bigger berries and less juice-to-skin ratio. It's crucial to pick at the right time, considering acid to fruit ripeness. Sometimes the acids are so high they need to be brought down, but there is a risk of over-ripeness. We pick some blocks from single vineyards early and others later to hedge our bets.

Wines made in big tanks are innocuous. The best Pinot noir is made in small fermentation lots so we have homogeneous lots to blend. Small batches of Pinot noir, Chardonnay, and Pinot Meunier give me complexity, richness, and fruity flavors. Pinot Meunier is a grape that adds a little spiciness and a bit of tannin to the wine. Our Carneros Chardonnay has characteristics similar to those of Burgundian white wine, since Burgundy is where my soul lies.

We handpick at night. The fruit is picked at 40°F, so when it hits the tank it's ready for a pretty cool fermentation. In 2012, Chandon introduced an optical sorting machine that takes high-speed photos to scan individual berries. It's the same machine Tom Tiburzi uses. The operator sets the parameters the winemaker is looking for, and the machine checks the shape and color of the berries as they ride down the conveyor belt. An air cannon shoots undesirable berries to a different belt and then into different bins. The sorter can check sixty tons rather than sixteen tons when grapes are sorted by hand. It's a game-changer. Grapes are delivered straight into stainless steel tanks. We can ferment less desirable grapes and sell that wine on the bulk market. It's particularly useful for Pinot and is a place where technology is good. It's certainly better to start with great fruit than to modify it with additives to get better wine.

Some winemakers guide and herd grapes for high extraction and then use more oak than the wine can handle. Every step along the way decides a wine's fate. I learned to wait and see rather than hurry an event that changes the wine. I want its character to develop by itself. I don't rack Pinot noir or Meunier, since lees protect wine from oxidation and add richness to the wine. Native malolactic fermentation lasts longer in a cool cellar, forming carbon dioxide and diminishing the need for sulfur dioxide. Most winemaker use $SO_2$ in high levels, but it doesn't fit with my desire for natural winemaking. I believe less sulfur leads to a better evolution of the wine, so we taste all the time and closely watch the numbers to avoid the risk of oxidation.

~ℓℓ~

## BURT'S GRILLED BEET SALAD WITH CHIMICHURRI PAIRED WITH DOMAINE CHANDON'S PINOT MEUNIER

Baguette, cut into four 1-inch-thick pieces on the diagonal
Four medium-sized beets
One avocado
A handful of arugula

CHIMICHURRI SAUCE

¼ cup of chopped Italian parsley
¼ cup of extra virgin olive oil (EVOO)
5 tbsp of red wine vinegar
One garlic clove
Pinch of dried crushed pepper (I like to crush whole tepin peppers)
¼ teaspoon of cumin
Salt to taste

Preheat oven to 400°F. Peel beets and then cut them in halves. Toss them in a small amount of EVOO and salt. Put beets into the oven and roast until tender; about 30 minutes. Prepare barbecue while the beets are roasting. When the beets are tender, smash them with a knife or other flat object, being careful not to burn yourself. The beets should be in the form of rough patties. Brush them with EVOO and place them on the barbecue in a spot that is not too hot. Cook for several minutes. Mark them like you would when you grill a burger with a quarter turn and grill on both sides. Brush the bread with EVOO and grill it on one side.

### CHIMICHURRI PREPARATION

This is a very easy sauce to make. It is spicy and tart and perfect for foods with earthy flavors. Combine the ingredients in a food processor, pulse and voila, it is done. Cool ingredients to room temperature. Toss some of the arugula in the chimichurri. Lay a layer of the arugula on one of the grilled baguettes. Top the arugula with grilled beet. Next, top the grilled beet with smashed avocado and drizzle with chimichurri. Eat with a knife and fork.

SERVES 4.

*This recipe is perfectly paired with Chandon's Pinot Meunier. The tangy and earthy flavors play off each other to provide the perfect complement to a summer evening. Think of this as a knife and fork salad.*

*Our Chardonnay is treated pretty much the same way. The wine isn't stirred a lot because that would make it advance in age. The wine goes into 20 percent new oak for less of an oaky character. I'm a big fan of Chablis and white Burgundy. I prefer a rich, not too fat wine with minerality, texture, and nervous tension that come from a backbone of acid.*

Burt comes from Modesto, California, and became interested in agriculture through his farming family.

*My mom is a good cook and passed on the Greek love of food. She never used processed products. Kids I grew up with wanted to eat at our house. They ate things like Kraft Singles while we had real cheese, something they thought was a real luxury. My grandfather made his own rub of oregano, garlic salt, and pepper for the lamb he barbecued over grape wood. I wanted to be like him, and today I grow and dry herbs like lavender, oregano, and dwarf curry. I harvest flowers before and after bloom for different flavors. I get earthy flavors when I add them at the start and aromatics when added at the end. My love of food sent me to work in restaurants. I worked my way up from dishwasher until I became a sous chef for a caterer. I knew about grapes from the family's vineyard and finally realized winemaking was a better fit for me. My next job was as wine buyer at Whole Foods, where I got to try a lot of wine and educated my palate. One harvest, I was the only employee at a small winery. Fresno State was my next step, but I wasn't interested in hi-tech winemaking and felt the university system teaches students how to make clean wine and how to deal with problems. I was more idealistic and wanted to make wine naturally. My first real wine-related job was doing research at Mondavi. It taught me how to conduct research and what numbers really mean. I also realized people who make products for wine conducted a lot of the research. I worked at Saintsbury Winery, where I learned not to fight the fruit. Some winemakers want to make bigger wines so they overextract and use additives to bulk up the structure. It's difficult to make an honest Pinot noir, a wine that needs to be pure, clean, and fresh. I get that with fewer additives and doing less work.*

*When I make wine I approach it from a food and flavor perspective. The main goal is balance of texture, body, flavors, richness, and aromas. Precise control of temperature changes the kinetics of fermentation with longer cold maceration because it extracts more color, flavors, and aromas. I need to see the trajectory of wine's amazing journey after a year and a half in barrel.*

*I'm amazed I can make wine the way I want. I'm allowed some latitude, since it's expensive to make my wine. It's a small program and I'm lucky the corporation doesn't want more production. Making high-quality wine in the Burgundy style is a blessing. Being able to learn and achieve my goals by the end of the year is satisfying: lowering SO$_2$ levels, making better wine, using my vision to take the wines where I want them to go. I avoid making trendy, hip wines that become yesterday's news, avoiding drastic choices that become a liability in the future. My wines must age gracefully along with my career. I'd eventually like to start my own label, focused on Pinot noir and*

Chardonnay. It's good to evolve a style and if it reaches perfection, start a new parallel style.

One of my personal quests is to enjoy wine. I go to wine-tastings, checking the zeitgeist of wines. I drink Domaine des Baumard's amazing botrytized Chenin blanc and Mona Lisa Chenins. I enjoy Cru Beaujolais, Cabernet franc from the Jure and orange-fermented whites.

## CATHY CORISON
### CORISON WINERY

One notable AVA is the Rutherford Bench, 2,500 acres stretching along 6 miles from Highway 29 west to the Mayacamas Mountains and north to St. Helena. The gravely, loamy alluvial soil of Rutherford Bench land is considered a perfect terroir for Cabernet Sauvignon. Cabernets from Rutherford are noted for intense dark fruit and a discernible taste of Rutherford Dust.

Spend time with Cathy Corison and you meet a strong, intensely focused winemaker who maintains she makes wines to suit herself, wines that totally represent her. The interview with Corison broke out of the gate when she said she liked the idea of *The Winemaker's Hand* and often uses the term. "The question of terroir versus the winemaker's hand is a complicated subject. Even when the grape source and other qualities based on terroir are consistent, there's no question an enologist's hand and personality can and should always be discernible."

Years before Corison bought the vineyard property on the west side of Route 29 on the Rutherford Bench land, long before her husband William designed the elegant Victorian-style barn to house her winemaking facility, she was bitten by the wine bug. John Haeger, a favorite college professor, introduced her to wine in noncredit wine appreciation class. "It shows the influence one person has on another. Wine grabbed me by the throat and ran with me. I studied biology at Pomona College in 1975 because I love living things. I discovered wine was a living system that was also delicious." After graduation, she headed straight to Napa with her father's gift of $200.

*My first job was at the Wine Garden, a wine shop and deli where local wine-makers gathered every Wednesday night. It was a fabulous experience for a young student.*

*I realized there are winemakers who don't have technical training, but I knew I had to learn all the aspects of winemaking. I chose the academic route as a better way for a woman to enter the field thirty years ago, when there were few women vintners. I fulfilled a required chemistry course at U.C. Davis, and the next year enrolled there for a master's program in enology. The formal degree gave me a good technical foundation, although I'm not aware of it any more. After that I worked at Chappellet for a decade and made wine for a lot of people during the '80's, I wanted to express my own winemaking voice.*

*I have two stylistic models for my wines. I admire the wines of St. Julien in Bordeaux that prove power and elegance can coexist in the same glass. Second, I appreciate Chianti Riservas, especially those made before the advent of Super Tuscans, when the best grapes are cherry-picked to adapt to an international style of wine. There are still good houses in Tuscany that make aromatic Riservas with beautiful balance.*

Corison maintains there is a close, undeniable link between terroir and the winemaker's hand.

*Terroir is undoubtedly a key factor, but it comes down to a winemaker's vision of how to work with the soil. Truly great, complex wine is a combination of a unique place meets the hand of an individual winemaker with passion and a personal vision. In the best case, the winemaker's hand becomes an integral part of the terroir. Wine is interesting to think about, beyond its use for washing down food. A consumer should become familiar with a recognizable, individual wine style. Someone who has never seen a Gauguin painting will always recognize his paintings, even though they may have only seen one. The same experience should be true of a particular wine. Good wine can be made by committee, but often too many hands, too many conflicting ideas muddle the results. Fortunately, there are occasions when, at large wineries, vintners are given the opportunity to make wine that reflects their ideas and attitudes. Ed Sbraga (winemaker emeritus), at Beringer Vineyards, comes to mind as an example when he had the license to use his hand. And then there are also times when a capable wine technician makes flawless wine without character and soul.*

~ℓℓ~

# CORISON BASQUE LAMB STEW

*A Corison twist has been added to a delicious basic stew.*

3½ lb lamb shoulder, cut into 2-inch pieces
6 cloves garlic, crushed and peeled
1 sprig fresh rosemary
½ cup dry white wine
2 tbsp extra virgin olive oil
1 large onion, peeled and chopped
Salt and freshly ground pepper
2 tsp sweet paprika
3 canned roasted red bell peppers, cut into ½-inch strips
1 large ripe tomato, peeled, seeded, and chopped
4–6 sprigs parsley, chopped
1 bay leaf
½ cup Corison Cabernet
½ cup chicken stock

Combine the lamb, 3 of the garlic cloves, rosemary, and white wine in a medium bowl. Let marinate for 2–3 hours. Drain the meat, discard the marinade, and pat dry with paper towels. Mince the remaining 3 garlic cloves and set aside.

Heat olive oil in a large, heavy-bottomed pan with lid, over medium-high heat. Working in batches, brown the meat on all sides, about 10 minutes per batch. Return all meat to the pot. Add onions, minced garlic, and salt and pepper to taste, and cook, scraping browned bits stuck to the bottom of the pot with a wooden spoon, until the onions are soft, about 5 minutes. Stir in paprika, add roasted peppers, tomatoes, parsley, bay leaf, and red wine. Bring to a boil, reduce heat to medium, and simmer until juices in pot reduce and thicken slightly, about 10–15 minutes.

Add chicken stock, cover, reduce heat to low, and simmer, stirring occasionally, until meat is very tender, 2–2½ hours. Adjust seasonings.

*Pair with our Cabernets. The lamb flavors melding with the sweet paprika, fresh herbs and roasted peppers highlight the delicious flavors of the wine.*

Terroir is emphasized today as an antidote to the current international standardized style of winemaking. Terroir makes sense when it is a consistent, unique factor in each vintage, as it has been for generations in Burgundy. But even there, house style can be so strong it often trumps the vineyard. It's why I needed to choose the right terroir to achieve the style I wanted before I made the first drop. Some of my favorite Cabernet Sauvignons come from the gravely, loamy alluvial soil of Rutherford Bench between Rutherford and St. Helena, a terroir that is perfect for Cabernet grapes. There's copious sun that *ripens them fully and the cool nights that produce dark color, complex flavor, and adequate natural acidity. The best vintages occur when the cooling fog rolls in each evening, clearing up by 9 or 10 A.M.*

"My brand was established in 1997 as the Corison Napa Valley Cabernet Sauvignon sourced from my Kronos vineyard," she said. She maintains she couldn't make her wines anywhere else in the world. Hers differs from her neighbors', a true example of a winemaker's personal choices, preferences, and attitudes.

*We each do something different at crucial junctures. Every decision nudges the wine stylistically, but the basic components of the wine come from the vineyard. My vineyard yields grapes that gush out color, great aromas, with concentrated flavors of blackberry, plum, and cassis. Our wines have a silky mouth feel, drinkable with hearty foods when young, but will continue to develop in the bottle for decades. I continue to make wine from gnarly 40-year-old vines on St. George rootstock that were here when I bought the vineyard. Banks consider vines to have a viable, commercially sustainable life of thirty years, so these old vines are amazing. After all these years, they know exactly what to do. I so value these old vines and I replant them vine by vine as they die. In 2010, only twenty-nine out of 4,000 vines were replaced.*

Corison casts a proud, maternal eye over her extraordinary vineyard stretching west behind the barn and explains the origin of the wines' names.

*Kronos is one of the three Titans, the sons of heaven and earth, who sit between earth and sky, just as, for me, wine sits between earth and sky. It's the timelessness of wine that I'm interested in, not necessarily Greek mythology specifically. The images on my bottle, cork, and box are Neolithic life symbols, one based on rain, the other based on a sprouting seed.*

*Grape prices have gone up frighteningly. I pay top dollar for some of the world's best grapes grown organically from three specific vineyards because great grapes make great wine. I deal with the owners on a handshake basis. I don't own the soil, but I'm involved in the farming at every stage, checking on the status and evolution of the vines.*

"Winemaking is the easiest thing I do," Corison says, tongue in cheek. "Farmers are always nervous. We're often dodging a bullet because every year, Mother Nature throws something different at us."

*Terroir is part of my hand. Together, we deliver a sense of place, power, and elegance, a wine that graces the table, one that achieves a balance between food and wine, each making the other better. I try to balance between a vine's green growth and its fruit. It's a struggle, but it's important to me to keep the alcohol level under 14 percent. Grapes picked too early have green flavors, but if picked too ripe, the wine loses the deep red, blue, and purple fruit characteristics I love in Cabernet. The result will have unsatisfying black and pruney flavors with high alcohol and low acidity. Grapes grown and picked correctly from the Rutherford Bench exhibit soft, ripe tannins that originate in the vineyard. It's not possible to remove bad tannins surgically in the winery, leaving only the good ones behind. Nine out of ten years, our tannins feel like velvet.*

*I have the power to blend with a consistent stylistic vision. Blending is very intuitive and changes year to year because of the weather. It's neither linear nor logical. A plus B doesn't equal A plus B. It's possible to blend for homogeneity, but why is that desirable? I sell off what doesn't fit my blend and it often goes into wines more expensive than mine.*

*I hope I've gotten better at what I do. I've become more intuitive about the way I make wine. The miracle of winemaking is underlined by experience. I don't need to measure sugars any more. I'm not interested in what's "in," like the current trend of boozy, very ripe, low-acid, sweet wine. I keep my radar focused through changes in fashion. I stick to my style because I've seen fashions come and go.*

*My wine isn't cheap, but it's a good value. I want to sell it and still be able to make the next vintage. The wine business has been tough for the last ten years. I don't delegate responsibility, so I juggle a lot of things, including family. I don't like shuffling papers and worrying about personnel. I prefer driving my tractor around the vineyard rather than worrying about the health of the business. My tractor is so tied to the soil and vines, and when I'm on it, stresses over issues disappear.*

She is interested in biodynamic farming and hopes to learn enough about it to do it well. "I question the way it's used for marketing wine. It's a big woo-woo factor that's done by a lot of people who dabble in it and throw the term around."

*What's left to accomplish? I can always make better wine with incremental changes, but I'm a lumper, not a splitter. It's why my main focus is on one wine, although from time to time, I need to make an interesting change, or I wouldn't keep going. I admire the wines from Alsace, so I make a dry Gewurtz-traminer in the Alsatian style from grapes harvested from Mendocino County. It's a goofing-around wine, fun to make, fun to drink, useful for our receptions and first courses at dinner. And sometimes I've bottled Syrah, Merlot, Rosé, and Cabernet Franc, limited production wines that don't meet the Corison blend requirements but that are lovely by themselves. They are sold under our second label, Helios, the sun god in Greek mythology.*

*I don't work to other people's goals and stylistic preferences, or to garner someone else's approval. I never put anything in a bottle I'm not proud of. All I have to sell is my integrity and my brand. I make wine I like, and count on others liking it.*

Corison's 1,500 to 2,000 cases of wine, with the final count depending on Mother Nature, are highly regarded "cult" wines. She defines a cult wine as one that is of limited quantity, that is hard to find, and that is praised by the critics. Although anyone who has enjoyed Corison wines knows she has earned the kudos, she demurs from the status.

*Critics like to pick everything apart. People who appreciate wine should be aware of the inflation of numerical and other kinds of ratings, especially if those ratings push winemakers to go for scores. In some cases, winemakers at certain producers are paid on the basis of high scores. Unfortunately, ratings influence people who are afraid of their own decisions. If they put their faith in scores, they have to believe them all, whether good or bad. My customers should get pleasure from my Cabernets without being too analytical. Professionally, I do a lot of formal blind tastings. I only need one description for the wine and food I love. "Yum."*

# BILL DYER

## DYER VINEYARD AND CONSULTANT

I met Bill Dyer well over two decades ago, when his wife Dawnine, winemaker at Domaine Chandon, invited me to a St. Patrick's Day party at her winery. Dawnine's job was to create sparkling wine for Moët Chandon's Napa off-shoot. Bill was Director of Winemaking at Sterling Winery, overseeing production of several varietals of still wine. Bill traveled a few minutes to his job down the steep road on Diamond Mountain Road while Dawnine drove up and down Highway 29 to its most southerly stretch to reach Domaine Chandon's facility in Yountville. In 1992, after twenty-five years, the couple abandoned corporate winemaking and purchased 12 acres in the Diamond Mountain Appellation. "We fenced in the property to keep out marauding, hungry deer. They can eat their way through a crop. We built our rammed earth house later in 1996," says Dyer.

*Diamond Mountain District has a reputation for powerful, dazzling blended reds, primarily based on Cabernet Sauvignon. Coastal hills, like ours, are an excellent place to grow wine grapes because of their interesting volcanic soils. We are located about 40 miles east of the Pacific Ocean and north of San Francisco Bay, with influences from San Pablo Bay. Our summer weather is quite easy to understand. The normal pattern is an on-shore flow with wind blowing from the northwest that brings fog to the coast. This keeps us quite cool. But every so often we have an offshore flow when the wind blows from the direction of Nevada, temporarily eliminating the effect of the cold ocean. Our climate of warm days and cool nights is sometimes described as Mediterranean, but I wonder where that idea comes from. In my experiences traveling* to Europe, the Mediterranean climate seems entirely different. It doesn't cool down at night there as it does in California.

I came out of my first college experience as a generalist. I was disinclined to specialize, so I ended up with a major in philosophy without a particular career path. I became interested in wine, first through tasting some interesting wines, like Ridge Zinfandel. Dawnine was still in school. We moved to Napa, where I visited wineries and became a cellar rat, the lowest flunkey in a winery. Then I joined Sterling. They sent me to school to learn winemaking.

Eventually, we wanted a house in the country after living for eighteen years in Calistoga. We weren't planning to have a vineyard when we started looking for land. I always liked Diamond Mountain from my Sterling days. We found this undeveloped site across the road from some of Diamond Mountain District's most eminent Cabernet producers—Reverie, Diamond Creek, and Von Strasser. We walked the property, turned over the soil with a shovel, and found beautiful gravel. It was the same caliber of vineyard land as those great wineries along the road. We decided to make a vineyard wine with our own label and cleared the land of trees. Some people buy rocky sites and spend $100,000 to cart the stones away. We live with the rocks on which our vines thrive. Our site at a 600-foot elevation seems to be an ancient rockslide from the hillside above. It was a Herculean task to rip out the largest rocks to get ready for planting. The vines struggle to thrive on what's left: streaks of gravel, chalky tuff, huge boulders, and red soil formed by volcanic activity eons ago. Our upland volcanic soils are more acidic than those on the valley floor. They also differ from the sedimentary sandstone and shale soils in the Spring Mountain District AVA immediately south of Diamond Mountain. The wines of the DMD typically show an intensity and concentration attributed to these deep but sparse volcanic soils.

The site made Bordeaux varietals an obvious choice. We planted the vineyard with Cabernet Sauvignon, Merlot, Cabernet Franc, and Petit Verdot. There's a lot of talk about a typical Bordeaux blend, but in reality there is no such thing. Bordeaux wines are a throwback to the time when wine made in that region came from a field blend. In earlier times, the varietal mix was different. Malbec dominated as number one, followed by Petit Verdot. Cabernet Sauvignon was way down the list. Today, the blend often starts with Cabernet Sauvignon or Merlot. A lot of permutations of this historic blend exist around the world.

Dyer Vineyard is planted on a grid with equal distances between rows. Planting decisions, like row direction, really depend on conclusions each *winemaker makes. There is no such thing as an ideal row direction, although some people argue passionately about a north–south or east–west plan. We use a V-trellis system that keeps shoots upright and spreads the canopy to provide a little protection from the sun. Our vines are planted north to south. The worst is east to west because the south side of the plant is in the sun all day long and the north side gets too much shade. Tweaking the north–south system a bit works the best at our vineyard to protect the vines from afternoon sun. Most vineyards were planted out of habit, with rows parallel or perpendicular to the entry road.*

*One wine differs from another because of all a winemaker's functions. It would be a real miracle if wines from two different winemakers tasted exactly the same. In a small operation, all the cards are in the owner's hands: site management, grape selection, attempts to manage biological processes of yeast and bacteria, decisions about barrels, and length of aging. I believe the best wines come from small estates where individual owners understand a season's idiosyncrasies and can take the long view.*

Bill's experience at Sterling Vineyard gave him an edge in selecting the varieties and clones to plant in the Dyer vineyard. "I developed the first single vineyard wines at Sterling, including a Diamond Mountain Ranch Cabernet in the early 1980's. I hand-selected the plant material, focusing on clones and rootstock that best matched our site and oversaw all the vineyard activities." Dyer expresses his ideas about the benefits of winemaking at a small winery and has distinct opinions about large corporations.

*I've come to the conclusion that large-scale corporations shouldn't own wineries. There's a huge difference between a small operation like Dyer Vineyards and one like Sterling Winery. We have the pleasures and difficulties of our own winery. Big businesses often take a short-term view, driven by the need to show quarterly profits to shareholders. Also, a large corporation maintains all the controls. In my experience, corporations are composed of decent, smart people who can collectively make bad decisions. A corporation can dig into their deep pockets to acquire vineyard land, expensive barrels, and other costly tools. At a big winery, a vineyard manager is in charge of ninety vineyards, so it's less likely that the winemaker sees the vineyard until the end of the season. Blending from ninety lots doesn't reflect a particular terroir. Corporations* have difficulty in understanding that grapes vary in yield and quality from season to season, sometimes by 20 percent or more. Such seasonal variations affect the quality and amount of wine, but variables aren't good for the bottom line.

In contrast, Dyer wines show off our vineyard site with our aim of achieving structure and balance paired with good aromatics. Our wines reflect this particular place, specific soil, aspect, and location of our vineyard. We planted the correct varietals in our vineyard to produce on average 400 cases of elegant Cabernet Sauvignon. We farm the plot the best we can, dealing with what each season gives us. We prefer our traditional approach, reflected in the continuum of all the things we do throughout the year. Our approach is to use tried-and-true methods rather than to follow the contemporary strategies of high-alcohol blockbuster wines. We stick to producing wines that reflect our personal approach to showcase the particular terroir of Diamond Mountain because styles change. We believe that strategy works well for us.

I used different blocks for the 100,000 cases of some reds when I worked at Sterling. Dyer wines are an entirely different project. Our blend from year to year is really simple. It is a vineyard wine. Basically, we pick on the ripeness of Cabernet Sauvignon. Then we do weighted samples from our 2,000 vines, 80 percent of which are Cabernet Sauvignon. The wine goes into one third new barrels and fifth-year used barrels. Dawnine and I are quite competent at blending. It was an essential part of our past winery associations, as it is now with our wines. Our vineyard is laid out so that we are able to co-ferment the varieties from the vineyard in proportion to the varieties we planted. Crop levels are low on our difficult site, with its five-degree slopes. Yield never exceeds two and a half tons per acre. Our vines are sustainably farmed and organic as a matter of principle. This is our front yard and it's also important that we are responsible stewards of the property. We don't want residual chemicals in our well, so we don't use herbicides. It's necessary to use sulfur, but it's an organic antimildew product. No one wants mildew in their wine. We can't avoid chemicals completely, but we use as little as possible if there's a severe problem. We go only as far as we're comfortable. Since 1996, we make Dyer Vineyard Estate Cabernet Sauvignon ourselves across the road at Rudy Von Strasser's winery.

Winemaking is based on hunches and perceptions. Deciding when to pick is the most important decision. We find it easy to make evaluations together. In our case, 80 percent of the wine comes from our vineyard. We make judgments together about barrels, playing to our individual experiences and strengths.

# BILL DYER'S WILD MUSHROOM RISOTTO

*It's good to have a forager in the family when you make this one. In a good year Bill will harvest and we will dry up to 40 lb of Boletus edulis, the mushroom that the Italians call* porcini *and the French call* cèpes. *But even if you have to buy the mushrooms, this is a great, rich, flavorful dish. The earthiness of the porcini is a classic unami, rich and dark and absolutely wonderful with a nicely aged Cabernet six years or older.*

*Making risotto is basically the same for all risottos. It's the "condiments" and the broth that provide the flavor.*

½–1 oz dried porcini
1 tbsp unsalted butter
1 tbsp olive oil (cooking quality—don't waste the good stuff!)
2 cups fresh mushrooms (these can be crimini or any available fresh wild mushroom)
¼ cup cream
Salt and pepper
2 tbsp olive oil
1 tbsp butter
½ cup onion, minced
1½ cup Arborio rice
4 cups broth (chicken or vegetarian—I make my own in the fall when we're drying the porcini and use the trimmings in the broth)
½ cup white wine or dry vermouth

In a small bowl cover the dried porcini with 1 cup boiling water. Let sit for 30 minutes. Drain the mushrooms, reserving the liquid. Chop both the fresh and rehydrated mushrooms. Keep them separate. Heat butter and olive oil in a skillet and add the fresh mushrooms as the oils begin to bubble. Sauté the fresh mushrooms for 3 minutes until soft and then add the porcini. Continue cooking for 2 minutes; then add cream. Salt and pepper to taste. Set aside.

Add the mushroom water and wine to the broth and bring to a simmer. Retain ¼ cup for the final step. Heat oil and butter in a heavy saucepan. Add onions and cook until soft. Add rice and stir (a wooden spoon is best) for a minute or two.

Add the broth, approximately ½ cup at a time, stirring frequently. When the rice is tender but still firm, about 18–20 minutes, add the mushroom mixture and the last ¼ cup of liquid and stir vigorously to combine.

Garnish liberally with Parmesan and chopped parsley.

*Pair with 2009 Dyer Vineyard Cabernet Sauvignon, Diamond Mountain District, Napa Valley.*

*I'm pretty familiar with barrels for Cabernet. We order medium-plus toast for our barrels. Heavy toasting is too much, and light toasting doesn't build enough character. Where whisky barrels are made with steam, wine barrels are held over a fire that determines the level of toast. Overtoasting gives off charred or tarry flavors, and astringency from the oak comes from undertoasting. We don't radically change what we taste once it is in the barrels.*

*Winemaking is fascinating because it sits at the intersection of many different disciplines and areas. It crosses over between many aspects of human life and nature. The work changes and flows with the seasons. A winemaker gets involved in the agriculture, production, marketing, and management. A winemaker's education involves many different courses, ranging from biological sciences to chemistry, engineering, agriculture, and sometimes business administration.*

*When I first started in the wine industry, there was a time when the process of making wine headed in the direction of more technology. A centrifuge is perhaps a good metaphor for this. In the mid-1970's, it seemed that everyone needed a centrifuge to clarify juice and wine quickly. Then we rediscovered things like gravity were quite reliable, and emulating traditional winemaking resulted in more interesting wines. We found we didn't need to be in such a hurry. Some improvements are not so much high tech, but rather are a result of more sensitivity and gentleness in handling grapes and wine. Within traditional methods there is room for improvement in some of the equipment we use. Old-style crushers ground the skins and produced harsh tannins. Today gentle rollers can be adjusted for any desired degree of crushing. The rollers can be bypassed to accommodate de-stemming. New tank presses allow much more gentle extraction, doing the job better than old-style continuous presses. A modernized old-fashioned basket press is making a return. Pumps are much gentler. We don't use genetically modified yeast at Dyer Vineyards. We prefer isolates from natural fermentations, or sometimes we prefer the yeast that occurs naturally on grapes. We believe talk of higher alcohols coming from specially bred super-yeasts is a fantasy.*

*Our understanding of grape maturity has gone through a major change. Instead of making picking decisions based on sugar content alone, we pay much more attention to other parameters such as tannin maturity, seed color, and other factors.*

Dyer is disdainful of the idea of a winemaker as an artist.

*Each year yields a different picture, but it's always consistent with a wine-maker's philosophy and taste. As to the winemaker as artist question, I think the term* artist *is overused. I believe we tend to confuse craftsman with artist. Calling winemaking an art is usually a self-serving way of bending the meaning of the word. Baseball players are sometimes considered artists, but they mostly chew sunflower seeds, spit, and scratch their groins. My definition of an artist is someone who works from imagination. In my opinion, there are a limited number of individuals in certain professions, like painters, writers, or cinematographers, who can truly be called artists. However, the idea takes us into some gray areas. Even some who are considered artists by my definition don't meet the criteria.*

Dyer consults with Miramar Torres of the famous Torres winemaking family for two decades and enjoys the challenge of working with Pinot noir in Sonoma.

*I find it stimulating to work in new areas. Each consulting role is unique, driven by differences in owners, available personnel, and location. You have to fit into your client's goals together with their limitations of resources and possibilities. Consulting is a challenge because each situation needs a different skill set. It's hard to get people on board for a consensus at a distance. There are some consultants who say, "My way or the highway," who probably don't vary their role much from client to client. I take a different approach. My job is advisory and I bring my experience to coach clients to make the best wine from their resources. Unfortunately, some clients think a consultant is there for every step during the year, but the reality is to be available to taste through the inventory for two or three days every two months. The rest of the time we connect by e-mail or phone.*

*There were no restrictions on crop yield or the kind of grapes until there was a push to make better wines in Mexico. Before the GATT Treaty in 1988 Mexico had little incentive to make good wine and had only a few technically proficient winemakers. Early efforts in the country created basic table wines, but by the 1980's Mexican winemakers wanted to produce world-class wine. They hired winemaking consultants from New Zealand and Australia who helped them switch to vinifera grapes.*

Dyer consults in Baja, Mexico, working with historic Italian Aglianico and Nebbiolo grapes.

*Nebbiolo is particularly challenging. The results in the New World don't match the success it has in Piedmont, but there are promising new stocks in the pipeline. The differences between working in Mexico might seem to be insurmountable, but the terroir doesn't present a problem, because the Sonora Desert extends with similar flora and fauna from Mexico through Walla Walla, Washington, right up into 15 miles above the Canadian border. Different zones along the stretch of desert resemble latitudes of Bordeaux, Burgundy, and Alsace. Harvest dates depend on differing length of days and seasons in both regions.*

*A few influential critics whom I consider evildoers encourage aberrant winemakers. The result? Ripeness is taken to absurd levels, making red wines more or less in the Amarone style. Wines with big scores have an easy time of it, but knowledgeable consumers seek out wines of good value and individual style. At Dyer Vineyard, our loyal customers walk the vineyard with us. Knowing Dawnine and me develops an intimacy that enhances the total wine experience. Strolling between the rows of vines in our vineyard puts people in touch with the vines and ultimately with our wines. Our customers buy when our wines are young and drink them after they have aged a few years.*

Dyer loves making wine, but he's a bookish sort of guy, someone who says he'd be a librarian if he weren't a winemaker. "I like to think and weigh ideas. I'd like to be president of the U.S. or a writer. At one point in my life, when I was tired of being a cellar worker at a winery at a time before I fell into making wine, I applied to library school. I thought it was a very rational idea. A college librarian must have a very stimulating job. What better place for someone who likes different ideas to read books and see movies? But I realized winemaking could provide me with a comfortable and ethical life." Dyer's' literary side turns up when he quotes from Buddhist sutras. Because their hands are often purple during the winemaking process he particularly likes the reference to a fabric dyer's stained hands in a quote from Shakespeare's Sonnet 111.

> Thence comes it that my name receives a brand,
> And almost thence my nature is subdued
> To what it works in, like the dyer's hand. . . .

On a trip to Tibet, the Dyers saw fantastic drawings of mountain scenes in Buddhist monasteries. "Our label comes from a painting from a sutra called Diamond Mountain we saw in Tibet. Our brother-in-law adapted the design for our label." The moment in Tibet was a fortuitous coincidence that matched Dyer's intellectualism and idealism.

*Making our own wine is very pure. Not only is it a part of our daily life, but it permits us to find our own niche in the wine world. We set our own goals. Each day begins with some project in the vineyard. If there are any discussions or disagreements, Dawnine and I compromise. Some people might say there can only be one winemaker in charge, but if you're compatible as a couple in other parts of your life, it extends to your work. Working together makes our life together special.*

# DAWNINE DYER
## DYER VINEYARD

Through the centuries, tradition maintained winemaking was an occupation for men only. Males held tight to the prerogative of converting grapes into wine. "No women need apply" was the general rule. Females were relegated to fieldwork—picking, sorting, and stomping on harvested grapes. History recorded the rare occasions when an occasional woman held the reins of business. One of the most notable was Mme. Veuve (*veuve* is the French word for "widow") Clicquot, who ran the family winery after her husband died in 1805. Her name on bright yellow labels of the company's Champagne bottles is a proud reminder of her major contributions to the development of sparkling wine. Almost two centuries elapsed before the institutionalized practice of male domination changed. By the mid-twentieth century, women took their place in all aspects of the industry, from sales and marketing to winemaking.

Around thirty years ago, Dawnine Dyer and I started our long friendship over the telephone. I was writing an article on women in the wine industry and I lucked out with an interview with Dawnine. She was one of a handful of female pioneers who cracked the industry's gender gap in the 1960's. The highly respected, well-liked winemaker at Domaine Chandon, the celebrated Napa Valley sparkling wine facility, was nicknamed Sainte Dawnine by her co-workers. My relationship with Dawnine affirms she is one of the most charming people in a business fraught with egomaniacs. Dyer says,

*I rarely felt held back when I began in the industry. My background in biology and microbiology led to an evolutionary path from the time I started as a lab*

*technician at Inglenook. At Robert Mondavi, I worked for Zelma Long, who to this day remains a close friend. Domaine Chandon liked my creds and ability to speak French. I worked alongside Edmund Maudière, the venerable consulting enologist who chose the vineyard site in Carneros and helped design the building that houses the winery and restaurant in Yountville. Maudière traveled six times a year from the winery's parent company in France. I was hired as a quality technician to set up Moët et Chandon's lab at their new winery. Maudière continued to travel from the winery's parent company in France to the States and consult at Domaine Chandon six times a year. Moët's consulting division was helpful to me. It was especially important because at the time U.C. Davis had a limited program for sparkling wine. In the beginning, I was a sponge. I absorbed a lot before I ventured my own opinions. I was very lucky to be included in tastings and blendings from the start at Chandon. It alerted me to the differences in flavors and characteristics in sparkling wine that are different from still wines. I worked for a couple of years and was promoted in 1980, when the winery needed a full-time winemaker with complete responsibility for the entire Domaine Chandon operation.*

Her ready smile and pleasant manner doesn't mean she can't get things done. She excelled at producing excellent sparkling wine. As an added fillip to her numerous talents, when called on to sabrage, or open a bottle with a saber in the Napoleonic tradition, Dyer does it with panache. "The trick is to find the weak part of the bottle's neck. I advise people not to try it at home."

*There came a time in 1989 when my husband Bill and I wanted to start our own label. We both worked sixty-hour weeks for large corporations and traveled a lot. Corporate situations make the winemaker part of a team, a small cog in a bigger wheel. The process is very collegial and takes constant consultation with innumerable people over many sessions. Each person on the team has an agenda. The marketing people talk about sales, and so it goes, from vineyard to bottling. When you own your own vineyard and bottle your own wine, there's a sense of independence and certainly fewer inputs. You are required to wear many hats. Innumerable internal conversations make you need to listen to your own voice. Yet it's surprising how hard it is to have a conversation with yourself. It's good to have a partner who is a collaborator.*

~ℓℓ~

# DYER'S DUCK AND WILD RICE SALAD

*Based on a recipe Mary Every, the winery chef at Simi in the '80's, shared with me. I no longer look at the recipe when I make it, so I guess I kind of own it. I use it at a luncheon or plated as a first course.*

2 whole boned duck breasts with skin (I use a fully cooked smoked duck breast that I get at the deli)
½ cup water, salt to taste
1 cup wild rice
3½ cups water
1 tsp salt
3 green onions, sliced
2 oz radicchio, chopped
2 heads Belgian endive
¼ cup toasted walnuts
2 tbsp walnut oil
2 tsp sherry vinegar

For the cracklings remove the skin with the fat from the meat and cut into pieces. Combine with ½ cup water in heavy skillet and cook over medium heat 45–60 minutes until fat is rendered and skin is golden (this works equally well for smoked or raw).

Bring rice, water, and salt to a boil. Reduce to a simmer and simmer for 45 minutes or until rice kernels begin to split open. Drain and place in bowl to cool.

If using smoked breasts you're done. If not, season the duck breasts with salt and pepper. Grill or sauté approximately 3 minutes per side. Let stand for 5 minutes and slice on the diagonal. Reserve a portion sliced and chop the rest.

Mix the rice, the green onion, the radicchio, walnut oil, sherry vinegar, and the chopped duck

Plate portions individually or serve it family style. The duck can be added warm or the whole dish can be cold. The endive is part of the base, and the duck slices, walnuts, and cracklings are arranged on top.

SERVES 4.

*I love the duck paired with young Cabs. It has bold and bright flavors, like the wines. The tannins from the walnuts, the wild rice, and the radicchio all blend beautifully with the natural tannins and fruits of our Diamond Mountain Cabernet Sauvignon.*

There was a huge harvest in '89. We stopped picking because we ran out of holding tanks. It was a moment of respite, until one Sunday. One Sunday Bill was at home in Calistoga lying in the hammock when someone next door started noisy work on a car repair. Later, two people had a loud argument. It all helped us make a decision to move. Bill said we needed to build a house. The property we liked for the house was covered with second-growth scrub wood. It wasn't our idea to start our own brand, but we reversed the order, since we knew more about vineyards than we did about houses. Bill cleared the land and watched the light and shading as it fell on the site of our proposed rammed earth home.

The vineyard became our first priority after we recognized Diamond Mountain's distinctive terroir. Some vineyards are so unique they point the way to the wine. Our vineyard cried out for the varietals that go into great red wines. Bordeaux vines thrive in deep, mineral-rich, not-too-fertile volcanic gravel with pockets of red soil. Fertile soils would give us huge vines. Instead we want the vines to have access to minerals that develop character in the wines.

Some people say it takes two people with differing skills to craft such different wines as Sauvignon blanc and Cabernet Sauvignon, while others maintain if you can make wine, you can make any wine. For me, having to switch from twenty-five years producing sparkling to still wine at Dyer Vineyard wasn't so difficult because sparkling wine begins as still wine. I made Pinot noir at Domaine Chandon for sale to consumers. I also did barrel sample tastings over the years with Bill that expanded my knowledge.

Diamond Mountain had an already established reputation for red wines, especially those crafted from Cabernet Sauvignon. Bill had worked with Diamond Mountain Cabernet at Sterling Winery and was particularly fond of fruit from the area. Its small berries produce firm tannins, a fairly dark color with black cherry, cassis, and blueberry, together with hints of cocoa, cedar, and anise characteristics. It is the most widely planted grape in the world and is the offspring of Cabernet Franc and Sauvignon blanc as analyzed by Carol Meredith in her U.C. Davis lab. It probably happened as an unintentional cross in a white vineyard where someone noticed the vine and the way it did well in certain places, an event that was probably replicated in many varietals around the world. So we went with Cabernet and planted Merlot in our vineyard, but it didn't set well because it requires soil with more clay.

Because it's such a small piece of land we focus on the vineyard itself. With such small quantities of each variety we follow the traditional practice of the three, picking them all on the same day and co-fermenting them. This gives us early complexity, but it does challenge us to coax the three varieties to ripen at the same time and to understand the blend in the field. We work hard to bring to bring the three varieties to maturity. It's a challenge to get the tannins supple. It's done by manipulating the crop in the vineyard and harvesting less green, more mature berries. For instance, we crop Petit Verdot as it tends to ripen later than Cabernet Sauvignon, and if it's still behind in véraison we *crop it again. We time pruning and tightly control crop levels to accomplish this. Over the years we've fine-tuned the ratio of these varieties in the vineyard to reflect the characteristics we want in the wine. Cabernet Franc, which is very attractive on Diamond Mountain, brings a floral, flinty note to the wine that lifts the aroma and complements the characteristics of the Cabernet. Over the years we have increased its percentage from 10 to 17 percent. Timing of different stages of fermentation, fermentation temperatures, and pumping over grape skins is what gives us color, flavors, and tannins.*

*The longer grapes are on the vine, the more character comes from the vineyard. Whether for still or sparkling wine, winemaking requires experience to understand that vineyards ripen at different times. We have a crew that helps us pick and prune. The entire harvest at our vineyard takes four to five hours, and we use Rudy Von Strasser's winery across the road to make 300 to 400 cases of wine. The last few years the number was closer to 300 because of difficulties with frost and rain.*

*Qualitative and quantitative criteria at harvest are different for still and sparkling wines. Ripeness in sparkling wine requires grapes to be picked early to get lower sugar levels. In sparkling wine we look for green apple and slight citrus flavors in Chardonnay and a little more berry, sassafras characteristics from Pinot noir. We watch for maturity and then confirm the findings with lab analyses. We look to pick at 18 to 20 rather than 24 to 26 degrees Brix. Acidity and brightness in flavors are crucial for sparkling wine. Red wines like Pinot noir and Pinot Meunier, a close varietal of Pinot noir, grow successfully in the cold hearts of Europe because their buds come late. Pinot Meunier's color stays a little bluer, so it's easier to extract color. It's also fresher and spicier than Pinot noir. Both Pinots add rose petal quality, fruit flavors, color, and depth. A good Rosé Champagne has a Chardonnay base with red wines blended in. It is the best Champagne for food, since fruit and food are a good combination, but then all Champagnes, including Blanc de blancs made with 100 percent Chardonnay, are perfect partners with food.*

*Winemaking is fascinating because there are no right answers. Wine can't be totally controlled because it's a natural product. Winemaking boils down to lots of plotting, strategies, trouble-shooting, and planning. Illusive qualities are always present. Very few decisions require split-second decisions. It's not like getting onto a freeway in thirty seconds. We make the case by walking our vineyard and taking many samples. Each year is different. Some years the fruit is good, sometimes not. Sometimes the bottles don't settle well and the wine requires a lot of finesse. It's impossible to get enough information into a com-*

*puter. A computer can make it easier, but it can't analyze all the variables or work out problems. Anyway, the gestalt of the process is more important than the computer analysis.*

When asked about ratings, Dyer says, "A great producer can have a poor year where the results won't be great. In a great vintage, every producer, from great to okay, can do a good job. Blanket endorsements and condemnations are frightening. Ratings deny a consumer's personal taste. Not everyone agrees about what's good. Your 84 might be my 97."

## MILJENKO "MIKE" GRGICH
### GRGICH HILLS ESTATE AND CROATIA
### (WITH COMMENTS BY VIOLET GRGICH)

Miljenko Grgich, the octogenarian better known as Mike, says, "The Bible says wine maketh glad the heart of man." His black beret, tilted at a rakish angle, makes him instantly recognizable. I have known Mike for many years. I went to his eightieth birthday party in New York City and congratulated him on his ninetieth in April 2013. I've interviewed him several times, once about his strong feelings as a Croatian during the past war between Serbia and his homeland. Grgich is as feisty today as he was when he left Croatia as a young man. He is the undisputed master of Grgich Hills Winery and continues to take part in crucial decisions at the winery. He is slowly passing the torch to his daughter Violet and his nephew Ivo Jeramaz.

Grgich seemed destined for a winemaking career from the time he was a toddler at the family winery in Desne, Croatia, a region with a long history of winemaking.

*My mama switched me from breast milk to wine when I was two and a half years old, the youngest of eleven children. I told Mama I would die without her milk, but she persisted. I don't know if I was born a happy child or if it was the wine that made me happy. Stomping on grapes wasn't like Lucille Ball's version. The only energy in those days was our hands and feet. There was no electricity or modern equipment at our winery. During the harvest of 1926, I was three years old. My family was busy bringing in the grapes. I was put into a large, empty wooden tank to be out of harm's way. Once in a while they dumped grapes in the tank. I was supposed to stomp the fruit, but when I was hungry, I ate grapes and drank the juice when I was thirsty. I was safe and the grapes supplied me with food and drink.*

Grgich studied enology and viticulture at the University of Zagreb in Croatia but felt strangled by Communism and conflicts with Serbs. "While I was studying at the university, Professor Sherman went to California on sabbatical for six months. When he returned to Zagreb we, his students, asked him how California looked. He answered, 'California, a Paradise with a climate comparable to Dalmatia.'" Grgich left family, friends, and the country he loved for the States. An exchange student program offered by the United Nations in 1954 sent him on a circuitous voyage that began in West Germany. A trip to Canada made it easier to enter the United States. "I was determined to start a career in California as a winemaker, but I was a nobody. I spoke no English. Some winemakers arriving in the U.S. brought vines with them. But I had nothing and so who would listen to me? I had to let my wines speak for me."

Grgich put an ad in the *Wine Institute Bulletin* asking for a job as a winemaker in California. Lee Stewart, owner and leading winemaker of Souverain Cellars, offered him a job as assistant winemaker. With visa in hand, he arrived in St. Helena, Napa Valley, on August 15, 1958, with $32 and a battered suitcase filled with wine books.

"My first job at Souverain was to wash empty barrels and tanks to prepare them for the coming harvest. It was easy to adjust because, as the professor said, the soil and climate of warm summers and rainy winters were like Croatia." Stewart taught him to establish a signature of wine that becomes the consistent fingerprint of a winery year after year.

*It was like the advice my late father gave me about the value of quality and consistency. Both add to the value and prestige of good wines. He always told me, "What you do today, do your best. And every day learn something new so that after 365 days each year you will be the winner and won't have to worry about your future." My experience and knowledge of ninety years helped me to feel and communicate with wines, guiding them to excellence and reliability from year to year. When I drink good wine and it goes down my throat, I want it to give me the urge for more. Every human has up to ten thousand taste buds. The more taste buds, the more sensitive one is to taste. A style in taste is developed through experience.*

After Souverain Cellars, Grgich worked with some of the most famous names in California's wine industry for nineteen years. "I was fortunate to have European roots and to have worked with Napa Valley icons. Brother Timothy at Christian Brothers, the legendary André Tchelistcheff at Beaulieu Vineyards, and Robert Mondavi. I worked with Mondavi in '69. He was crucial because of his personality and willingness to share improvements with others. My history, family, and the Napa experience shaped my style. Every year I try something new. My wines have traces of all these geniuses. I pass this on to Violet and Ivo."

Mike's reference to Violet brought to mind several conversations I've had with his daughter and how her passion for Grgich Hills intersects with her love of music. Violet's comments about the relationship between music, art, and wine are too interesting to omit. At Grgich Hills Estate she spent years working in the cellar and participating in wine tasting in addition to bottling and lab analysis, and found time to get a Master of Fine Arts, specializing in the harpsichord.

*I love to make comparisons between winemaking as a combination of science and art. For us at Grgich Hills, the emphasis is on art. Winemaking blends art, intellect, and science. The highest quality occurs when these elements are in synch. The comparison between art, music, and wine is valid because the best composers, musicians, artists, and winemakers go the extra step to infuse their work with genius. Great wine, like great art and sublime music, should transport you to another world. Artists or vintners need to rely on personal explorations. It is impossible for a musician to play a composition exactly the same way every time. Nor can a winemaker exactly replicate wine from year to year. The best soloists and symphony conductors are famous for their individual interpretations, and, like them, winemakers bring their specific talents and goals to the task of making different wine from their neighbors. The best one person can do is to strive for some measure of balance and control. Critics have a profound effect on perceptions about art and music as well as wine. Comments and numerical ratings impact on a consumer's judgment about wine, a painting, or a concert. Consumers have to rely on their individual dis-*

## GRGICH'S SPIT-ROASTED LAMB

**1 40-lb lamb**
**Kosher salt**

Prepare charcoal fire into four piles on the ground or on concrete—no need to dig a pit. With a knife, cut holes into both shoulders and both legs and pour salt into the holes. Liberally salt the inside cavity of the lamb with kosher salt. Rub salt into the outside skin.

Utilizing a large commercial spit-roaster, tie and truss the lamb firmly to the bar. Arrange the charcoal so each pile is under the shoulders and under the legs. There should be no charcoal under the belly. The charcoal is placed under the thickest parts, so that the entire lamb is done perfectly at the same time.

Roast for 5–6 hours, until thoroughly done, not pink. It is important to rotate the lamb very slowly at the beginning. The lamb should be well roasted, with a deep, rich color, crispy skin, and succulent, tender flesh.

*Carve and serve with Grgich Hills Estate Zinfandel or Grgic Vina Plavac Mali! The spicy characteristics are a marvelous complement to the lamb.*

---

*cernment and observations on wine, art, or music. Winemaking requires care and dedication to small details, like any work of art. Wine helps us see the magic, beauty, and joy of being alive. Variation is good in all aspects of life. No one wants to eat the same meal every day. A different wine can be a soul mate to a change of moods.*

But back to Mike Grgich. . . .

In 1969, Grgich was projected into the spotlight when the Mondavi Cabernet he crafted won first place in a prestigious, tradition-shattering competition. The Paris Tasting in 1976 was a blind-tasting contest between French and American wines in Paris. American wines were to salute the two-hundredth anniversary of American Independence. It was a French attempt to teach American upstarts a lesson in humility. French judges shocked France by giving each of the highest awards to an American red and a white. It was Grgich's Chateau Montelena Chardonnay that pummeled the best of the great white French Burgundies. The unexpected win turned the wine world upside down and floored the gas pedal for the American wine industry.

"The Judgment of Paris was the biggest excitement of my life," says Grgich. "I felt I was born again. My wine scored 132; the French, 126. The French believed only French soil could produce great wine. The *New York Times* published my picture and interviewed me. Telephone calls from Germany and France added to the excitement. My victory over the best French Chardonnay created a great historical moment for Croatia, California winemaking, and me." The win put Grgich on the map as a world-class winemaker and led him to fulfill a dream of owning his own winery. In 1977, he formed a partnership with Austin Hills and Mary Lee Strebel of the Hills Bros. coffee family. Hills's business experience matched Grgich's vinification skills.

Grgich cast his eye on 20 acres in Rutherford and went through all the problems associated with a new venture: construction difficulties, rights of way, legal compliances, and a host of other unforeseen challenges. When the problems were cleared away, the real work began. In 1979, the winery acquired 79 acres in Yountville that were once part of a Mexican land grant. Loamy soil, pebbly gravel, and exposure to sun were all Grgich had hoped for. His years of toil at other wineries schooled him in Napa Valley terroirs and where and how to plant his new vines correctly. "I picked Rutherford because André Tschelistcheff claimed its microclimate was the best for Cabernet Sauvignon. He said Rutherford dust separates and upgrades Rutherford Cabernet from the rest in Napa Valley." Next, he bought land in Carneros, an outstanding cool-weather site for Chardonnay. In 1980, the Grgich Hills 1977 Chardonnay was acclaimed the best among 221 wines from around the world in The Great Chicago Showdown, another of the winery's countless awards. Grgich Hills Estate produces 70,000 cases of noteworthy whites and reds from 366 acres of their own certified organic and biodynamic acres.

*I was born a farmer and am a farmer. Working with Mother Nature is so much fun. My winery is designed to produce the healthiest and best wine. Growing grapes is like growing kids. Overfed kids by age four are obese. I correlate the same idea with grapes. Biodynamics can produce obese grapes because it adds too many nutrients. Don't overfeed kids or a vineyard. Every innovation isn't better. Vines are the chefs when they absorb nutrients from water and soil. Biodynamics is an add-on to organic wine but isn't necessary. Organic and biodynamic processes are good for grapes lacking life, but once they achieve balance, they don't need more help. I believe a winemaker should find quality in simplicity. A quality product comes from the human touch combined with passion and art, not machinery. After fermentation my wines are moved to oak barrels to mature and get aromas and extractives from oak. When wines are bottled they are moved to the "Honeymoon Suite" for one year to marry aromas and flavors from grapes with extractives and aromas from oak into a bouquet.*

*I look for consistency in quality, for balance and longevity. The winemaker creates the balance between body, acid, alcohol, and tannins. They support each other like members of a family.*

Grgich is fixated on the origins of American Zinfandel.

*On my first day in Napa Valley, I saw a certain grape in the States everyone called Zinfandel. Intuition told me they originally came from Croatia. Then I read a book on American grape varieties and noticed that nobody knows how Zinfandel came to the United States. I recognized those grapes and leaves and became convinced Zinfandel is the same as, or at least a cousin to, Plavac Mali, red grapes, grown on Peninsula Peljesac in Croatia. I was sure California Zinfandel came originally from there. Years later, Dr. Carol Meredith of the University of California, Davis, Professor Ivan Peic, and Professor Edi Maletic did DNA testing to prove Croatia is the origin of Zinfandel. I never gave up. The varietal detection they performed in 2000 proved I was correct. The Crljenak Kaštelanski grape crossed with another local grape and became a new clone with better color and body called Plavac Mali.*

Grgich developed a consuming interest in jumpstarting the Croatian wine industry after the fall of Communism in 1990 at the age when most people consider retirement.

*I didn't go back for personal business, but I wanted to share my knowledge. Under Tito, the industry produced bulk rather than quality wine. They couldn't make good white wine, but made oxidized wines like sherry. Then the industry fell further behind as a result of the Serbian-Croatian War. When I*

*returned for the first time in thirty-six years, Croatian President Frano Tudj-*
*man suggested I do in Croatia what I had done in America. I brought back the*
*knowledge and experience I gained in California's wine industry.*

In 1996, Grgich decided to build a winery on Peninsula Peljesac near
the island of Korcula, where Marco Polo was born.

*Ancient Greeks, Romans, and modern Italians inhabited the island over the*
*centuries. Wine was produced on the island for fifteen hundred years. It is a*
*phenomenal, lovely place, second only to Dubrovnik. In the old days, cus-*
*tomers came with their own bottles. We didn't pull out old vineyards, but*
*cultivated them better. I bought a stone building at auction, originally used*
*by the military as a* karaula, *or border post. It was broken-down after the*
*war, without a roof or windows. I wanted it because it was the best area for*
*grapes. I planted a local red grape, Plavac Mali. We christened the winery*
*Grgic Vina (Grgich Winery). I outfitted the building with modern equip-*
*ment—the best jacketed fermentation tanks made in Santa Rosa, California,*
*an automatic bottling line, a microfilter for sterile bottling, an air-condition-*
*ing unit for the entire winery to ensure proper temperature control, and a*
*complete laboratory setup. The cellar was stocked with new French oak bar-*
*rels. We experimented with natural yeasts, finding a natural way to make*
*better wine.*

*The first crush at Grgic Vina took place in 1996. My goal was to produce*
*world-class wines. So far, the winery has been a great success. Many new win-*
*eries in the area follow my example, although at first local winemakers derided*
*my innovations. They thought my white wine was too watery. I have great sat-*
*isfaction to see the quality of my Croatian wines rise and was honored with*
*the award of Vrhunska Vina, or top premium wines. The new winery pro-*
*duces 3,000 cases, half white, half red. The recession scared some people into*
*buying cheap wine. Even now with the recession, we're quality-oriented in*
*business and wine.*

Grgich appreciates the countless medals he received for his California
wines, but the accolades for his Croatian wines are equally meaningful. The
growth of the Croatian wine industry, in conjunction with Roots of Peace,
an organization dedicated to removing minefields and restoring land for
agricultural purposes, is part of his philosophy to share lessons he has

learned over the years with others. Croatia's ten centuries of winemaking are continuing with one hundred wineries making good wine with better equipment and education. A stone monument in Croatia bears his name in recognition of the contribution he made to the land of his birth.

In March 7, 2008, Mike Grgich was inducted into the Vintner's Hall of Fame in the Culinary Institute of America in St. Helena, California. In November 19, 2012, the Smithsonian Institute's Museum of American History in Washington, D.C., inaugurated a two-year exhibit on food and wine that included a hand-crafted bottle of Grgich's 1973 Chateau Montelena Chardonnay, the small cardboard suitcase he carried when he left Croatia, his original beret, and wine books he used at the University of Zagreb.

To sum up, Grgich says, "Winemaking is an art you are not born knowing. It is the continuous story of striving to do things better and to learn how each vintage helps you make the best wines possible. It's all about setting your heart and mind to doing it right despite the odds." Grgich continues to charm guests as he hosts wine-tasting dinners. He advises guests to seek the wine that says "More!" as it goes down your throat. Then he raises a glass and makes the classic Croatian toast. "Zivili!"

## CHRIS PHELPS
### SWANSON VINEYARDS AND AD VIVUM

Chris Phelps and I met for breakfast one morning at Sara Beth's Restaurant near New York City's Central Park. It was our first encounter. Over bowls of oatmeal and an order of eggs he immediately struck me as a gentle man who might have been a poet or a college professor rather than a thoughtful winemaker.

Two events set Phelps on his future path to viticulture.

*In 1957, when I was little, my parents moved to vineyard-covered Livermore Valley, California. They became friends with our neighbors, the Concannons of the eponymous winery. My folks usually drank local wines and Italian varieties like Pinot grigio at the time when Americans relegated wine to the back seat, preferring cocktails and gin and tonics. Mom and Dad became so enamored of wine they purchased between half a ton and a ton of grapes and made Zinfandel and Cabernet Sauvignon at home. As a teenager, I liked digging in the ground for old bottles for my collection, so my parents had me dig a wine cellar like I was their indentured servant. During those winemaking experiments at home, my dad and I were curious as to why some wine tasted good, some bad, and most interestingly, why they never tasted the same from one year to the next.*

Phelps's choice of summer jobs was an indication of his sense of adventure.

*I put myself through college as a seasonal firefighter. A helicopter once dropped my crew and me into a fire in the Sierra Nevada Mountains. We thought we'd put out the fire quickly, but the winds were strong and five of us huddled to-*

*gether surrounded by the fire. At best, we only had a fifty-fifty chance of making it out. Fortunately, our captain knew the best exit and we escaped. A second time, while fighting a fire in Idaho, I met another college kid who was a wine geek. He answered my questions about wine. I suggested he consider the viticulture and enology program at California's U.C. Davis. Sure enough he did. At the time, I was registered at school intent on a degree in geriatrics, until the same guy talked me into the program, where I studied viticulture and French. I took six months off to work with Louis Martini, my first mentor, and after graduation, I spent two years in Bordeaux, taking every winemaking course offered. It was tough at first to understand technical French, but I got through it.*

After the course work in France, Phelps was offered three jobs in Bordeaux while he and his fiancée were vacationing in Nice. One offer came from the highly regarded Chateau Petrus. He sent his acceptance to the winery on a postcard. "I went back to Petrus sure I had the job, but all the positions were filled. It turned out they never noticed the postcard." But after a good laugh about his acceptance of a job with such a casual response, they found a place for him.

*I interned with Christian Moeuix, the proprietor and winemaker at Petrus during the great vintage of 1982. Not long after, I was given a job at a winery supervising forty fermenting tanks. I was a kid, completely on my own, but I worked day and night. My only assistant, Claude, took a two-hour lunch break and left work promptly at six. I was in charge of everything from picking decisions to winemaking. I still can't believe what I accomplished in three months with the help of another mentor, master enologist Jean-Claude Berrouet. I honed my skills in making Bordeaux-style reds. All the time, they were checking me out. Christian offered me a position as founding winemaker at Dominus, the new Moueix winery in Napa. I was penniless and still can't believe I had the gall to reject the offer of a small salary. I also wasn't sure I had the experience. Christian upped the ante, told me to get married and come back to live at Chateau Petrus for the winter. All we needed to do was answer the phone on weekends. What an experience for a Francophile!*

After twelve years at Dominus, Phelps spent seven years at Caymus Vineyards, managing all red winemaking from 1999 through 2002. Swanson

Vineyards persuaded him to join them as winemaker, where he helped lead the winery to its current success.

*I incorporate all my experiences into a full, rich life. I'd be a different wine-maker without my Bordeaux experience. I don't do what other people do, but I'm open to input. Being open-minded is important. Making wine isn't rocket science. Rather, it comes from years and years of experience. Winemaking is 80 percent art and 20 percent science. It's based on your senses, intellect, gut reactions, and emotions, although you need to stay aware of science. You can't be ignorant of chemistry because the wine will suffer. A lot of winemaking is intuition. Women are better at using their intuition and going with their guts, yet I feel I'm more intuitive myself. I think it's better to trust your judgment and your feel over numbers from the lab. You need an instinctive sense of what needs to be done, from planting and farming in the vineyard to harvest, to the steps of making wine, then to bottling and release. There's a learning curve to see where a grape varietal does well, since blanket statements don't cover every vineyard.*

*We have lots of choices during each vintage today. Length of maceration is one factor. We can get residual sugar by arresting fermentation. We can re-move alcohol by reverse osmosis, although I've never done this for reds. We can choose different clones. French clones ripen earlier, necessary in the cooler climate and short growing season in Bordeaux. But we don't need those clones in sunny California, where a golden vintage goes on until October. Swanson isn't dry-farmed. In very rainy seasons, water stays in the soil, so watering is held off until August. However, lack of water develops high extraction and high alcohol.*

*I'm disturbed by current techniques of manipulation in winemaking. Co-dependency between critics and producers creates fads in wine. The tendency to shape styles to please the critics and get good scores is significant and shock-ing. Some winery owners sell their soul to achieve a great score. It's why con-sumers' reliance on critics' scores is problematic. Tasting wine is a very per-sonal thing. Consumers shouldn't hesitate to trust their own judgments. They can go the route of "the devil you know is better than the devil you don't know" and stick with the same old favorite stand-bys. I suggest trying different wines because the discovery of wine is so exciting. It's important to pay atten-tion when tasting red wine, to notice if it's too smooth in tannins or has too much sweetness in the finish. It's best when there is some sense of tannins, texture, and body in the wine. It's also essential to recognize that the alcohol*

# TRI-TIP MARINADE

8 lb top round,
bottom round or
sirloin tip beef
(The recipe adapts
to a lesser amount
of meat)
⅓ cup Worcestershire
Sauce
1⅓ cups water
⅓ cup maple syrup
½ cup red wine
½ cup olive oil
⅓ cup balsamic
vinegar
1⅓ cups soy sauce
2½ oz (or 72 grams)
of ground coffee
1½ tbsp crushed
garlic
1 tsp black pepper

Trim most of the fat from the meat. Combine all ingredients. Marinate 5–7 days in a covered container in the refrigerator. BBQ is good; smoked is best. Direct-heat smoking takes 200°–225°F. Remove at 140°F. internal temperature, wrap in foil, and place in a hot box for at least one hour. Slice thinly and serve at once. Ladle jus over sliced meat. This recipe may be adapted for 24 or 100 lb meat. Adjust ingredients and time accordingly.

*Phelps's recommended wine is a good 2009 Napa Valley Cabernet Sauvignon, specifically the 2009 Swanson Alexis Napa Valley Cabernet Sauvignon. The smoky, plumy, coffee-laced aromas and flavor of the meat meld perfectly with the rich blackcurrant, espresso, and black cherry notes of the wine. The silky tannins in the wine work very nicely with the nearly al-dente texture of the meat. Invite lots of folks to share this experience with you. Serve copious amounts of wine and you will have friends for life.*

This secret recipe, comes from Boy Scouts Troop 1, St. Helena, California.

level can have a wider range than what's printed on the label. It can vary as much as one degree in either direction.

A winemaker only gets a chance to use his skills once a year. I feel, in the last few years, that my job comes down to channeling what the grapes want me to do. My winemaking is based on how the vineyard is handled. I know sunlight, variations in temperature, and water are three important factors that influence vines. Too many or too few leaves affect photosynthesis. With too many leaves, the grapes won't ripen properly, developing off-flavors. Too few leaves also influence flavors. I might be provincial about ripeness, but my goal is to achieve ripe tannins in the vineyard. That concept never fails me.

We need to taste in the vineyard every day to check the correct time for harvesting. What and when to harvest create major moments of anxiety. The crucial decisions in our cyclical enterprise, and winemaking is definitely a cyclical enterprise, occur at harvest. You can check the level of brix, but the *final judgment is based on how the grapes taste. My most important decision is to judge when the grapes are ripe. It can be that only half of the vines are ready in a particular block in a vineyard. For example, unripe Cabernet grapes have too much acid and unripe tannins. Grapes with too much hang-time on the vine develop less fruit and more raisiny flavors, making the wine taste like Port. I want fruit, not raisiny flavors, so my goal is the opposite of long hang-time. My objective is to shape wines of great balance, refined texture with singular aromatic and flavor profiles that evoke their place of origin. When I make a Cabernet Sauvignon–Merlot wine, I want it to have balanced acidity, ripe tannins, and flavors that melt in the mouth.*

*Many of today's wines are overoaked and too high in alcohol. It's fairly common to add extracts of oak or grape tannins to wine. Concentration adds tannins to wine, adjusts astringency, and adds color. Some wineries use oak chips instead of barrels for an oaky flavor. Adjusting sweetness is achieved with concentrate when wines are overextracted. Sometimes winemakers add water to wine to cut alcohol. We joke these are "Jesus units." I'm old school and believe it's unnatural, exploitative, and cheating. I avoid those techniques as dishonest. I don't want to fight a wine to drink it. A good wine should reflect where it comes from without manipulation. In the end, honesty will win out.*

Besides his full-time job at Swanson, Phelps, at the urging of his entrepreneurial son, releases his own wine.

*I was hesitant to take the leap because I always worked for someone. But I made the leap and produce a new wine called Ad Vivum. Viv is the Latin root for both "life" and "wine," so Ad Vivum is the journey where life and wine meet. It is the equivalent of L'Chaim, the Hebrew term for "to life." In 1990, I met Larry Bettinelli, a grape-grower in Napa who for years gave me a ton or two of different grapes that helped me learn more about a vineyard. In 2005, I made wine from the former Reese Vineyard. It's now Sleeping Lady Vineyard. It's set right on a bench against the Mayacamas Mountains. I knew right away these wines had a different twist that makes them tantalizingly different from other Napa Cabernets. In 2007, at crush, there was a Eureka moment because of the wine's color, richness, and overriding distinction of aromas and flavor signatures. I knew then I wanted it to be my own wine. At the start, I made it for friends and for communion wine. Now it's four vintages with an output of 900 bottles.*

Asked about how wine is priced, Phelps recalls a high school media class that taught him about snob appeal.

*I decided it was important to price carefully. It's comparable to negotiating a salary. If you negotiate too low, you can't go back and change your mind. Wine must be separated from passion. It has to make money and guarantee a return on your investment. High costs—land, federal and state permits, label design, and barrels—make the venture capital-intensive.*

*Since a composite of significant details adds up to an excellent finished product, it's important to tread a true line with integrity. Wines I've made in the past thirty years straddle that line. Wine should be good at release and still taste good in fifteen years. If a wine tastes the same from beginning to the end, it's like listening to a symphony without dynamics or different tempos. A wine should be like a person who wants to make a good impression.*

Phelps offers this advice: "Don't look for a wine's flaws before seeing the good points. Find the positive and give the wine a chance. The same is true when you meet people." Those words confirmed he was indeed a poet and a gentle man.

# MICHAEL SCHOLZ
## ST. SUPÉRY WINERY

It's said you can't go home again, but winemaker Michael Scholz returned to St. Supéry after an eight-year hiatus. Scholz's profound impact on the winery was enough for St. Supéry to invite him back. "I left in good spirits and never thought I'd be back," says Scholz. "Then I saw the opportunity to bring my personal vision to St. Supéry's portfolio of Napa Valley Estate wines. I look back fondly on the period from 1996 to 2001 as a time of great accomplishment for St. Supéry and me. I am thrilled to work again with the two estate vineyards and the St. Supéry team to see where we can take the winery in the future."

Scholz's accent shows his Australian roots as the sixth generation to grow up on the family's vineyard in the Barossa Valley.

*My great-great-great grandfather came to Australia not as a convict, but for religious freedom. He settled in a large German community in the Barossa Valley, where he had bought property sight unseen. My mother and winemaker brother and I run the winery today. Five generations of my family are doctors, but my high school teacher decided medicine wasn't for me. It was easy for me to find a career in winemaking. It was all around me, with many family and friends in the business. I studied winemaking and liked the concept. I found it's been a good gig.*

*St. Supéry's good, clean portfolio includes several classic wines. At St. Supéry we are an estate winery, meaning we make wines using only grapes from our own 500 acres of vineyards. We're pretty centered here with what we do, selling popular varietals. Sauvignon blanc and Cabernet Sauvignon are at the core of the winery's program of about 90,000 cases every year. We have a Bordeaux focus with a desire to make quality wine that is round, centered,* and charming. The winery makes several primarily Cabernet Sauvignon wines each vintage. Our Bordeaux-style red Élu is dominated by Cabernet Sauvignon. It is a special, limited-edition Bordeaux blend from our Dollarhide estate. It is blended with Merlot and some other red varietals we grow, like Petit Verdot, Malbec, and Cabernet Franc that are also Bordeaux varietals. St. Supéry also has two more Cabernets in its portfolio. Our ringers are Moscato and Chardonnay.

Cab can be a big, bold, robust wine with tremendous appearance of big colors and hue of reds and purples, especially when it's young. These wines have a lot of texture because of the tannins, and when they're young, they may be hard to drink. I think those characteristics are typical of Cabernet. It can be quite a brute without toning down. A little bit of Merlot does the job, and other times it's Malbec. Typically, the aromatics follow through to the flavor and will evolve in mouth-feel as well. Aromatics of ripe berry, blackcurrant, or cassis are fairly consistent in Napa Valley.

Cabernets need patience, which is also part of the varietal's tradition. They may be slightly immature as a three-year-old wine and should develop interesting characteristics as a six-, seven-, or eight-year-old wine. I want a wine to be drinkable in three years, but I also want it to have the ability to improve, which it will do in the bottle. Those who choose to drink Cabernet should recognize they can drink it early, but if they cellar it for two extra years, the difference will be dramatic. The wine will have softened a little but will still have great structure and increased complexity.

Sauvignon blanc is another exciting varietal, especially here in California. Ours is a true expression of this variety. First, we do a terrific job growing grapes at our Dollarhide estate. I try to harvest Sauvignon blanc at the point of optimum flavors. We take a simple approach to making this wine, fermenting it in stainless steel. The grapes have good flavor when we harvest, and our challenge is to capture that flavor in the wine. I don't mind a hint of a grassy component together with grapefruit and citrus aromas and flavors. The grassy component is part of the varietal characteristic. In California, in the '80s, Sauvignon blanc was produced a little on the ripe side and it was fashionable for it to see a little oak. Overoaked Sauvignon blanc can taste a bit like Chardonnay. St. Supéry Sauvignon blanc style leans toward the Southern Hemisphere style, yet with the stamp of our Napa Valley vineyards. Our style is very expressive, crisp, and clean. Sauvignon blanc is a great spring and summer drink, and works well with food such as salads with vinaigrette dressings, lighter dishes prepared with fish, shellfish, and white meat. It's really a terrific *wine. Virtú is a Sauvignon blanc and Semillon blend. In addition, there is a 100 percent estate Fumée blanc style that sees a tiny bit of oak. A third white is a blend of Sauvignon blanc and Semillon, sometimes Semillon dominates. To get exactly what we want, we start and continue to blend and adjust.*

*It's surprising to see the number of people who don't want a dry wine. Many of our visitors prefer a sweet wine, so we make a Moscato that began as a wine for the winery's visitor's center. Moscato is one of the hottest items we sell here on site. Our Moscato, made from Muscat Canelli, is not complicated, but an expressive, rich, light wine excellent with a basket of fruit aromatics that burst out of the glass. If you pour a glass of Moscato, you can catch all the aromas without lifting the glass because the wine's nose is quite vibrant. Some vintners pick to get 3 percent sugar, but our style is a bit sweeter. It's not a late-harvest wine, but the grapes hang on the vine a little longer to achieve our style. We maintain acidity so the wine doesn't appear thick and cloying. Our Moscato is quite clean and crisp, great with some food and always with dessert, sorbets, or fruits and with a few Asian dishes. Otherwise try it as an aperitif on a summer's night. With only 10 or 11 percent alcohol, it's not a big wine, but it's very impressive.*

*Every vintner wants to take nature's raw materials and come up with a product that is significantly personal. Yet as much as I like to be creative, the terroir of an individual vineyard, the soil and climate where it's located, dictates the core and heart of the wine. Our terroirs are crucial. A similar topography exists in some regions around the world and grapes can grow quite the same over vast distances. Yet, here in Napa Valley, the terroir of Oakville, for example, is different from that of nearby Rutherford. Therefore, my time is worth as much in the vineyard as it is in the winery making wine. If I use two different vineyards, my wines will not be as identical as if I used only one.*

*The way wine turns out is based on terroir, our vineyard management decisions, barrel plans, and countless other factors. I do a lot of things to give me more options. For example, oak selection is very important to wine and it's one of several factors over which the winemaker has some control. Because variations between barrel suppliers differ immensely, I need to keep my style similar all the time, so I do trials and choose what performs best for St. Supéry. Some winemakers may choose American barrels, but I'm using French oak from terrific forest sources that work for me. Every year, I buy a handful of barrels in small lots of two to four to try, and I search for new opportunities. If one of my suppliers starts to slip, I already have a good idea about where*

## SCHOLZ'S FOIE GRAS FRENCH TOAST
## WITH MOSCATO APRICOT GLAZE

8 oz foie gras
8-day-old baguette
  slices, 1 inch thick
3 large eggs
2 tbsp butter
¼ cup milk or cream
Kosher salt
Freshly ground white
  pepper
½ cup apricot
  preserves
½ cup St. Supéry
  Moscato

Slice the foie gras into 8 1-oz slices and season lightly with salt and pepper on both sides. Heat a small sauté pan over high heat. Sear liver slices for about 30 seconds per side. Remove from pan. Slice each baguette piece down the center, not cutting all the way through, to create a "pocket." Place a piece of foie gras inside each bread slice.

In a shallow bowl, beat eggs well and incorporate milk. Add about ¼ tsp of salt and ⅛ tsp of white pepper. Dip each bread slice into egg mixture until well coated. Heat a sauté pan and add the butter. Cook the toast on each side until golden, about 3–4 minutes.

Combine apricot preserves and Moscato in a small pot. Cook over medium-low heat and stir until well combined and the mixture attains a syrupy consistency. To serve, place two pieces of toast on each plate. Drizzle apricot glaze over top.

SERVES 4.

*Serve with St. Supéry Moscato. A dry wine would throw off the flavors of the sweet preserves and delicious wine.*

*I can go for replacements, since numerous options exist among barrel suppliers. There are other style parameters, such as fermentation temperatures and maceration time on skins. You have to multiply all these factors on a probability chart to understand the effects on wine.*

*Winemakers are strongly linked to the potential of the vineyard and their own winemaking goals. It's important to respect what nature gives. Ultimately, it comes back to the vineyard coupled with a winemaker's goal in choices made about vinification. Variations in wine take place around color, flavor, and structure. Harvest decisions are a very important factor when it comes to flavor.*

I asked Scholz how he handles all the varietals. He explained there is a chronology to harvest.

At harvest we're working like crazy, and I start knocking off the dominoes in the order they come in: Sauvignon blanc is the earliest and biggest part of our production. Then Semillon rolls in. Then Moscato. By the end of September, we're done with whites but we've barely started with reds. Vintners differ dramatically about the correct time to pick reds. We pick our reds through October. So managing harvest is easy because it lays itself out. Tasting grapes determines when I call for a harvest. I make sure I'm also familiar with all the numbers from the lab. Brix tells you what's happening in the field and is a guide to flavors in the vineyard. Some wineries pick at 23 degrees brix, while vintners looking for rich, ripe wines pick at 27–30 degrees brix. Each decision leads to totally different goals. There's a great difference between 23 and superripe 28 degrees. All the factors tell me what to pay attention to.

I haven't studied organic versus nonorganic grapes in any scientific model, so I find it difficult to say if organic is better. The biodynamic approach to viticulture with farming to phases of the moon is similar to what some older-generation farmers in the Barossa Valley have always followed and one must respect those guys with their vast experience. Here at St. Supéry we have earth-friendly ethics and both of our vineyards are Napa Green certified. Although we spray our vineyards to maintain quality, we do not use synthetic or nonbiodegradable products. The reality is that sustainable farming produces healthy vines and leads to better fruit.

Many winemakers in Napa Valley are going for a specific vineyard or appellation designation more and more frequently. Today we are well informed about specific appellations, like those in Bordeaux and Napa, and we strive to learn more about site-specific, vineyard-designated locations. I think knowledge about wine is burgeoning and buyers find it interesting to spin that knowledge down from district to district, and then vineyard to vineyard. Some consumers find this confusing, whereas others strive to use the information to expand their appreciation. Visitors to Napa Valley who want to learn more about grape growing and winemaking are encouraged to visit the St. Supéry Estate Vineyards & Winery and its education center in Rutherford.

Dramatic results occur as a result of terroir, but if three different winemakers craft wine from the same blocks, each will come up with a wine that shows the profound influence of their vision. It's what The Winemaker's Hand is all about—the personal artistry of winemaking. Wherever we winemakers work, our attitudes from vintage to vintage are like a collection of short stories with a common theme. As a winemaker, I have ideas of what appeals to me. I take a unique approach to my wines. I bring all my knowledge and tools I've *learned over the years to craft wine. Completing harvest and getting through tenuous times are very rewarding.*

When asked if he had a favorite wine to produce, Scholz says,

*I'm not sure I decided on a favorite variety to produce. If I had to pick one variety, in Australia it would be Shiraz. But in Napa Valley, the exciting and challenging variety is Cabernet Sauvignon. I hesitate to say which wine is my favorite to drink because I find all wines interesting. I enjoy doing different projects all through the year. Going into the vineyards is a big part of what I enjoy, while paperwork and administration is a fine part of the job, but less exciting. I look forward to upgrading our cellar and implementing some new features. I am fortunate to have the ability to craft the styles the winery has today. Some of our wines illustrate their varietal expression while others are thoughtful blends.*

## Spring Mountain District

Look for signs of ancient trails used by American Indians and early settlers to crisscross the steep terraces of the Mayacamas Mountains. The rugged region, replete with meadows and woods, is named for its many springs rather than for the time of year. It is situated between Napa, Sonoma, and the Santa Rosa Plain. Spring Mountain, perched on the western side of Napa Valley, seems to be a distant outpost, removed in time and lifestyle from the sophisticated environment of some Napa Valley AVAs. It's not near enough to jog to town for a newspaper or carton of milk from any of the relatively small wineries. The Pacific Ocean and San Francisco Bay exert a profound influence on the area, and it is the wettest, coolest appellation in Napa Valley. Local vintners overcome the demands of Spring Mountain's difficult terroir, where grapevines struggle to survive in steep hillsides, higher elevations, and harsher weather of the Mayacamas Mountains. Fog plays an important role in the region known for its emphasis on red wines grown on a mix of sedimentary and volcanic soils with low fertility that yield small crops. Ironically, grapevines in inhospitable environments often produce wines of concentrated flavors, well-balanced tannins, and good acidity. Cabernet Sauvignon represents 90 percent of production, followed by smaller plantings of Merlot, Cabernet Franc, and Petit Verdot. Chardonnay makes up 50 percent of white wine production.

The first vineyards on Spring Mountain were planted around the time of the Civil War. As happened in many wine regions, the double whammy of Prohibition and phylloxera put a damper on the growth of the entire American wine industry, including Spring Mountain wineries. By the late 1960's and 1970's, several wineries revived winemaking on Spring Mountain. In this rough-hewn area, winemakers eschew corporate methods and mass production.

Even though it was one of the earliest districts to make wine, Spring Mountain District AVA waited until 1983 to be officially established as an American Viticulture Area. Only about one sixth of the area is vineyards, 80 percent planted in red grapes. Given the small crop yields on hillsides, around thirty winegrowers produce less than 2 percent of Napa Valley wines.

It takes nerves of steel to drive up the rugged, winding roads along patches of deep woods where only a few scruffy wooden signs point to wineries off the narrow road. Finally, you reach the rustic Smith-Madrone Winery and its tasting room at the highest point in the district.

## STUART SMITH
### SMITH-MADRONE VINEYARDS AND WINERY

I sized up big, bearded Stu Smith as a guy you would trust to get you out of the woods and away from the big, bad wolf if you were lost. Stu is clearly a product of the 1960's. Right away you sense he is absolutely unafraid to voice his opinions. The former captain of his high school football team, a shot-putter and volleyball player, a lifeguard on a Santa Monica beach, where he made the princely sum of $2.96 an hour, has a reputation as a contrarian with strong viewpoints.

*I grew up at the pre-Cuisinart, pre-wine time. There wasn't even a pizza joint in Napa and only one good restaurant, called the Grapevine. During those years, everyone cooked roast beef until it was gray. Ditto for vegetables. Monterey Jack was an exotic cheese. We never had wine on the table, but my folks had a couple of pops of perfect Manhattans every night. My father had two double martinis at lunch and played golf until the end of his life. Our stepmother spooned a Manhattan cocktail into him in the hospice, and he died with a smile on his face at ninety-four and a half.*

Smith studied economics at U.C. Berkeley in the mid-1960's during two important events—the protest against the war in Vietnam and the revolution in food and wine that erupted in San Francisco. The revolution in food and his burgeoning interest in wine pushed him into an introductory viticulture and enology class at U.C. Davis.

*I didn't cook well, but I learned to love wine. I had to play catch-up in a science program in plant physiology and chemistry in order to go to graduate* school. I was a student with no money when my brother Charlie and I syndicated a partnership with family and friends to start Smith-Madrone Winery. We chose the name as a tribute to the Smith family and to the evergreen Madrone trees on our property that bear lily-of-the-valley-like flower clusters in spring and orange-red berries in fall. My relationship with my brother is like a good marriage. He's often off to play croquet for a week. I'm into canoeing and camping. We agree, or if we disagree, we resolve it.

Making wine is a lot like cooking fish. Start with bad fish, and there's no amount of money or time that can make it good. It's why Charlie and I needed to be in Napa. It is the place to make world-class wines, a great American viticultural area where it's possible to make the best of the best. We searched and finally found the perfect site on the highest point in the Spring Mountain appellation above St. Helena in 1971. We chose the highest point because Bacchus loved the hills.

Smith says growing great grapes can be compared with a three-legged stool that collapses if one leg is missing.

The right terroir for grapes to flourish is the first leg. California is obviously better than Alaska. The terroirs must be differentiated more closely, which is the reason for specific appellations. Second, grapes need appropriate soil. Soils with moderate fertility and depth are perfect for premium wines. The mountains provide us with good grapes grown on specific slopes with different exposures. Poorer soils on our steep mountain limit the grape production to a few tons per acre, with smaller berries, higher leaf-to-cluster ratio, and higher skin-to-pulp ratio. In contrast, deep, rich soils produce grapes without character and flavor, producing many tons of low-cost, ordinary wine per acre. Most winemakers agree that vines that struggle produce more concentrated flavors in grapes and thus more flavorful wines. Third, a grower needs to be clear about his goals to maximize grapes for quantity or quality. It's why a very good grower can mitigate some of those issues.

Unlike other farmers, who produce one crop a year, vines will produce for decades.Many growers who want more grapes per ton irrigate. We agree with Mark Twain who said whiskey is for drinking, water is for fighting over. We dry-farm most of our vineyards but use drip irrigation on newly replanted blocks for about five or six years. Then it's tough love for the vines. Our philosophy is a good practice in a world where water is often in short supply for over seven billion people. *Too often it's people with a plentiful supply who don't recognize the importance of a commodity like water.*

*I learned to make wine by drinking Cabernet Sauvignon from Bordeaux, Pinot noir from Burgundy, and Riesling from Germany's Rheingau or the Moselle. Then we started by planting the four great grapes: Chardonnay, Cabernet Sauvignon, Riesling, and Pinot noir, which continue to be the universal standard for quality today. Napa does better than Bordeaux in blended reds, and we make Chardonnay and Riesling as good as anywhere in the world. Riesling is not only a great white, but one of the great wines of the world. At Smith-Madrone we understand the requirements for growing great Riesling grapes. Riesling in German climates has a long and cool growing season. We grow our Riesling vines on southern slopes, so grapes can benefit from the greatest amount of heat and sunlight, because our climate on Spring Mountain is cooler than the Napa Valley floor.*

*Making Pinot noir is like the search for the Holy Grail. Pinot is one of the best and also one of the most difficult grapes to work with. When Pinots are good . . . wow! On the other hand, our American idea to make Pinot noir got lost in the wilderness. In California, you can do just about anything you want, but because you can do it doesn't mean you should. We didn't want to make as bad a Pinot as many French or California wineries do. It became impossible to rationalize producing Pinot from a business point of view. We eventually gave up on it and grafted the vines over.*

*My philosophy of making wine is to get whatever nature imparts to the grape into the glass. The concept of uniqueness derives from a specific terroir and sense of place. Wines from smaller properties reflect a winemaker's personal vision and artistry. My goal is to make wine true to myself, not because the marketplace demands new styles of wine. I want to get the best each vintage offers with certain hallmarks of good wine—a balance between acidity, tannin, and alcohol. If one characteristic dominates, complexity is lost and the wine is too one-dimensional. Complexity is a result of many little things. Results are bad when these characteristics are delivered in large quantities.*

"At Smith-Madrone we accentuate our positives. We don't mimic other terroirs, sites, or styles." Smith experimented with blending red and white wines.

*I tried blending Riesling with Chardonnay. I got down to 2 percent of Riesling in the blend, dropped it to 1 percent, but it still dominated the Chardonnay.*

# SMITH-MADRONE SPRING MOUNTAIN
## RED WINE RISOTTO

*The experience of watching Stu set up his Scout camp stove to heat the pot of broth and also cook the enormous pan for the risotto is hard to capture in a home kitchen.*

2 sticks of unsalted butter
8 oz olive oil
2 onions, minced
6 quarts chicken broth
2 lb Carnaroli or Arborio rice
½ bottle Smith-Madrone Cabernet Sauvignon
Minced fresh Italian parsley
Freshly grated Parmesan cheese

Pour chicken broth into a large pot and heat over a medium flame. Bring almost to the boiling point. The broth should be hot and steaming, but not boiling. Place a ladle nearby.

Melt butter in a large pan, then add olive oil and gently heat. Add chopped onions and sauté until soft. Add the rice and stir, coating all the grains with the oil/butter mixture. Add the wine and stir until it's absorbed and the rice grains take on a pinkish hue. Now add ladlefuls of the hot broth, stirring constantly. Only add another ladle when the previous one has been absorbed and there is no excess liquid in the pan. This will take about 30–35 minutes. After 25 minutes, start tasting until the grains of rice reach the softness you like in a risotto. (Some people prefer risotto soft or al dente.)

Garnish with finely minced Italian parsley and Parmesan cheese.

*This hearty risotto is a perfect partner for Smith-Madrone Cabernet Sauvignon, not only because that wine is part of the dish. The richness of the finished rice and cheese contrast with the power and finesse of the Cabernet flavors. The play of tannin and acid goes well with the richness.*

Now our Rieslings and Chardonnays are 100 percent of each varietal. We ultimately came up with styles perfectly suited to our winery that reflect the terroir of our vineyards and us as grape growers and winemakers. In some viticultural areas, Chardonnay requires a lot of manipulation, but it's in the right place at Smith-Madrone. It does well without blending. We ferment the grape juice and age it in barrels where it "does its thing" until it's bottled. We planted some Merlot as an option for blending in our Cabernet Sauvignon, but ultimately realized that Cabernet Franc made us happier than Merlot. Merlot has its place, but it proved to be more prominent in the blend

## SMITH-MADRONE GRILLED BUTTERFLIED
## LEG OF LAMB

*Try to serve at an elevation of 1,900 feet if you can.*

1 (4–5-lb) butterflied
leg of lamb,
trimmed of excess
fat and sinew from
one 6½-lb bone-in
leg of lamb
Olive oil
Fresh herbs
Salt and pepper
Bottle of red wine,
preferably
Smith-Madrone
Cabernet
Sauvignon

The day before: Rub the lamb with olive oil and place in a container large enough to hold it with several branches of fresh rosemary, sprigs of fresh thyme, one roughly sliced onion, one roughly sliced orange, pepper, salt, a bottle of Smith-Madrone Cabernet Sauvignon. Marinate in the refrigerator overnight. Let lamb stand at room temperature 1 hour before grilling.

Prepare barbecue (medium-high heat). Place lamb on grill rack. Cover barbecue and open vents; grill lamb until instant-read thermometer inserted into meat registers 130°F for medium-rare, turning occasionally, about 25 minutes.

Transfer lamb to cutting board; let rest 10 minutes. Cut lamb crosswise into ½-inch-thick slices. Transfer to platter.

SERVES 10 TO 12.

*Pair with the 2009 Smith-Madrone Cabernet Sauvignon.*

than we anticipated. Cabernet Franc is cleaner and more precise and gives us interesting flavors and aromas.

Consumers need to recognize that good wine isn't made in a factory where consistency is the goal. Some wineries, particularly big ones, maintain a reliable style from year to year. Smith-Madrone is subject to Mother Nature's whims, both good and bad, making it impossible to reproduce wine exactly the same from one year to the next. It causes adventures in the vineyards and the winery. Anyway, I think consistency is the hobgoblin of little minds. Winemaking is challenging because each vintage is unique and often hard to repeat, even with the same grape variety.

Smith, like every vintner, has gone through a few difficult times at the winery.

*Heat made the '84 vintage the most difficult. It was physically exhausting to work twenty-four hours, seven back-to-back days. It added up to 127 hours. In 2008, because of smoke taint from nearby forest fires, we sold off our entire red wine vintage. The most psychologically stressful was 2010, when rain and cold held back ripening. Luckily, it warmed up in October. If it had been a normal, cool October, we'd have been toast.*

*Phylloxera is making it necessary to replant the vineyard. Some white blocks and all of the red blocks are being replanted block by block, especially if we want to change the spacing, row direction, or varietal. It is a slow process to replace the individual vineyard blocks destroyed by phylloxera. It's a slow process stretching out as much as fifteen years. Working slowly allows us to replant vine by vine, to change spacing and start new blocks of white grapes. Going slow is the most difficult way, but it's cheaper than doing our entire 38 acres all at once, especially since it allows us to keep going with production of 4,000 cases.*

The wine business is expanding in California and throughout the world. Smith is watching wealthy boys and girls who come into his industry and think they are in a glamorous business without understanding all the hard work it takes to be successful. "It's the reason there is more overly complicated and more atrocious wine today than I remember in all my forty years in the business." Smith rejects new French oak, high-alcohol wines, the high prices of Napa wines, irrigation, and numerical ratings of wines from wine writers like Robert Parker. He holds Robert Parker and some wine critics partly to blame for pushing winemakers to create the currently popular style of high-alcohol, low-acid wines in order to achieve good ratings.

*Forcing grapes to achieve high alcohol is like trying to put a round peg in a square hole. Parker's standards for high-alcohol wines violate the first law of wine and lead to overripe prune and raisins flavors. I call this the Porthos or Three Musketeers style in a flagon of red wine—flat, simple, and boring, lacking brightness of fruit or good aromas. We should give up vintage dating if, for the sake of good ratings, winemakers aim for continual similarity.*

*Perhaps there are absolute standards for quality, but standards have soft edges. Wine quality has unfixed parameters. It's the reason it's hard to articulate why a wine is good. Numerical ratings in magazines lead consumers by* the nose. Many people are afraid to admit they don't know everything about wine. It would be far better for the average consumer to know it's okay to make a subjective response as to what they like and if a wine tastes good or bad.

A small group of sophisticated wine aficionados finds the idea of terroir and the entire winemaking process interesting. They are curious about brix levels, blends, fermentation, yeasts, and barrels. But I think all that information is too specific and unnecessary to the enjoyment of wine, like asking how many angels dance on the head of a pin.

Rather than relying on other people's judgments, Smith recommends wine lovers organize a vertical selection of one winery's offerings.

It's a way of getting an overview of a terroir and the diversity between vintages. I suggest organizing a personal tasting by brown-bagging a selection of wine recommended by Robert Parker or any other self-exalted wine critic who grades wine for a magazine. That way it's possible to judge if a rating system is in accord with your sensibilities. It's a way of finding if your personal judgment is compatible with a critic's high, middle, and low marks. Everyone is afraid to be wrong in a blind tasting, but it's human nature to be fallible. We're not robots. What tastes great in the morning after a good night's sleep may not taste the same way after a fight with your wife. The most important thing is to trust your taste. When I was in school, we had tastings in black glasses. It's hard even for experienced vintners to tell a Bordeaux from a Burgundy when poured into a black glass.

Asked when was the last time he mixed two wines up, Smith replied, "Not since lunch."

Biodynamic principles based on the preaching of Rudolph Steiner, the German Theosophist, gets Smith's back up.

Many principles of organic farming Steiner proposed in 1924 go beyond organic ideas. Some famous vineyards, including Zind Humbrecht in Alsace, Burgundy's hallowed Romanée-Conti, and Mike Grgich use at least some of the Steiner techniques. My blog, biodynamicsisahoax.com, unequivocally throws down the gauntlet at fans of Rudolph Steiner's theories. Steiner had no experience in agriculture. Steiner was a flim-flam man like Timothy Leary and P. T. Barnum. One of his claims, planting by phases of the moon, worked *for the ancients before there were calendars. Today we rely on satellites and technology for information about weather. Burying manure in cow horns to enrich the soil can't hurt, but it creates a false idea that biodynamics has an exalted status over organic and sustainable farming. People today make all sorts of assertions with little or no connection to the truth, and biodynamics is added to the list. It's poppycock, a whacky cult, a hoax built on magic dust, as worthless as animal sacrifice. It deserves the same level of respect we give to witchcraft. I put Steiner in the same category as gremlins and Lemurians. I'm schooled in science, so I'm intolerant of claims that biodynamics is an ancient peasant custom used to heal the earth and make better wine. It boils down to Faith vs. Reason. Show me scientific evidence biodynamic soils and vines are healthier and biodynamic wines are better. Unfortunately, no scientific studies prove the theory's efficacy. And, to go one step further, it's equally possible to have good soil and make bad wine. If the Steiner assertions are true, I'm sure many of us would consider converting to biodynamics. At best, it's a great marketing tool because it sounds important to consumers.*

*All wineries, particularly in times of recession find it difficult to sell wines. A distributor does what is good for his business. A salesperson doesn't have a special interest in a particular winery, but tries to make sales unemotionally. A restaurant has unlimited choices about what to put on a wine list and retailers can carry sixty to seventy bottles. By contrast, a winery has to take a more personal approach. A good, distinctive wine needs a story. Ours is simple. We've been farming for four decades, so we're the real deal, not baloney artists. Some customers tell us to raise our prices. Several decades ago, a waiter urged us to raise our prices because the restaurant staff gets bigger tips on higher-priced wines. A restaurateur couldn't sell our Riesling because it seemed too inexpensive. Until Riesling prices rise, customers think it lacks quality and pass it up.*

Wherever Smith travels around the country, he is heartened to see wine on almost every table. "Right now, there is more knowledgeable appreciation of wine than ever before. Americans are head and shoulders above where they were thirty years ago in terms of wine appreciation. Movies, television, and advertisements make wine part of our culture."

Smith has a life beyond wine. The Boy Scouts have played a constant, significant role in his life since he was an Eagle Scout. The former Scoutmaster likes the role of paternalistic grandfather in the movement. He is proud his sons went through the program. "Scouting is more important today than ever before for young men between the ages of eleven and eighteen who are evolving into manhood. Scouting separates a boy from his mother, especially today when too many mothers 'helicopter' over their children, depriving their kids of a sense of independence. Unfortunately, there are fewer rules for guidance today, so scouting is important because it emphasizes leadership, responsibility, community service as well as the pleasures and skills of outdoor life. These are important issues when so many kids are parked in front of the computer."

Smith is an active member of G.O.N.A.D.S., the Gastronomical Order for Nonsensical and Dissipatory Society, whose vintner-members meet monthly for lunch. "I love our industry even though I often disagree with some of its issues. I am privileged to be part of a process that has gone on for eons." He treats guests to barbecues cooked on a camp stove of Smith-Madrone Cabernet-marinated butterflied lamb and risotto. "I believe food gives us life, but wine enhances it. Wine is proof God loves us and wants us to be happy."

# DAVID STEVENS
CONSULTANT

I've known David Stevens for a couple of decades, since his days at Domaine Chandon and Bouchaine Winery in Napa Valley. He's a really fun, garrulous, quick-witted guy with a wide range of interests and substantial winemaking skills. David and I can get together and pick up on any one of a dozen topics from politics to literature to gossip as though our conversation survived a mere hiccup of an interruption. He can turn a mean phrase and should he leave winemaking, he'd make a terrific writer.

*I'm consulting now, and the lessons I learned from my main mentor, Brad Webb, have stuck with me since the beginning of my career. Webb was a politically savvy, clever winemaker with a holistic approach. I think of Webb as the unsung hero, the real father of the California wine industry. He was the first to use stainless steel tanks and good French oak along with fine filtration, filled headspaces in barrels and neutral gas, plus forty-five other things. He taught me making wine is a game of balance and elegance, not a game of power. I learned from him to be calm, to understand that things work out. Those ideas and my past experience with sparkling wine transfer to producing still wine.*

*There are all kinds of consulting possibilities and all kinds of consultants. My fit is project-based. There are clients who buy land who need someone to facilitate their vision. Not all consultants tell their clients the frightening cost of going from grape to bottle. Some are good at extracting money from clients. I need five clients to maintain a good lifestyle. It's hard to maintain even relationships with all of them. If one client gets a rating of 98.... Whoa! It's a no-win game for the consultant.*

*A majority of consultants take on wealthy clients who want to have their own $150 Cabernet Sauvignon. The job is to help them go from a dream to a bottle, an action that is like catching fireflies in a jar. It's a noble cause, but few people understand the virtue of patience. In an era of overnight delivery from Fed Ex and instant communication, people often fail to understand how long projects take.*

Stevens takes on a number of related winemaking tasks. His company, Devon International, was started with two colleagues as a group consultancy. Each partner brought a distinct specialty to the organization. Stevens contributed winemaking expertise. After he left full-time work at a winery, he discovered freedom from a full-time job led to consulting in countries like Macedonia and work with lawyers and insurance companies helping to settle cases related to wine industry problems. He also is called on to judge wine competitions.

I always find Stevens's take on winemaking very unique.

*Modern winemaking is more about power than about balance and grace. Lots of consumers like the current trend toward high alcohol because alcohol, which is sweet, will cover some of a wine's bitterness and astringency. It's like a pinch of salt that corrects off-flavors in beer or quinine water. The problem of high alcohol can be solved with different yeasts and better vinification. Different techniques reduce alcohol. It can be distilled or boiled, which evaporates the alcohol out. There is also vacuum distillation and reverse osmosis (ultrafiltration) that filters water and alcohol out of the wine. I used this process recently for a wine in the United Kingdom. Unfortunately, if you take away too much alcohol you're left with too much bitterness and tannins.*

*I believe that there should be absolutely no sense of the winemaker in the wine. I've worked in Macedonia with the Vranic grape they sell to other Balkan states and European countries. This varietal is a zaftic, or heavy cousin of Zinfandel. They were making wines simply, in big concrete tanks, churning out wines that were lovely when young. It was an interesting experience because winemakers there aren't as collegial as they are in the United States, France, or Spain, nor do they work with French barrels or commercial yeasts. I invited every winemaker to meet with me and was accepted because I wasn't there to compete. As an outside agent, I was successful because I wasn't making money from their product. It took a long time and a lot of explanation to help local* winemakers to understand the world expectation for wine. It was well and good to get them to give up traditional procedures if they wanted to compete on the world stage, producing wine the world would understand. Once they got the message, they invested in new laboratories, processes, and equipment. I advised them not to pull out their vineyards or to plant varieties like Cabernet Sauvignon and Merlot, but rather to continue to use great local varietals made in a high-quality way. That way, there wouldn't be a standardization of fruit, but wine with its own palate of flavors.

Stevens also takes a different stand from many of his peers who laud terroir as the defining influence in vine cultivation.

The consulting experience led me to disagree with U.C. Davis that terroir is based on physical environment, including soil and climate issues, because grapes don't care where they grow. Rather, terroir is cultural. Grapes are like rats in their omnivorous habits. Vines originally grew where a tree fell on the forest floor and provided a light gap. A vine's only interest is sunlight and water. They are able to grow on every type of soil. A vine isn't designed by nature to be trained on trellises. Hope and stubbornness help grapes do well on any kind of soil. Witness how they acclimatize to different soils. For example, they do well in the clay of Carneros; the deep top soils in Walla Walla, Washington; and sandy soils on Long Island. Soils in France vary widely, even within regions like Bordeaux and Burgundy. Grapevines stretch from one end of Italy to the next, adapting to whatever conditions of soil and terroir they grow in. Viticulture isn't about the soil, so there's no need to worry about it.

My fondest memory was making wines from Pinot noir grapes from the Carneros region. It's every winemaker's secret dream to craft a great Pinot. I have wonderful memories of working with Dawnine Dyer, another great mentor, at Napa's Domaine Chandon. It was my first experience with Pinot noir, where it was often paired with Chardonnay as a component in sparkling wine. I'm a totally converted Pinot person because it's fun to make, fun to drink. It's a wine with mystique. It's light and goes with a lot of food. When I get to drink a good one I say, "Oh goody, I drank a Pinot noir." The public consciousness of Pinot noir will be raised when wine drinkers learn about the fruit-driven versatility of the grape. Pinot is a joy, intellectually complex. If a beautiful Pinot were a painting, it would be a wonderful Renaissance work of art with dazzling perspective. Those rich canvases make you wonder how the painters managed to get so much in each work of art. Both the paintings and

## MY DAD'S FILL-THE-KITCHEN-WITH-SMOKE, BUT OTHERWISE PERFECT, HAMBURGERS

*Stevens's note: There is no higher form of hubris than a recipe for a food that has been widely loved since childhood. For most of us, certain iconic foods will never be as good as the ones served on the tables of our youth. Below is just such a faux pas. If this humble outline does not live up to the burgers of one's youth, the author encourages a free substitution of any ingredients and/or techniques.*

1½ lb ground beef
(75% lean)
¾ tsp Cavender's
Greek Seasoning
1 tsp peanut oil
Sliced sharp cheddar
cheese, to taste
4 "Brioche-like"
hamburger buns,
toasted to taste

CONDIMENTS

Thick-sliced raw Walla
Walla Sweet onions
Thick-sliced beefsteak
tomatoes
Mayonnaise
Butter lettuce

Mix the ground beef and Cavender's Greek Seasoning. Loosely form 4 round patties, approximately ¾ inch thick. Make a deep dent in the center of each patty with your knuckle. Heat, on high, a large, well-seasoned cast-iron frying pan. Add the peanut oil. When the surface of the oil begins to quiver, add the patties dented side up. Cook until browned on one side (there will be smoke). Try to avoid the urge to squash the patties into the pan with the spatula. Flip patties once and only once and cook until slightly underdone or to your taste (there will be more smoke). Add cheese. Quickly remove patties from pan and put on a plate and tent with foil. Allow patties to rest for 30 seconds. Place patties in buns and serve with listed condiments (if available).

SERVES 4.

*Pair with lots of a very cold, fruit-forward sparkling wine like Chandon rosé, Pinot noir rosé, or Blanc de noirs. The sparkling wine suggestion is based on the almost magic counterplay of the cold, high-acid wine and the warm, slightly greasy sandwich.*

*the wines are about complexity and balance, not seeking color or powerful imagery.*

*Making Pinot is like walking a tightrope every vintage. That's true of every wine to some extent, but truer for Pinot. An old wives' tale says Pinot is hard to grow, but in truth, it's no more difficult than good Chardonnay if you have the correct climate. Pinot is about balance. It can be funky, but with proper attention it's no harder to produce than Cabernet. Well-crafted Pinot isn't* blended, but it's treated as something virginal and pure. A great Pinot is very different from a poor one. Cheaper Pinots can have poor color because the tannins and phenols that make red wine red are different in Pinot. They aren't stable. When this happens, Pinot often handles like a grape varietal from Mars. When they are pallid, they are blended with Zinfandel, Malbec, or Syrah for extra color. There is an obsession with color in Pinots, but color is an independent variable. We equate quality with darkness of color, but a dark Pinot isn't always good. Extraction simply for color can have negative effects on taste and aromas.

Winemaking is attention to detail. I think of winemaking as a sport with rigid rules determined by science. Winemaking is a science that requires constant planning. The right staff is crucial, the growers have to be on board and the materials all lined up. My goal as winemaker is to play the hand nature deals me the best way I can. Terroir plays a big role in a wine's character, so the deck is stacked for and sometimes against the winemaker. A winemaker has to do the homework—picking cleanly without leaves, choosing the brix level, punching down the skins to keep the cap wet, adding sulfur dioxide, and choosing the right barrels. Finding a good cooper is as difficult as finding a wife. Yeasts are crucial because natural yeasts found on grapes don't do the job.

I was trained to believe diversity is the key to complex and high-quality wines. Sometimes wine is about a specific place. Some of my colleagues are excited when cases roll off the line, or when they see their label in a restaurant. Not me. I'm totally turned on by the creative process. Using grapes from several local vineyards, and selecting new versus used wood helps to achieve desirable diversity. Decisions about early or late blending also make a huge difference. If wines are blended, I blend early, so the wines get to know each other in the barrel. Plus it gives me more time to blend later if needed.

At the moment, it's all about indigenous versus genetically enhanced yeasts. Some yeasts are delicate dancers, leaving flowery, fermentation-based flavors. Other yeasts are like sledgehammers. Yeast, in its infinite wisdom, produces a ton of heat. Yeasts have no brain and if left to their own devices would pasteurize themselves. That's a form of a stuck fermentation. It's not always as easy to correct by adding more yeast. In the old days, there was no way to control the heat. Some wineries use Bentonite because it can remove flavors. Winemakers in the past always hoped Mother Nature turned cold once the grapes are harvested to keep the freshness and characteristics of the grape. It's the way it worked in regions like Germany's Moselle.

Modern winemaking is the poor stepchild of World War II. Industrial compressors were used on liberty ships to cool engines and keep food fresh. After the war, surplus compressors were used to control the temperature of fermentation in white wine. The new technology worked wonders in regions like California's Central Valley. Winemaking is an accumulation of a million small choices and about twenty big ones. It boils down not just to the critical decisions about when to harvest, how fermentation temperature affects sugar to convert to alcohol, when to press off, how to get extraction from the skins, pulp, and seeds. It's all a miraculous change. Tasting a young wine is not even remotely like what it will be like in two or ten years. It's like a long pass in football or like flying by the seat of your pants. It pays to remember Nature bats last.

There are always downsides and surprises to producing wine. Sometimes the winemaker's role is to find out why grapes from a vineyard that has historically produced good wine suddenly make a left-hand turn. Haywire fermentation is often fixable with an inoculation of new fresh yeast. Not all problems are fixable, but we can try with a variety of solutions. I say the solution to pollution is dilution. One moderately undesirable solution is to add a poorer wine to a blend and sell it off as bulk wine. Or it can find a home in a second label.

In my opinion, it doesn't take much to produce a muy macho wine blazing with tannins. Some cult Cabernets that demand major prices are as far from fermented fruit juice as shoe polish. A fork stuck in it would remain upright because the wine is full of bitter, astringent compounds: grape seed and skin tannins, oak tannins, leaves, and stems combined with ethanol to smooth them out. That's the kind of wine I call muy macho.

I appreciate the challenge of crafting a fine drinkable wine. Coca-Cola and Sprite producers capitalize on the consumer's love of fruit flavors. Coca-Cola is basically fruit flavored and high acid—it doesn't look all that appetizing, because it's sludge-colored. The magic ingredients of Coke are lime and lemon essence coupled with a dash of a cinnamon-like spice and a few other simple ingredients. I see wine as an excuse to drink up-market fruit juice on the adult beverage side. The best Pinot noirs walk the line between their fruity nature and tremendous accessibility. These wines are very drinkable, especially Pinot from the southernmost Napa Valley region of Carneros, where they flourish in hot summer days and cool nights. A long ripening season avoids a lot of vegetative notes while accumulating sugar and fruit characteristics of berry, cherry, strawberry jam, and occasionally, a subtle huckleberry flavor in the final ripening stages during the growing season.

*I feel that Pinots are best when drunk young, two to three years after pro-
duction, when they have a bluish, purplish hue and a taste of fruit after the
wine settled down a bit. Wines change in the bottle. Some experienced Pinot
lovers might say the only classic Pinots are produced in Burgundy. A Pinot
from the Carneros district, the perfect environment for growing this varietal,
is fabulous and different from its French counterpart. In some ways, the Champagne district in France is a horrible place to grow grapes—far north, where
there are no moderating oceanic or lake effects, without enough heat to ripen
the sugar needed for traditional still wine. Burgundians who live in the cool
climate often make up for poor growing conditions by chapitalizing with a
little sugar. It's not something they tell consumers.*

*Merlot and Chardonnay are still today's hot wines. Cabernet, at this mo-
ment, is the king of red wines, but wine drinkers who order it are looking for a
big, powerful red wine. Pinot is boxing it out with Sauvignon blanc for fifth or
sixth place. Pinots come in all price ranges, but there are very good Pinots that
sell for $40. The fruit characteristics are there, complemented by interesting
acids, background flavors, and characteristics that come from cooperage or
yeast. Only an occasional Zinfandel or Syrah has some of the same pleasant
characteristics of Pinot. But it's Pinot's complexity and fruit characteristics
that always fill the bill for me.*

*There are, unfortunately, bad Pinots, just as there are bad wines of other
varietals. Consumers who are really interested in this varietal can follow the
trail of Pinot noir zealots, who, like Star Trek groupies, attend meetings like
the annual international Pinot noir celebration. These folks enjoy unraveling
the puzzle embedded in its taste.*

*It's not necessary to open a bottle early or decant young wines. Opening a
bottle several hours early doesn't do anything, since the oxygen barely gets
beyond the top couple of millimeters in the neck of the bottle. I see nothing
wrong with putting most reds in the refrigerator for about half an hour and
serving them slightly chilled.*

Stevens also professes a love for crafting brandy and Port.

*When Domaine Chandon first set up the new winery and vineyards, they
planted a couple of varietals like Folle blanche that didn't make good sparkling wine. They were grapes used to make cognac in France. So they were
distilled and sat in warehouses to age in cognac barrels. Dawnine Dyer did
one control project. I worked with her, spent a lot of time with other brandy*

*producers and found blending brandies to be a wonderful educational experi-ence. At Bouchaine, I made a white Port from Viognier, one of the best things I ever produced. I sourced half a ton of lovely Viognier. Port is also very inter-esting because it is a way of preserving sweet wine. Halfway through fermen-tation, when there are a lot of natural sugars left, a raw distillate of eau de vie stops fermentation. White grapes make white Port, and conversely red grapes make red Port. I once made a Zinfandel Port for a friend's wedding.*

*Consulting fits my personality. It satisfies my boundless curiosity and al-lows me to do something different every day. My motto is, "Have tongue, will travel."*

## TOM TIBURZI
### DOMAINE CHANDON

My long-standing affection for Domaine Chandon, its architecture, beautiful grounds, and complement of sparkling and still wines goes back over two decades. I've attended wine-blending sessions and enjoyed innumerable lunches and dinners at the highly esteemed Étoile restaurant. At a St. Patrick's Day party we attended, sparkling wine was dosed with green food coloring. Chandon's facility never fails to live up to my memory of its excellence. Sparkling wine was its major focus when I first got to know Domaine Chandon. Moët et Chandon, the French parent company of the California winery in Napa Valley, spared no expense to make the American bubbly rise to the top of the bunch. A team of French Champagne experts headed by Edmund Maudière supervised and made suggestions. In the ensuing years, Americans, including Dawnine Dyer, whose chapter appears in *The Winemaker's Hand*, headed the house of bubbles in Yountville.

Today Tom Tiburzi is chief winemaker, responsible for the creation of several hundred thousand cases of a range of sparkling wines. I chatted with Tom over a fabulous lunch at Étoile, topped off with a tour of the winery. Tiburzi spoke of his Old World Italian background. His father immigrated from Italy in 1921. His first job was to help to distribute bootleg liquor with his cousin Ciurli. He went on to be part owner of a hotel where he ran a restaurant and speakeasy. After Prohibition ended, the family moved from Minnesota. His father received one of the first liquor licenses in the state. During World War II the family moved to San Diego. He was too old to join the Navy but wanted to help with the war effort, so he went to work riveting airplane wings. Afterward, he went into wine and spirits distribution, and started a family.

Tom Tiburzi wanted to be an environmentalist and biologist in the 1970's.

*I was a work-study student to pay the bills at Berkeley. It was a time of political change. President Reagan's EPA blacklisted environmentalists. I needed to find a new direction and went into environmental research. I graduated and got married in 1978. My wife Sherri was a cook and worked for chef Philippe Jeanty as a pastry chef at Domaine Chandon before I was hired into the winery. I got caught up in food and wine. I followed an impulse. I dropped off an application for a seasonal harvesting job at Chandon. I told Dawnine Dyer this is where I belong. I followed my bliss. It's a lesson as to why one should listen to intuition.*

*My scientific background, methodology, and experience in conducting research level analysis helped me to understand the ramifications of evaluating grape-growing trials. The trials related to replanting vineyards infected with phylloxera, including issues of vine and row spacing, canopy management, and other crucial decisions. My experience between algae and bacteria cultures and wine are similar, at least in a purely scientific sense, because wine is a yeast and bacteria culture. It was an easy transition for me. Making the research wines as a seasonal employee got my foot in the door, and I made the transition to permanent staff member. My first job was as a lab assistant, then enologist. From there I moved to staff microbiologist, then took over managing the second fermentation in the bottle. My next job was in primary fermentations. Each step brought me closer to being a winemaker. I learned the art of blending from Dawnine Dyer, Edmund Maudière, then blender of Dom Perignon, and his successor, Richard Geoffroy. I made the jump from science to support-winemaking to the craft of winemaking. The art of winemaking was handed down from master to apprentice since the mid-1700's at Moët et Chandon and I've had the fortune to receive this knowledge.*

*I wasn't trained as an enologist, but working with wine, especially base wines for sparkling wine came very naturally to me. After being hired at Domaine Chandon, I took technical courses at U.C. Davis. I headed the microbiology committee at CERA, the California Environmental Research Association for several years. I was a member of the small-scale winemaking committee doing winemaking trials. One particular CERA project stands out. Each*

# TIBURZI'S SEARED SALMON WITH ROASTED BEETS

4 red beets, washed
4 golden beets, washed
3 tbsp butter, plus 2 tbsp
3 large onions, thinly sliced
½ cup cream
¼ teaspoon ground cloves
Salt to taste
1 tbsp extra virgin olive oil, plus 2 tbsp
3 slices bacon, cut into ¼-inch matchsticks
10 cippolini onions, peeled and cut into quarters
¼ cup vegetable stock or canned low-sodium vegetable broth
Freshly ground pepper
4 salmon fillets (5 to 6 oz each)

Preheat the oven to 400°F. Place the beets on a baking pan, cover them with a sheet of aluminium foil (crimping it loosely around the pan), and roast in the oven until they can be pierced easily with a fork, about 1 hour. Remove the beets from the oven, take off the aluminium foil, and set aside until cool enough to handle. Peel the beets using a carrot peeler or sharp paring knife. Cut into large dice, between ¼ and ½ inch square, and set aside. In a large sauté pan or skillet, melt 3 tbsp butter over medium heat. Add the sliced onions, increase the heat to medium-high, and stir to coat with the butter. Continue to sauté, stirring occasionally to prevent browning, until the onions are fully wilted, about 30 minutes. Add the cream and the cloves, lower heat to medium, and continue to cook for 5 minutes, stirring occasionally. Add salt to taste. Transfer the onions to a blender or food processor and puree until smooth. Set aside.

Preheat the oven again to 400°F.

In another large sauté pan, heat 1 tbsp olive oil over high heat and add the bacon. Cook until crisp, about 3 minutes. Add the cippolini onions, reduce heat to medium, and sauté until soft, about 10 minutes. Add the beets, vegetable stock, and remaining 2 tbsp butter. Reduce heat to medium-low, stir gently to incorporate the butter and let cook until the liquid has evaporated, about 15 minutes. Remove from heat and cover to keep warm.

While the beets and cippolini onions are simmering, lightly oil a baking dish or pan with 1 of the remaining tablespoons olive oil. Salt and pepper the salmon fillets and drizzle them with the last tablespoon olive oil. Place the fillets on the pan, skin side down, and bake in the oven until opaque throughout, about 15 minutes.

When the salmon is done, remove it from the oven and set aside. In a saucepan, quickly reheat the onion purée over medium heat. Spread a 6- to 7-inch wide circle of the warm purée in the center of each dinner plate. Arrange the beets and onions on top of the purée. Place the salmon fillets at an angle leaning against the beets.

SERVES 4.

*Pair with Pinot noir or Pinot Meunier. Our Pinot noir made with grapes grown in Los Carneros is a silky-textured wine with fresh fruit flavors that perfectly mimic the richness of salmon, making the match perfect.*

# DUNGENESS CRAB SALAD WITH ASPARAGUS, SORREL, CARA CARA ORANGE, AND VIOLETS

## CRAB SALAD

1 lb Dungeness crab
  meat
2 shallots, minced
1 tbsp olive oil
1 tbsp lemon juice
2 tbsp crème fraiche
2 tbsp chopped chives
Salt and pepper

## ASPARAGUS

20 white asparagus
  tips
2 tbsp extra-virgin
  olive oil
2 tbsp Meyer lemon
  juice
1 tbsp lemon juice
Salt to taste

## ARUGULA PUREE

2 cups packed
  arugula leaves
1 tbsp extra virgin
  olive oil
¼ cup crushed ice

## GARNISH

20 segments Cara
  Cara oranges
4 stalks green
  asparagus, shaved
  into thin slices with
  a vegetable peeler
16 arugula leaves
16 red-vein sorrel
  leaves
16 violets

*For the salad:* Mix together all ingredients and fold together, salt and pepper to taste. Refrigerate until ready to use.

*For the asparagus:* Fill a large bowl with ice and water. Bring a pot of water to a boil. Add the asparagus tips and cook for 1 minute. Transfer immediately to the bowl with ice water using a slotted spoon. Drain and transfer the asparagus to a bowl. Add the extra-virgin olive oil, add lemon juices, and season to taste with salt.

*For the arugula puree:* Fill a large bowl with ice and water. Bring a pot of water to a boil. Add half of the arugula and cook until tender, about 30 seconds. Transfer to the bowl with ice water using a slotted spoon. Drain and squeeze out any excess moisture.

*Pair with étoile Brut.*

member of the team, from different wineries, had a special part of the project, taking the same grapes from the same vineyard block with the aim for each of us to conduct various trials along with a control wine, using the same protocols. We eventually learned using the same protocols and grape source that resulted in wines very different from each other. It took four years of repeating the trial before the control wines were even close to being the same. We had to use yeast and bacteria from the exact same cultures, and the same equipment, including de-stemmers, crushers, shape of fermentation vessels, and punching tools to arrive at the same wine. We learned that differences in tools had a much greater impact on wine style than we had thought. It was clear that it is necessary to understand and control equipment and tools, since slight differences have major impact on end results. Importantly, to fulfill creative stylistic goals, the right winemaking tools are as crucial to a winemaker as the right brush to an artist.

I see wine as akin to conceptual art, something to be consumed and made again. Tastes in art and literature evolve and change. Styles may change incrementally over many years. I can't make wine for everyone. At Chandon we make eight different sparkling wines with different profiles. Chandon doesn't focus on a commodity brand, although I have a lot of respect for commodity products. Some consumers read sophisticated literature. Other people read comic books. I hope consumers will move to a higher level in regard to both wine and literature.

Perception is key to the art of winemaking and the enjoyment of wine. When you're in love and drink a wine, it may become your favorite for the rest of your life. We believe we all taste and feel things the same way, but we don't all respond to sounds and shades of color, temperature, textures, and tastes identically. The number of our individual taste buds and the amount of saliva we make alters our perception of taste. Some of us have more sensitivity to certain aromas and tastes. It's why we use our taste buds, brains, and science as the supporting characters to the art of winemaking. This concept is helpful when our blending team works together. In blending, everyone nominates a wine and explains why it is good for the blend. We add more of this and that to get on track. We have to be cautious to avoid directing the blend to what tastes good. Rather, we need to keep the stylistic goal that we are trying to achieve in mind. Working within structure will overpower personal feelings. As we blend and we see we're on the right course, the variations become smaller until everyone agrees the wine is on the right course. Once the blending formula is set, the cellar creates the blend.

*Then comes the magic. An apocryphal story relates how Dom Perignon, a monastery cellar master, opened a bottle and exclaimed he tasted the stars. Fermentation way back in time was an uncontrolled process. It sometimes stopped and started, producing gas and bubbles that broke the fragile bottles. At first, the bubbles were considered a serious defect in the wine. It took decades before winemakers unlocked the secret of how bubbles became the dominant characteristic of sparkling wine. It took more time to understand how yeasts appearing naturally on grapes create carbon dioxide that carbonated the wine. It took time to solve the problem of exploding bottles by designing heavier glass bottles and stoppers to replace inadequate hemp closures. It was necessary to find a way of getting rid of unsightly remnants of yeast in the wine. Madame Veuve Clicquot invented a system of riddling, or turning each bottle by hand to slowly deposit the dead yeast cells to the neck of the bottle.*

*Chandon turned to mechanical riddling in 1989. Bottles are placed on a palette and revolved by computer. At first the results of mechanical riddling were inconsistent and were corrected with hand riddling. Three to five days of mechanical riddling as opposed to two weeks of hand riddling is cost effective and efficient. It's not a big deal for me. I like it to be noneventful and quick.*

Several elements play a crucial role in sparkling wine.

*Different yeasts determine characteristics in the wine. Some will show fruit flavors; others add creaminess. Dosage is the addition of sugar and wine after the yeast particles have been removed and before the final corking. In the past, dosage was used to mask flaws in the wine. Now dosage tweaks the style we want, creating a balancing act against acidity and sour notes. The amount of sugar can vary in concentration from 400 to 650 grams of sugar per liter. We typically end up between 9 and 12 grams of sugar per liter for a Brut-style sparkling wine. It's a lot of work for the lab to create the many dosage trials we winemakers ask for, but the quality end result is worth the effort. Consumers rarely understand or appreciate the importance of developing the dosage liqueur in the sparkling wine process, I guess it is our little secret.*

*People often ask about the importance of science versus the craft in winemaking. Science helps us be efficient. It makes our efforts reproducible and supports quality control so that the wines have good shelf life. But foremost, it is the winemaker's skills at sensory evaluation and creative instinct that makes the finest wines.*

*Our wines are made from the classic Champagne grapes: Chardonnay, Pinot noir, and Pinot Meunier. The classic tier includes a Blanc de noirs tinged with shades of rose and copper. Brut Classic is our standard bearer, creamy with bright flavor and acidity, Chandon Rosé has a rich mouth feel and depth of flavor, and Riche is aromatic with a lush pallet made with a touch of Moscato. Chandon's Étoile Brut and Rosé exemplify the finesse and elegance that comes with a focused blend developed by four to five years on the yeast in the bottle.*

*In still wine production, the aim is to showcase a varietal from a particular place at specific years. Sparkling wine and Champagne most often are a blend of different vintages. Rather than showcasing a particular vintage, the huge challenge for Chandon's sparkling wine is to produce a consistent wine style profile from year to year. We accomplish that through a judicious use of reserve wines that helps us develop our style. The trick to making sparkling wines is to understand what the base wine blend, or cuvée, tastes like now and how it will evolve in two to seven years so we can create similar wines every year. Wines from previous harvests are available to us when our group is at a blending table. Notes on aromas and other descriptors tell us which base wines should complement each of our sparkling wines. For example, to blend the Blanc de blanc we decide which base wines will be nominated for the blend. The DNA of the Chandon brand is its compatibility with food, so it stands to reason that we talk about food and wine pairings during blending. Our close affiliation with Chandon's restaurant, Étoile, is an added advantage other winemakers don't have because we construct the blends with food in mind after consulting with our chef. For example, a wine has to be delicate enough to stand up to sushi yet strong enough to stand up to wasabi.*

After lunch Tiburzi took me on a tour of the winery with endless rows of stainless steel and concrete tanks. "I keep my eye on new technology," he said, leading me to a complicated electrodialysis machine, an engineering advancement that draws potassium ions from still wines through a membrane to stabilize them when they are exposed to cold temperatures. "This environmentally green process reduces energy consumption as compared with conventional methods. In the winery we focus on safety, quality, and efficiency." He gave an example of cost-efficient, energy-saving ideas like the electrodialysis machine and mechanical as compared with hand riddling.

Tiburzi listed the characteristics of a good winemaker. "First, it's not about the person, but about the wine. Marketing can make a celebrity out of a winemaker, but it shouldn't go to your head. A good winemaker needs a solid grip on the science and art of winemaking. The question reminds me of a remark I think was made by Matisse. 'Creativity and art take courage. It's not always important to do what is safe.' We all want to get to the top, but it's a question of which path we take."

# ERNIE WEIR

## HAGAFEN CELLARS

Ernie Weir radiates Mr. Nice Guy when you meet him at Hagafen Cellars. The winery isn't the fanciest in Napa Valley. Rather, it's a homey, unpretentious place, not one of the flashy, high-end wineries featured in glossy architecture and wine magazines. The tasting room off Napa's Silverado Trail has a small counter surrounded by stacks of wine cartons. Weir maintains he prefers to put his limited resources into vineyards and wine rather than focusing on flash and panache.

Visitors sample a few tots from Hagafen Cellars's wide range of single varietals and blends. "It's a jolly atmosphere, where everyone walks out with a modestly priced purchase. Our shop at the winery is our best sales outlet where we sell 50 percent of our yearly production of 8,000 to 10,000 cases from our 20 acres less than a mile south of the famed Stags leap District and 20 yards from the Oak Knoll District," says Weir. "Our customers want to know more about wine as their sophistication about food grows. My customers come in the door to ask questions, and I want them to feel comfortable with our wine. They often want a relationship with growers, producers, and their products, and they like our casual approach. It's not necessary to be too analytical, although there's room for that too. I want wine to be fun. They feel comfortable wearing sandals and shorts when they smell and taste a variety of wines, and they get to meet a winemaker like me in wine country."

Weir took a serendipitous right-angle journey into winemaking after taking a degree in sociology from UCLA.

*That begat my interest in socialism, which begat my interest in how children are reared, which led to an interest in Bruno Bettelheim, the famous educator who lived in Israel. I went to Israel, learned the language, and traveled through the Mediterranean and Europe. I learned more than I bargained for. My journey opened my eyes to wine and food. I switched to a totally different career path. I honestly believe the grapes picked me. I came back to the States and headed for Sonoma and Napa. I registered at Napa College and took my second bachelor's degree, in enology and viticulture at U.C. Davis. Incidentally, my mother was upset by my preference for agriculture. She wanted her son to be a doctor or lawyer, not a farmer.*

Weir started his new career joining the all-star winemaking team as a propagation manager—viticulturist at the celebrated Domaine Chandon sparkling wine facility in Yountville, a small town and one of Napa Valley's appellations. "Napa is a very cooperative place in terms of sharing information and equipment. I learned marketing from Michaela Rodeno, who became the CEO of St. Supéry Winery. Dawnine Dyer, the winery's admirable winemaker, showed me the subtleties of flavor analysis. Zack Berkowitz and I learned viticulture from Will Nord, the vineyard manager. Working with this talented group was like going to graduate school. Those were heady days, but eventually we all went off in our own direction."

Weir and his wife Irit founded Hagafen Cellars in 1979. Hagafen is the Hebrew word for "vine." The couple's connection to their religion provided an opportunity to create an excellent wine that would also fulfill the ancient Judaic requirement to assure purity of wine.

*My family is an ethnic mix of Ashkenazi, or Eastern European Jews, and Sephardim, who have a heritage that stretches back to the expulsion of Jews from Spain in 1492. We enjoy the mix of cultural influences.*

*The 1970's marked the ascension of cultural pride. We could have gone into winemaking without the headaches of rabbinic supervision, but kosher wine was a wonderful way to address our history. Judaism considers wine a revered beverage. We coupled Hagafen with tradition and excellence. Rules and laws, known as Kashrut, require rabbinic supervision to ensure the wines' purity, which includes the cultivation of grapes through all the steps, from pressing,* and fermentation until the wine is bottled. In some wineries today wine is boiled as it was in ancient times to separate it from wines used for idol worship. Modern requirements for kosher wines changed, so rather than boiling, wine is flash-pasteurized to 185° and then quickly chilled, retaining its flavor in the same way that pasteurized orange juice and milk do. Flash pasteurization fulfills the religious requirement without affecting the wine's flavors. As an aside, some Australians winemakers who aren't affected by religious proscrtptions also flash-pasteurize.

Wine certified as kosher indicates that the regulations were adhered to scrupulously. Both non-kosher and kosher wines accompany Jewish prayers and religious occasions. Three prayers welcome the Sabbath, including one thanking God for the fruit of the vine. A Jewish bride and groom declare their commitment by sharing a glass of wine. More stringent rules govern Passover wine that are an integral part of a Seder. The Seder calls for four glasses to be drunk at the holiday dinner during the reading of the Haggadah, a millennia-old story that celebrates the Jews' escape from Egyptian bondage. Dishes served at a Seder dinner have symbolic meaning. Charoset, a dish of chopped nuts and apples mixed with sweet wine, represents the mortar Jews used when building the pyramids. Dinner, depending on a family's heritage, often begins with gefilte fish, a dish that resembles French quenelles. Some families serve fish fried in turmeric followed by chicken soup with matzo balls. It's often followed by a lengthy meal of pot roast, lamb, or turkey with sweet dried fruits, potato kugel, or pudding and honey cake.

We serve Sauvignon blanc at the start, followed by a rich Chardonnay, an elegant Merlot or Syrah, or Cabernet Sauvignon. There's no harm in adding a fifth glass of intensely sweet late-harvest Sauvignon blanc with dessert. Wine, as always, enhances the meal."

Weir dons separate hats for growing grapes and the humble work of winemaking.

My attention to the two sides of wine production ensures the superb quality of o.ur wines. Fine wine starts in the vineyard with careful vineyard management. I do the best I can, making as few compromises as possible without affecting quality. I interfere as little as possible with the soil, creating a balance that minimizes the impact of chemicals and erosion, matching modern farming

## BRAISED LAMB SHANKS IN CABERNET WINE SAUCE

6 small lamb
shanks—visible
fat trimmed
Salt and pepper—
to taste
3 tbsp olive oil
½ lb brown
mushrooms—
stemmed
½ lb shiitake
mushrooms
10 cloves garlic—split
6 large shallots—split
3 cups chicken stock
(or low-sodium
chicken broth)
1 cup port wine
1 tbsp chopped fresh
rosemary
2 bay leaves

Season shanks with salt and pepper to taste. Heat olive oil in roasting pan just large enough to hold shanks in single layer over medium-high heat.

Add shanks and sear on all sides, for 58 minutes. Transfer to platter. Halve or quarter mushrooms, if large. Add brown and shiitake mushrooms, garlic, and shallots into roasting pan. Cook, stirring occasionally, until lightly browned, about 2 minutes.

Add stock, port, rosemary and bay leaves. Bring to boil, scraping any bits sticking to pan. Add shanks. Cover with tight-fitting lid or foil. Bake at 350 degrees 45 minutes, then turn shanks. Continue baking until meat is tender and just starting to loosen from bone, 45–75 minutes.

Set pan on counter until meat is cool enough to handle. De-fat cooking juices by pouring into fat separator or skimming the top layer after pouring juices into bowl and refrigerating until fat solidifies. Pour some of sauce over shanks and arrange mushrooms on and around meat.

*Pair with Hagafen Estate Bottled Napa Valley Cabernet Sauvignon and enjoy!*

techniques while maintaining the age-old wisdom and traditional values of conservation and land stewardship. I never seek to change what nature provides. It takes restraint and confidence to stand back rather than to think that if some changes are good, more will be better.

In California, there are some better and worse vintages. Protection from frost is a continual headache. There is a window from March 15 to May 15 when fog rolls in from San Francisco Bay, affecting some vines. Whatever the conditions, I strive to take maximum advantage of Napa Valley's natural geology and climate to produce the wine varietals best suited for our terroir.

My job is to let the natural fruit flavors express themselves, but not at the expense of extreme alcohol and tannins. We train our Cabernet Sauvignon grapes in a special trellising system. The vines hang from the trellis in two "curtains" for maximum sun exposure. We're in transition to be certified organic, but I think biodynamic farming is a grandmother's fairy tale.

*We originally bought grapes from a nearby vineyard, but today our own vines grow on well-drained soil perfect for our 8,000 cases of small lot, artisanal, intensely fruity wines. Our first commercially released vintage was harvested in 1980. The winery is a long golf shot away from the Stags' Leap District and a mere hop, step, and jump away from the Oak Knoll District, both lauded for a number of highly successful wineries and excellent terroirs. I am negotiating for an American Viticultural Area (AVA) designation that would include Hagafen Cellars, since consumers are increasingly aware of the added value of appellation designations.*

*I'm always experimenting. I get bored and like the challenge of producing a number of wines, looking for specific qualities in each varietal. I grow our own Cabernet Sauvignon, Syrah, and Cabernet Franc. I make two styles of Riesling, some from grapes sourced from other properties. I always use the same hock bottle because it's familiar to our consumers. I produce different white wines from nearby vineyards. I make a wonderful crisp Rhone blend of Roussanne and Marsanne. Some of these varietals are new to most Americans, so each bottle has to be sold individually at the winery. Years ago a vineyard worker gave me the nickname Don Ernesto, and it appears on the label of our Vin gris, Rosés, and our white and red table wines. A neighbor's Chardonnay grapes touched with Botrytis became my first late-harvest wine. The following year, Botrytis attacked the Sauvignon blanc grapes and I made my second late-harvest wine. Crescendo is the name of our mostly Cabernet Sauvignon Bordeaux blend, and our reserve line is called Prix. Hagafen's sparkling wine, made in the traditional méthode champenoise, is 80 percent Pinot noir and 20 percent Chardonnay. A Rosé bubbly is 85 percent Pinot noir and 15 percent Chardonnay. The sparkling wines are finished it at a facility called Rack and Riddle in Hopland.*

Weir's confidence grew to the point where he walks in the vineyard to consider the potential of the vintage, different fermentation temperatures, and future blending. "Sometimes the harvest comes in calmly and slowly. Other times it needs triage. But it's always important to decide what to pick and what to leave in the field. There's room for intuition, training, artistry, and chemistry," he adds. "Once harvest is complete, I begin the second part of my job. It's when I make wine." Weir, like many vintners, works in the lab with scientific analyses and numbers to measure sugar, acids, pH levels, and other components.

*Barrel selection at Hagafen is important. I don't subscribe to making or drink-*
*ing oaky Chardonnay or high-alcohol fruit bombs. We sometimes use a hybrid*
*barrel with narrow wooden staves wood that form the sides of a cask made*
*from American wood matched with French heads, or French barrels from local*
*Napa producers. Bottling is the hardest time, the hell we pay for the good times*
*the rest of the year. It's always an interesting challenge since each year the grow-*
*ing season and harvest are unique.*

*Our customers come from a wide variety of backgrounds, yet kosher certi-*
*fication isn't an issue because they see how often our wines are awarded gold*
*medals, coupled with the excellent prices of our wines. In the end, consumers*
*consider flash pasteurization a zero issue. There are times when being kosher*
*works in Hagafen's favor. Since 1980 our wines have been served on numerous*
*occasions at the White House to visiting foreign dignitaries. Hagafen wines*
*were served at the first Passover Seder hosted at the White House by President*
*Obama.*

Ernie and his family spent the winter months of 2010–2011 on the
edge of the Mediterranean Sea in Caesarea, Israel. He always enjoys visiting friends, family, and local wineries. "When you find a passion, it is
much less of a chore to go to work. For me making or selling wine is better than the worst day doing anything else. It's only fun to sell wine honestly and with a straight face. Wine is about passion and celebrating the
good things of life with relatives and friends. As for the winemaking part
of the equation, Weir says, "If you love this way of life you will love the
way a wine expresses itself, whether in California or Israel. It is a way of
life that brings joy to all of us."

## JOHN WILLIAMS
FROG'S LEAP WINERY

John Williams comes to farming naturally. He was raised on the family farm in the hamlet of Clymer in the Finger Lakes region of upper New York State. "My grandfather loved his dairy and his herd, but my father suffered the economic realities of small family dairies." Williams thought he had left the life of a farmer behind when he enrolled at nearby Cornell University. One summer during college, he worked at Welch's Grape Juice Company. Until then grape juice was the closest relationship Williams had with the fruit of the vine. The grape bug bit him, the first step in the direction of his life's work. During his sophomore year, he worked at Taylor Wine Company, the giant winery in the Finger Lakes region.

*When I started to work, New York State regional wines were generally poor products made from native grape varietals, sometimes produced with an admixture of cheap California wines. Even so, by the end of the first day, I loved everything about the wine business. I knew it was for me. As my path veered serendipitously into the world of wine, I was sure that making wine had little to do with farming. Nothing I studied at Cornell and later at U.C. Davis changed that view. Practical studies were confined to laboratory techniques and the use of new analytical tools. Even when we studied soil science or plant pathology, every discussion was far removed from the realities of field and farm. After almost four decades of making wine, I realized my initial judgment was wrong. The heart and soul of a great wine is deeply rooted in the care and cultivation of the soil.*

Fortunately, during his years at Cornell, some wineries began to concentrate on better- quality wines. It took Williams a while to discern the differences between quality and quantity. In the 1970's he developed a relationship with Peter Johnstone, founder of Heron Hill Winery, who brought him into contact with weekly tastings of great wines that showed potential for excellence in winemaking. The next phase of Williams's winemaking career began in 1975, when he and a friend took a bus to Napa Valley. The magic of the burgeoning wine region quickly worked its charm on him. In 1977 he joined the start-up Glenora Wine Cellars as winemaker at a time when consumers were poised to buy handcrafted, quality wines. "I didn't know if I should have told them I didn't know how to make wine or not," Williams said. "I was intrigued by the fact that these guys, the founders of Glenora, didn't know what they were doing, but they had money, great vineyards, and were willing to trust me with everything. I could really shape it."

Soon favorable reviews launched Williams's career. He hooked up with Dr. Larry Turley, who introduced him to Warren Winarski, owner/winemaker of Napa's Stag Leap's Winery, who bolted to fame in the 1976 Paris competition between Napa Valley and French wines. Williams joined forces with Turley and was making wine with grapes from the doctor's vineyard. An old ledger revealed that Turley's vineyard once was a farm that sold frogs for 33 cents a dozen to San Francisco restaurants at the end of the nineteenth century. The duo jocularly called their new enterprise Frog's Leap. Eventually, the partners split up and Williams moved his share of the business to Rutherford at the Adamson Winery's historic 1884 red barn. The renovated barn sports a weather vane with a frog patterned after the winery's iconic logo. It houses William's distinctive square stainless steel fermentation tanks.

Currently, Frog's Leap crafts an average annual production of 60,000 cases of Sauvignon blanc, Cabernet Sauvignon, Chardonnay, Merlot, Rutherford, and Zinfandel, together with a small amount of Rosé. "We dry-farm and nourish the vineyards with cover crops and compost to retain moisture from winter rains. We are committed to traditional winemaking with the use of native yeasts and bacteria for primary fermentation and malolactic conversion. We harvest at natural ripeness to achieve freshness and wide-ranging, harmonious flavors. The wines are handled minimally, fined and filtered sparingly. It makes our wines lower in alcohol, higher in acidity, and lighter on the palate. Neutral oak allows us to preserve delicate elements."

Williams speaks passionately about Rutherford's terroir. "The most special wines reflect their climate and soil from grapevines deeply connected to their soil. We say our Cabernet's special characteristics come from the alluvial fans of the Napa Valley, with their well-drained, gravelly soils that warm quickly in the spring sun. We call this special quality 'Rutherford Dust' because the essence of this place is captured in our distinctive rich, dark red wine flavors. It is the perfect environment for Cabernet Sauvignon in particular, which must have warm, dry 'feet' *aka* roots if it is to develop the deep, rich black flavors we know and love."

*I believe terroir has the power to transport you back into time and place. Our Rutherford Cabernet Sauvignon is an example of the best qualities in an appellation noted for the quality of its cabs. My most noble goal is to make a wine that smells and tastes like where it comes from. Wines should be prized for their elegance, balance, ability to age, and most of all, to reveal the truth of the place where they were grown.*

*Since I settled in Rutherford, I've tried to unravel its terroir, the sense of how this unique place is part of our wine. It's always exciting when I taste Rutherford Dust in other wines from our appellation and find it disappointing when I don't. The dust has a unique earthy, dusty smell and a distinctive mouth-feel that is like rubbing velvet against its nap. Rutherford is an integral part of my body. It's in the water I drink, the food I eat, the wine I make and drink. Every winemaker should want to feel those intense qualities. I'm tuned in to aromas and flavors. Olfactory experience, the powerful chemistry of smell, can be an out-of-body experience, in the same way certain odors remind me of Christmas candy. My Sauvignon blanc reminds me of the aroma of rain on a slate roof in Ithaca, New York. It's the place in my head where I go for aromas of Sauvignon blanc. I summon up the Rutherford terroir in the same way.*

*The concept behind great wine is its terroir. Every molecule of the grape is connected to the wine. Organic farming with compost, grape pumice, and cover crops like vetch, legumes, and mustard helps soil to hold water and, importantly, provides flavor to the grapes. Our soil is as rich and malleable as chocolate cake. One pound of healthy soil at Frog's Leap can hold 9 pounds of water. We get 35 inches of rain in Napa Valley, but zero rainfall from May to*

October, so it's important for the subsoils to hold water. A grapevine's job is to send down deep roots to extract flavors from the soil as it seeks water. A vineyard without organic material can't encourage strong root growth, so vines lose their ability to provide water to the plant. Consequently, the grapes lose their ability to get flavors from the terroir. When a farmer uses fertilizers and drip irrigation, the vines keep their roots closer to the surface, until they sometimes reach the size of a basketball. Fertilizer and irrigation are like candy and Coke to a kid. The more vines proliferate like weeds, the more the wine tastes like weeds. Ecological farming with organic materials such as cover crops and compost enriches the soil and puts energy back into the environment. Fungicides, herbicides, and other chemicals are banished at our vineyards to protect the universe. Honest farming leads to beautiful wines.

Vines adapt to many conditions, so a winemaker has to decide whether to be a master manipulator or a co-conspirator. There needs to be a correct balance between our needs and nature's requirements. It's part of an ongoing process that starts in the vineyard as a series of thoughts and actions that deepen the relationship between grapes and wine. We can submit vines and grapes to our will, but our goal should maintain the vines' natural balance with proper trellising, correct row alignment, and protection from insect pests and predatory animals.

I believe the winemaker's duty is to stand aside and let Mother Nature determine the natural beauty of the grapes. One single precept motivates me beyond all others and leads me to follow a natural path to winemaking. It is the Taoist principle that expresses the practice of not-doing. Standing back sounds easy to do, but in fact, it is the most difficult way to make wine. I prefer to work within nature's patterns and rhythms rather than to take actions that follow man-made paths and conventions. I never undertake a procedure merely for its own sake. Decisions about winemaking should respect Nature's natural order rather than a human time schedule. I don't believe in forcing fermentation to fit my schedule, or racking based on time rather than taste. We use oak barrel aging to subtly enhance flavors in some wines, rather than to disguise or overwhelm the wine. Current wine styles favor overextracted wines produced by winemakers with big egos who push for 16 percent alcohol using all sorts of manipulative techniques. The Taoist concept makes you deal with what is given to you to work with. Otherwise, the natural process is stifled. My goal is to work with purity of purpose to craft fine wines in a more traditional style. Accepting this premise takes me down all sorts of remarkable winemaking paths.

## WILLIAMS'S SEASONAL SAVORY PORK ROAST

*At our house we prefer to cook by method rather than to a specific recipe. This allows for seasonal changes and the whim of the chef. We make this dish with everything from figs to apricots with a host of herbs clipped from the garden, although we seem to have a weakness for tart cherries. We like to serve the roast with an arugula salad, braised winter greens, and roasted seasonal vegetables. This makes a delicious company meal to accompany our Merlot.*

3–5 lb boneless pork roast, butterflied
Several slices of Provolone cheese
Several slices of pancetta
Chopped herbs, fruit, jam, or conserves to taste
Minced garlic
Salt and black pepper

Let the meat stand until it reaches room temperature. Unroll into a flat sheet and then layer with pancetta, provolone cheese, and chopped fruits and herbs of your choosing. Add garlic and black pepper. Reroll the roast and tie with butcher's string to secure the stuffing and hold the meat firmly in place. Brown the roast on all sides in a few tablespoons of olive oil. Place in a heavy roasting pan and glaze with fruit jam or conserves. We like a mixture of jam and hot pepper sauce for a sweet and spicy effect. Roast in a medium oven at 350°F until the internal temperature of the roast reaches 155°F. Remove and let stand 10 minutes before slicing and serving with the accumulated juices.

*Pair with Frog's Leap Merlot.*

But the process of winemaking occurs over a long continuum, so there are moments when Williams needs to take action. "I hope I have no significance in the winemaking process at all. My dream is to make my hand invisible. Mine is a fairly rare attitude in winemaking, but I believe it leads to distinctive wines." Williams shares the purist approach of André Tchelistcheff, who advised a strong handshake relationship with every vine in a vineyard as the path to good winemaking and ultimately to excellent wines.

*It's a paternalistic attitude, like one has for children or animals. When I walk into a vineyard, I can sense a vibe of discord or mischief. When a vine goes in the wrong direction, it requires love and discipline, much like the troublesome* child who requires the most attention. Yet, a burr in the saddle is like stress on the vines and is important to the wine's ultimate character and depth.

Frog's Leap also crafts a Zinfandel. Some Zin grapes come from the Gonzales vineyard south of the town of St. Helena in the heart of Napa Valley. The vineyard lies in a band of special Zin ground stretching across the valley between the Mayacamas and Vaca Mountains.

Williams has a long, affectionate, and productive relationship with the Gonzales family, who planted the eight-acre vineyard seventy years ago. Today it is planted with Zinfandel, Petite Sirah, and Carignan vines.

*Our Zinfandel is made in the ancient tradition of a field blend of grapes picked by hand and fermented together in one tank. We New World winemakers followed the lead of Old World winemakers. A few generations in the past set our path, so we're not exactly sailing alone without charts. Other people's efforts are our roadmaps for developing Chardonnay and Riesling, for example. Petit Syrah [note the different spelling] in France is usually made there as a single varietal. Frank Leeds, our vineyardist, took sage advice from his beloved Uncle Roy Chavez, who spotted a three-acre streak of gravel in the newly purchased Galleron Vineyard. Uncle Roy counseled us to plant some Petit Sirah on that gravel. The grape and the specific site are a match made in heaven. Petit Sirah produces tiny berries with intense color that led us to believe it would make a big wine. We made it that way until we took a different approach and started to treat it delicately, almost like a Pinot noir. Gentle maceration, less oak, and ten months in barrel rather than the more typical two years emphasizes its fruity qualities and gives us a wine with grace and delicacy. We use Petit Sirah as a component in Zinfandel to add succulent qualities. Petit Sirah left over from the Zinfandel blend is bottled into about 800 cases of a delicious single varietal wine.*

Winemakers face many hazards like their fellow farmers throughout the agricultural industry.

*Our early spring months of February, March, and April are the loveliest in Napa Valley. The hillsides are green, the vineyards are covered with brilliant yellow mustard, the songbirds are in full throat, and there is all the joy and expectations of the nascent vintage. Behind all this beauty lurks a potent danger of spring frost—perhaps the most serious threat we will face all year. Once* the new buds emerge, they are under constant threat of nighttime temperatures dipping below the freezing point and destroying the coming year's crop and even the vine itself. Large propeller-windmill type machines are scattered around the vineyard to fight off frost. Most deadly frosts in the wine country come when cold air is trapped by warm air above and settles on the vines. The large machines mix up the warm and cool air to avert the damage. Common, if less visible, are sprinkler heads positioned above the canopy. At the first sign of freezing, the vineyard manager turns on the sprinklers. Many growers believe sprinklers provide the highest degree of protection from the frost. Less common now, but very dramatic while in use, are vineyard heaters, once called smudge pots, that burn diesel fuel to warm the air and protect the vines. It's common for vineyard managers to show up at vineyards many predawn hours to address problems. On most mornings in this critical battle of the elements, the threat disappears with the rising sun.

The grapes know to start ripening to get ready for winter. Developing flavors in the wine isn't a stop-and-start process. Many winemakers in Napa let grapes have longer hang-time on the vines at harvest to achieve more sugar. They pick at 28 brix, resulting in alcohol levels of 16 percent. In contrast, we pick at on average between 22 and 23 brix. Until two weeks before harvest, the grapes have no acid. Then the berries produce tartaric and malic acids. The berries start to consume themselves and convert malic acid into a by-product. It's all about sex. The berries recognize their seeds are mature enough to procreate, and the grapes become palatable to birds and foxes, who deposit the seeds to make new plants. The fruit is harvested at a dynamic moment when sugars and acids are in balance.

After sorting, de-stemming, and pressing the grapes, Williams marvels at the complexity of fermentation.

Every vintage has its challenges, and each time harvest conditions gives character to the vintage. The years that present some difficulty often provide the most exciting wines, defining great vineyard locations, superior farming, and the skill of the cellar team. These are the wines that ultimately define a serious producer's reputation.

Polymer corks leave a bigger carbon footprint than natural cork because it's made from petroleum products. In addition, they don't act well as an excellent hermetic seal. They're very unsuitable for reds because they don't last longer than five years. They work fine on Sauvignon blanc bottles so we use it for

20,000 cases, or a quarter of a million bottles, or 40 percent of Frog Leap's to-tal production. Natural corks can have mold, mildew, or other problems, causing damage to around 3 to 4 percent of bottles, representing a tremendous loss of income. We're renewing our efforts for quality corks in our other wines and will eventually go back to corks for the Sauvignon blanc. Cork suppliers are getting better, beginning with how they farm cork. Our enologist is fabu-lously sensitive to odors, sniffing out even low levels of TCA, the technical term for the corky smell in wine, in tests of every batch of cork. We've cut our loss to 1 percent, or 2,500 bad bottles, but that is still bad for business. A con-sumer who tries one bad bottle may not risk another purchase. Ditto for a storeowner when a bottle is returned, and so on down the line to a distributor. Everyone loses. Consumers in a restaurant who find an off-tasting bottle should discuss it with the sommelier, rather than be unhappy. Justified com-plaints are helpful to everyone.

Williams advises telling the sommelier to charge for the undrinkable bottle. "It lets the sommelier know you're not playing games."

I believe making wines to impress doesn't work. I make wine everyone can enjoy, but I also want to be appreciated by those who perceive Frog's Leap with love and attention. Frog's Leap respects its sense of place and delivers the glo-ries of its natural flavors for maximum pleasure. Consumers will be happiest when they cultivate a special discernment about particular characteristics in a wine's soul. It's good to develop a relationship with a few wines to find char-acteristics that will evoke particular memories of tastes and aromas. On the other hand, wine can be enjoyed without going that deep. As with art or mu-sic, more understanding enhances enjoyment. I believe we are richer humans when we rise to the next levels of appreciation with focus, making decisions based on our own individual judgments.

Williams disdains numerical ratings that lead to prejudgments based on a stranger's opinion because it undervalues personal assessments. "No doubt about it, critics' opinions and ratings can force changes in taste, and unfortunately, sometimes in winemaking styles. Pundits and prognosticators line up to declare the quality of infant wines. How dare these people proclaim the quality of nascent wines?" In the fall of 2010, Williams gave a tongue–in–cheek lecture at the Awahnee Lodge in

Yosemite National Park. He called it "The 'Worst' Wine-Tasting Ever: A Retrospective Tasting of the Five 'Worst' Vintages of the Last Thirty Years." He presented Frog's Leap Cabernet Sauvignons from 1988, 1989, 1998, 2000, and 2003—all vintages that were for the most part panned by critics. "These wines have proven to be some of our favorite and most treasured vintages, still developing beautifully in our wine cellar."

Williams is dedicated to the three E's of sustainability: economic vitality, environmental responsibility, and social equity. "Responsibility to society requires concern for our agricultural workers. At Frog's Leap, we cross-train our workers to prune, tie, sucker, and harvest. When they go through the hire/fire/hire/fire periods of work, we help to find them jobs at other wineries. Care for our workers is something I learned from my grandfather at his farm." Williams's concern extended to the new hospitality center built in 1995, certified green by LEED (Leadership in energy and environmental Design). Frog's Leap was one of the first Napa wineries to install solar panels that deliver electricity throughout the winery, with excess production sold to the local energy company.

Frog's Leap's organic program extends to the gardens and orchards around the winery. Master gardener Degge Hayes produces bounties of fifty different kinds of fruits and vegetables. Honey, olive oils, jams, and preserves are sold to local restaurants and at the winery. "Incorporating biodiversity of plant and animal life in our farming systems is in itself a bigger payoff. No one species can dominate for good or ill," says Williams.

One of the wine world's best mottos defines Frog's Leap and Williams's sense of humor: "Time's fun when you're having flies."

## Los Carneros

Los Carneros AVA stretches across the southern parts of the two major wine regions of Sonoma and Napa counties in California. The larger section of the region falls into the Sonoma AVA, and the smaller into the Napa AVA. Carneros covers 90 square miles stretching from the Mayacamas Mountain Range and San Francisco Bay. Both maritime and mountainous influences affect the Carneros terroir, making it cooler and more moderate than Napa and Sonoma Valleys to the north. Cool climate grapes, particularly Pinot noir and Chardonnay, two of the three varietals favored by the French, are heavily planted in the region for still and sparkling wines. Pinot noir is a problematic grape, but it thrives in the region's predominately clay, thin, and shallow soils with poor drainage that encourage vines to struggle. Crops are often small, but the berries develop desirable intense flavors of Pinot noir and Chardonnay.

Carneros exists side by side with Napa. Both were once part of a Mexican land grant and are essentially farming communities but with markedly distinct qualities. Carneros is more bucolic, almost as though it belongs to an earlier time. In Carneros, pick-up trucks are more likely to be seen on the roads that pass dusty cattle farms and quiet vineyards. Megamansions dot the hills and valleys of Napa, where Mercedes Benz and high-end sports cars with vanity plates zip along the two main roads.

The 1970's and 1980's saw a wave of investment in the growth of wineries in Carneros. The region's reputation caught the eyes of local growers like Louis Martini. Foreign investors grabbed the opportunity to create a sparkling wine facility in America. The French company Moët & Chandon built Domaine Chandon's handsome winery and restaurant in the small Napa Valley town of Yountville, where they produce world-class sparkling wine and lesser quantities of still wines and have done so since 1973. Taittinger, another premier Champagne house, built Domaine Carneros, an impressive chateau-style building with a commanding view of the Carneros hills. Then disaster struck in the 1980's with an infestation of phylloxera that eventually required extensive replanting.

## ARMANDO CEJA
### CEJA VINEYARDS

The Ceja family is a poster image for Hispanic immigrants who achieved the American dream. Five decades ago the Cejas and Morán families arrived in Napa Valley from Mexico in desperate need of work and a place to live. "My father, Felipe Morán, offered Armando Ceja's father and his family a job harvesting grapes in Oakville in 1967," says Amelia Morán Ceja, the first Mexican-American president of a wine company.

The brothers Armando and Pedro Ceja met Amelia Morán in September, 1967, when they were kids picking grapes at Mondavi's Oakville Winery, where Amelia's father Felipe Morán was a vineyard foreman. "He helped growers like us in the valley. We were a large family and moved from one rental home to another, all located in vineyards," Armando Ceja says. "Each season, from beginning to end, the whole family worked. My wine-making career began with harvesting grapes when I was seven. We dreaded working weekends and after school. We pruned, fertilized, and picked at harvest. It was exhausting."

Soon the Ceja family found permanent work through the U.S. Government's Bracero Program, from the Spanish word for "strong arm." It came to mean someone who did manual labor. The Bracero program was a response to the need for agricultural and other laborers during World War II. From the original few hundred Mexicans who came to harvest in California, the work force from south of the border spread throughout much of the country.

*We were always on the lookout for the opportunity to develop our own wine brand. The owners of the land that is now our winery had financial difficulties* and needed to downsize. When the property came on the market in 1980, the Morán and Ceja families jumped in together. We worked out a deal to swap our old houses in exchange for the land. At the time, like much of the area from the early 1930's up to the 1950's, this parcel was essentially orchard country. We kept a couple of pear trees from the old orchard near a small, historic red barn on the property. The trees still gift the family with fruit.

We qualified for an adjustable-rate loan when rates were extremely high— a 13.9 percent starting rate with a cap of 18.9 percent. It was a major challenge to make the monthly payments, especially because I was still in college and my parents lost their jobs. They put the property up for sale, but no one made them an offer. This situation forced us to move back to Napa and live in a small studio attached to our parents' house to save the property. From that point on, all the properties we acquired were owner-financed and we paid off the balance in installments.

Once we got the land, we were able to grow our own grapes and make wine. We started by making with between ten and thirty barrels of wine for family and friends every year. It was beautiful wine, but we weren't ready to take it to the market. Our family enterprise grew from one to five vineyards, four in Carneros and one in Petaluma. We produce about 10,000 cases of Sauvignon blanc, Chardonnay, Vino de Casa blanco, Pinot noir, Merlot, Cabernet Sauvignon, Syrah, and Vino de Casa rosso. A new dessert wine, Dulce Beso (Sweet Kiss), and a Rosé called Bella Rosa, blended with Syrah and Pinot noir, round out our portfolio.

We're lucky to be in a great area for the kind of grapes we grow. We grow Vienza Arnez, a grape equivalent to Italian Chardonnay, to add fragrance and fruitiness to the wine. Our Chardonnay is fully matured and barrel-fermented with special yeasts. We play around with a blend of Merlot and Cabernet for our Cabernet program. We grow Syrah on our gorgeous land on the east side of Petaluma. Pinot noir is a fickle, finicky variety, a moody adolescent that can go through funky stages. One moment it's great and then it changes. You ask it what's happening, and then it suddenly decides to clear up and settle. Our silky Pinot noir is loaded with fruit and spice, richer than many other Pinots. We get deeper color with the appropriate manipulation of the cap and other techniques.

I believe in healthy vines, green foliage, gold and purple fruit. Good, healthy, well-balanced vines achieve the best quality, so we practice sustainable agricultural management with cover crops of legumes, peas, and beans mowed in to build up the soil. We have some problems with vines because Carneros Creek,

## AMELIA MORÁN CEJA'S FRESH, SPICY TUNA

8 oz ahi tuna steak
4 tbsp extra virgin
    olive oil
1 large avocado,
    peeled, pitted,
    diced
2 minced Serrano
    chilies
⅓ cup chopped fresh
    cilantro
⅓ cup chopped red
    onion
1 tsp fresh grated
    ginger
1 tbsp fresh lime juice
2 tsp chopped fresh
    oregano
Salt and pepper

Heat ½ tbsp of oil in a heavy small skillet over high heat for 2 minutes. Brush tuna with ½ tbsp olive oil; sprinkle with salt and pepper. Place in skillet and sear until slightly brown outside and almost opaque in center, about 2 minutes per side. Cool tuna and dice finely. Combine tuna, remaining 3 tbsp oil, and all remaining ingredients in medium bowl. Using fork, mix just to blend. Season the tuna tartar taste with salt and pepper and chill. Serve with chips or with a small corn tostada.

SERVE ALONE OR AS AN APPETIZER. SERVES 6–8.

*Ceja Vineyards Pinot noir pairs perfectly with this dish.*

only 150 yards from us, is a breeding ground for the troublesome blue-green sharpshooters. These insects are a huge problem because bacteria from their saliva glands suck out sap, nutrients, and water, and destroy the vines. Pierce's disease causes another ugly death for vines. Sometimes disease-stressed vines struggle and are able to produce grapes with excellent flavors, but too much stress is dangerous. We need to manage diseases with different rootstocks and other methods.

Good wine is captured by what our vineyard gives us. We start with a green thumb and use a gentle hand during vinification. We take charge of all the steps in winemaking from choice of rootstock until bottling. With our help and guidance, our wines express themselves. We conscientiously work to get the wines at a suitable level of alcohol to make our wines food-friendly. The finishing steps continue in the cellar with decisions about barrels, yeasts, and aging. Barrel aging enriches the wine with layers of fruit, minerals, and viscosity. Careful overall treatment enhances fruit flavors and aromatics.

Ceja wines reflect our respect and dedication to our vineyards. Our wines reflect our philosophy and respect we have for farming and how grateful we are to our parents for having brought us here. Our label reflects our family heritage. Pedro was instrumental in choosing the bell as integral to the design. Our ancestors were in the transportation business in Mexico and ran teams of horses and mules wearing bells. We also focused on the historic Spanish missions in California, where the first wines were introduced. Parallel wavy lines on our label represent the river of life, a design that was found on many mission doors. Three Latin words on our winery's bell, Vinus, Cantus, Amor—wine, song, love—were written by a Mexican in his foundry in San Jose.

We are a classic American success story, blending two wonderful cultures. Three generations of the family work together in jobs that range from winemaking to marketing. Our website, Salud Napa Valley, is recorded in Spanish and English. The website focuses on our wine and our rich Mexican culinary heritage that goes way beyond tacos, burritos, and refried beans.

We have a lot of bosses and sparks fly when we get together. We are all equal, although when push comes to shove, sometimes one of us ends up on the floor. There's a lot of sibling rivalry, but it is obviously working out okay. The success of Ceja Vineyards is due to our family's collective effort and unabashed loyalty. We succeed because our wines reflect our culture, our winemaking practices, and our passion to bring our products to the public. A good marketing plan, especially for a small producer, requires pursuing both wholesale sales and direct sales to consumers. We found our own American dream in the work we do in a place we love.

# STÉPHANE VIVIER
## HDV WINERY AND VIVIER WINES

Janus, the god of beginnings and transitions, has two heads facing opposite directions: one faces eastward and the other looks west. Symbolically, they look to the future and the past. Janus may be the perfect symbol for Stéphane Vivier, who divides his time as winemaker for HdV Winery and his personal enterprise, the eponymous Vivier Winery. The young vintner adapts his past French training, experience, and sensibilities to winemaking in America. He works in Carneros with Chardonnay and Pinot noir, the two grapes that surrounded him when he grew up in the tiny village of Meloisey, where three hundred souls live in 5 square miles circumscribed by the great historic vineyards of Burgundy. "The vineyards were my childhood playground and from an early age I learned to love winemaking. By any measure, my Burgundy maintains its reputation as one of France's blueblood viticultural regions. The air, the very culture of its historic heritage are infused with wine, from flowering of vines to harvest, from pressing of the grapes to bottling. The region's major varietals, Pinot noir and Chardonnay, are accorded stratospheric praise."

Like many French children practically weaned on wine, Vivier tasted a celebratory glass of a 1974 Richebourgh Grand Cru on his tenth birthday. "It gave me a sense of what great wine can be and set me on a path to become a winemaker." Three years later, an eighty-three-year-old neighbor, in spite of the seventy-year age gap, took the thirteen-year-old in hand for his first lesson in winemaking, providing the youngster subtle lessons that can only be gleaned from an experienced winemaker. Then other neighbors led him through other steps to his future career. "Those relationships were quite a beginning. They inspired me to become a winemaker, not an easy feat in France for someone who doesn't come from a winemaking family. Most of all, I learned great respect for simple, but precise, viticulture in a centuries-old vineyard that was finely tuned by generations of growers. It was a style influenced by Burgundian tradition."

Vivier formalized his education with a degree in biochemistry, followed by advanced degrees in enology and viticulture at the Université de Bourgogne in Dijon. In 1999, the twenty-five-year-old was sidelined into a job selling oak barrels, the only job he could find, and one that wasn't at the top of his list of preferable occupations. He reluctantly left Burgundy and took a position in a Swiss research lab working with Pinot Noirnoir's phenolic compounds. He switched to work in the vineyards and cellars of Pommard, Meursault, and Chassagne-Montrachet. The twin siren calls of wine and Rugby, the national sport of New Zealand, drew him "down under." But he felt too far from family and friends. With a small stipend from his parents, he found work in California where he began to learn important lessons crafting New World wines. His enthusiasm for expressing the individuality of both the vineyards and wines were extremely alluring and free from the restrictions of tradition or AOC restrictions imposed on most European vintners.

Destiny brought Vivier, with his skills in vineyard management and winemaking, to work in Napa with families with deep roots in the wine industry. He became the winemaker at HdV (Hyde de Villaine) in 2002. Once again he was under the tutelage of a great Burgundian winemaker, Aubert de Villaine, co-owner and co-director of the Domaine de la Romanée-Conti, one of the world's most prestigious wines. De Villaine had joined forces with Larry Hyde, a highly regarded winemaker/winegrower who had come to Napa Valley over four decades earlier to pursue a passion for grape cultivation and wine. Hyde and de Villaine forged a natural bond between vineyard manager and winemaker, and brought a confluence of experience from France and California to their new enterprise. The relationship between Larry and Aubert was further solidified when de Villaine married Hyde's cousin, Pamela. Hyde and Pamela are descendants of the historic Californian winemaking de la Guerra family. Ergo, the de la Guerras' coat of arms, together with *H* for "Hyde" and *de V* for "de Villaine," are combined in the winery's logo, standing for tradition, family, and winemaking history.

Vivier became the third contributor who adds balances and stability to the HdV enterprise. He made his first vintage for the company in 2002, bringing his broad experience and French sensibilities to the winery. He oversees all aspects of crafting the winery's 6,000 cases of Chardonnay, Syrah. and a Bordeaux-style red, Belle Cousine.

*The wine is named for Pamela de Villaine, who is the "Beautiful Cousin." It is a blend of Merlot and Cabernet Sauvignon, rather than Cabernet Franc in the Pomerol style of Bordeaux.*

*Hyde's single vineyard grapes express the unique microclimate of Carneros. The 150 acres of vines yield carefully managed, limited quantities of intense fruit from the Carneros region. Eighteen acres of selected vines are dedicated to HdV. It takes a lot of work to understand the site. Our terroir—a cool climate with well-draining, shallow soils of sedimentary terraces, loamy soils, bedrock. and clay—demands respect as well as an opportunity to express itself. The vines struggle to find an eventual crack in the impenetrable hard clay pan for water, and their roots often grow wide rather than down. Older vines struggle in the vineyard, extracting minerality, salty, flinty characteristics enhanced by morning fog from San Francisco Bay and by ocean breezes in the afternoon. We encourage a healthy microbial ecosystem and a naturally balanced substructure for the root of our vines.*

Vivier notes Hyde green-farming foregoes chemicals in favor of natural methods to fight destructive insects. He farms sustainably, although the vineyards are not certified organic.

*We try to dry-farm, since clay retains enough moisture from winter rains. A long growing season brings both intensity and balance to our wines. Plentiful sunshine, coupled with careful pruning and good ripening, is a great set-up for Cabernet and Merlot, with yields of intense black fruit, black currant, and spice. These factors encourage the vines to maximize their potential.*

*Our wines are linked to the site's terroir. Our philosophy incorporates four concerns. First, the geology of the soil. Second, the microclimate influences on the plants. Then the choice of vines, the wood stock, and clones need to match the site. Fourth, we must ask what humans bring to the process What do we make of the terroir? How do we interpret and respect the other three issues?*

# VIVIER'S CHICKEN STIR-FRY WITH ASPARAGUS AND CASHEWS

*Cashews are packed with oleic acid, the mono-unsaturated fat that makes olive oil so heart healthy. This chicken–cashew stir-fry is a lighter take on a dish that Vivier orders at Rin's Thai in Sonoma, California. Its Asian flavors come from a bright mix of fish sauce, oyster sauce, and basil—and just a little oil.*

½ cup raw cashews
1½ lb skinless, boneless chicken breasts, cut into1½-inch pieces
2 tbsp Asian fish sauce
2 tbsp vegetable oil
½ cup chicken stock or low-sodium broth
1 lb asparagus, sliced on the diagonal, 1 inch thick
1 tbsp oyster sauce
1 tbsp fresh lime juice
1 tsp cayenne pepper
½ cup chopped basil
¼ cup chopped chives
Freshly ground black pepper

Preheat the oven to 350°F. Spread the cashews in a pie plate and toast in the oven for about 8 minutes, until they are nicely browned and fragrant. Let cool. In a medium bowl, toss the chicken with 1 tbsp of the fish sauce. In a wok or large skillet heat the oil until shimmering.

Add the chicken in an even layer and cook over high heat, turning once, until browned and just cooked throughout, about 4 minutes. Using a slotted spoon, transfer the chicken to a clean bowl. Pour the chicken stock into the wok and bring to a simmer, scraping up any browned bits stuck to the bottom of the wok.

Add the asparagus slices, cover, and cook over moderate heat until they are crisp-tender, about 3 minutes. Using a slotted spoon, transfer the asparagus to the bowl along with the chicken. Add the remaining 1 tbsp of fish sauce to the wok along with the oyster sauce, lime juice, and cayenne pepper. Simmer until the sauce is reduced to ½ cup, about 2 minutes.

Return the chicken pieces and sliced asparagus to the wok and toss to heat through. Remove the wok from the heat and stir in the cashews, basil, and chives. Season the stir-fry with black pepper and serve right away. Serve with steamed rice.

*Vivier offers two choices of wines to pair with the dish. A 2010 Hyde de Villaine Chardonnay or a 2011 Vivier Gap's Crown Pinot noir Sonoma Coast. Chardonnay is a great addition to chicken for its textural and fresh opulence in this dish. The Pinot noir will provide the spice and fruit components, completing this already multilayered recipe.*

There is no scientific evidence that proves the effect of terroir on grapes. Nevertheless, we work hard on a lot of little things in the vineyard to produce grapes that don't need a lot of work in the winery. For sure, there is a difference from year to year. Many factors can change in the course of a season: the climate, the soil, the vines get older. We change also. I believe in minimum handling to get to the end, but it takes a lot of work coupled with training and intuition to do no work, to be simple. My job is more about research into vines and then into myself in order to better understand what needs to be done. In the end, the grapes have to do the talking.

The amount of time spent in the vineyard is the key to great wine. We create teamwork and partnership with our vines. We constantly monitor their health to avoid tragedy. We can't afford to overlook one thing. I harvest by taste, but my background in biochemistry is an aid to determine sugar, acid, and tannin levels. Chemistry and science are helpful, but in the end, decisions about these special artisanal wines come from my heart and taste buds.

I believe winemaking is not about an individual's statement but rather for the winemaker to be there to interpret grapes, vines, and land, ultimately creating a sense of place in a bottle. I embrace a winemaking style that respects the traditions of Burgundy, which means allowing the vineyard to speak. We want to bottle a picture of the vineyards, not a portrait of the winemaker. From my beginnings in Burgundy and my experience in different regions and through different vintages, I appreciate that in wine, as in life, it is difficult to stay simple.

Wine isn't a competitive occupation. My competition is to understand the vineyard. For me that is the most important thing. As competitive as I am, I'm satisfied when I see a bottle of HdV on a restaurant table. It's hard sometimes not to get the gold medal, especially if you want a chance to explain why you think the wine deserves one. I want consumers to meet the HdV team in order to know our wines and understand we craft enjoyment. People can certainly live without wine, but wine creates good times and memories of life's key moments. It can create a powerful beacon in life with a capacity to shape memories of an event.

Freedom is the best part of my work. I don't have a job. I don't go to work in the morning. I go to my passion. I work with the plants because wine lives in the vineyards. You give to the vines and they give back to you. To be around with living things teaches you a lot about yourself, how to learn from your mistakes and successes. We live in a fast world where people want immediate rewards, but I'm lucky to stop and look back at the bigger picture. Our society *rarely allows people to reflect on what they are doing. It's a quality that is very rewarding for me. It's one of the things I love about what I do. I consider myself very lucky.*

Recently, Vivier and his wife Dana started a side project, something they want for themselves.

*We started it without investors, without rich uncles. It was like jumping off a cliff. We do everything on our own. Dana has an MBA and good business acumen. I do everything else, including making wine deliveries. It's an idea to create Pinot noir from California with a Burgundian feel. We source our grapes for our 300 cases from young, three- to four-year-old vineyards on the Sonoma coast and from one vineyard from the Willamette Valley in Oregon. The grapes come from cool regions where the vines have to work hard. We get to know the vineyards and understand the potential of the vines and fruit. We subtly guide the developing wines with a classic light touch. Luckily, HdV has gone along with our project.*

*With Vivier wines, we can blend our respect for tradition and our enthusiasm for emerging winegrowing regions into our love of Pinot noir, both red and pink. So far we've made 300 cases of complex Pinots and 100 cases of Rosé.*

A wine called Sexton Vivier is named to honor special things in his life. Vivier couldn't resist the pull to make a wine in the style of his beloved Pineau. Fully aware of Dana's skepticism, he and his crew poured their hearts into making this, stirring it with care, and tasting it one drop at a time from the palms of their hands. "This wine is magical and it's like nothing you've tasted from California. Winemakers only get thirty-five or forty chances in their lives to make wine. I am already thinking ahead. I'm planning to share some vintages I am especially proud of with my grandkids." An endearing remark considering his and Dana's first child, Lucile, was born in 2010 and a baby boy joined the family in spring of 2013. He certainly does think ahead. America's gain is Burgundy's loss.

# Mendocino County

Spanish explorer Lorenzo Suárez de Mendoza explored the Mendocino coast. Like Amerigo Vespucio, after whom America was named, Mendoza's last name became attached to Mendocino County. The region was sparsely settled until California's Gold Rush in the 1850's brought immigrants to it. Prospecting did not always pay off, so newcomers turned to farming. California's rich and varied terrains proved extremely hospitable to a wide variety of agriculture, including grape cultivation. Grape vines were first planted in Mendocino County on rugged hillsides north of San Francisco. Mountains divide the region into a wide variety of terroirs. Ten American Viticultural Areas have been established in the county, where grape growers and winemakers experiment with new vineyard practices, a frequent commitment to organic viticultural methods and grape varietals. Prohibition decimated the original small wineries. Orchards and walnut trees replaced vines. Then a budding interest in winemaking during the 1960's spurred a revival of old vineyards and ancillary growth of new ones.

# JOHN CHIARITO
## CHIARITO VINEYARD

The phone rang at 8:15 one morning, a bit early for a late riser like me. It was 5:15 in California, time for farmers and winemakers to begin their day. John Chiarito was on the line, returning my call. I had reached out to him because of his particular interest in Sicilian grapes. While winemakers all over the world are introducing new varietals to complement or replace their indigenous grapes, Chiarito grew Nero d'Avola in Mendocino County in Talmage near Ukiah. He followed his parents, who had moved there when he was twenty-five years old. Chiarito had tackled all the jobs at his 5-acre vineyard, where he produced 1,000 cases of estate-grown wines.

*I've been making wine since 1995, although I started my winery in 2002. Up to then, I worked as a general contractor building single-family homes. I built my own house and with a thousand-foot winery cellar on an abandoned walnut orchard. I removed all but the perimeter trees in the orchard and planted grapes twenty years ago.*

*My Italian heritage speaks loudly to me, so my first release included Nero d'Avola and Negroamaro, two varietals that flourish in southern Italy. I liked to think of it as homage to my maternal and paternal grandparents, who came from small villages in the southern Italian regions of Campagna and Basilicata. As a child, I spent nearly every Sunday at the home of my grandparents on my father's side. My grandmother and mother would cook homemade orecchiette and a fabulous ragu, served with braciole topped with grated ricotta salata. I was drawn to Sicily and traveled there a number of times. One day, I realized Mendocino's hot summers and cool evenings were perfect for what I consider to be the island's incomparable varietal, Nero d'Avola.*

Chiarito recounted the chronicle of his grandfather and father, Americo Donato and Antonio Chiarito. After the Chiarito family immigrated to America, Americo was the first of the family's children born in the United States. They lived in Hartford, Connecticut, like many other Italian families. "The family saga says the Chiaritos moved back to Italy before World War I, ostensibly to show off their American-born son. In truth, they were probably disappointed because the streets in the U.S. weren't paved with gold, and as immigrants they faced tremendous prejudice." Americo's father fought for the Italians in World War I, but the family returned to the United States in 1926, when Americo was thirteen.

"The next part of our family chronicle is filled with irony." After college, Americo enlisted in the United States Army during World War II, landing near Salerno in the first wave of the invasion of Italy. John remembers his father's recounting a favorite story about his war experiences.

*My father found himself in a fig orchard as the world was exploding around him. Not knowing whether he was going to live or die, Americo climbed one of the trees filled with figs and slowly devoured the fruit as bombs crashed and exploded around him.*

*My father was my accountant and my best helper until he died one month shy of 97 in 2010. I really got to know him when we worked together every day. He kept up his schedule at the winery through his last year, harvesting, bottling, pasting labels, and operating the corker on the bottling line. He always asked what more was there for him to do. I valued him so much. His beautiful signature was on our label. The hand on the label signifies the tremendous work we had put into each vintage and into every bottle. Our motto is Fatto a mano, "made by hand." A cliché says good wines come from a good, well-tended vineyard. In truth, it took a tremendous amount of work to make our 1,000 cases of wine.*

*I spent most of my time outdoors, but I preferred it to cellar work. I left enough space between rows so I can ride the tractor in all four directions between the rows. Our soil is a pretty deep, gravelly loam, organically dry-farmed, relying only on winter rain. The vines are head-trained in an older style and tied with willow. I like to think of this as a Roman tradition. My customers never understand that every vine was handled at least six times a season.*

*We harvested the grapes by hand in 30-pound lugs early in the morning, when the temperature was in the 40's. The fruit was brought into the winery in half-ton food-grade plastic picking bins and dumped on the sorting table,*

## CHIARITO'S BRACIOLE CON ORECCHIETTE

*Beef rolls with little ear-shaped pasta*
*("My mouth is already watering," says Chiarito.)*

½ lb beef round, carne asada or flank steak sliced thin and lightly pounded to ¼ inch or less.
1 garlic clove, minced
⅓ cup grated Pecorino Romano or Parmegiano cheese
¼ cup chopped fresh Italian parsley leaves
¼ lb diced pancetta or salt pork
4 tbsp olive oil
Grated ricotta salata to taste
1 small can crushed Italian tomatoes
Pinch of red pepper flakes

Mix parsley, garlic, and cheese together. On each slice of beef place the parsley, garlic, and cheese mixture. Roll up each slice and either tie with string or secure the filling with a toothpick. Brown the braciole in olive oil in a heavy, deep pan, turning often. Add crushed tomatoes, salt, and a pinch of hot red pepper flakes. Add sausage or pork to the ragu for a tastier sauce. Simmer for 1½ to 2 hours on the top of the stove or in a 350°F oven.

Serve the sauce with pasta. My family enjoyed it with home-made orecchiette topped with grated ricotta salata. The braciole was served as the second course with cooked greens or with small stuffed artichokes and a salad.

*Pair with Negroamaro, a wine with great acidity.*

hand-sorted and run through the de-stemmer/crusher immediately. I had a small press with a water-filled bladder that pressed gently and pumped juice from the berries. The press is very gentle, and so I combined both the pressed and free-run juice. The free-run juice was pumped into a tank. I always did a second pressing on the remaining skins. I usually fermented half a ton of grapes at a time. I didn't want heat to kill the yeasts, so I punched down the cap with my hands three times a day. I felt the warm spots to make sure the juice never got really hot.

Our Nero d'Avola was bottled as a single varietal. I was the first to petition to get this varietal approved by the federal government. Zinfandel was grown in the Ukiah Valley for a long time, but I only blended Zinfandel and Petite Syrah after several blending trials. First, I tasted all the Zin, then I added 5 percent Petite Syrah. I worked my way up, smelling and tasting, adding or subtracting Petite Syrah until the final blend. In 2007, the Zin was the best ever when it arrived straight from the vineyard and needed no blending.

We did all the bottling in the cellar as well. We used a small six-bottle filler. Every bottle was placed on the filler and when full, was handed to the person doing the corking at an electric corker that created a vacuum. Four of us bottled 300 cases a day without labels and foils. Each bottle was dealt with individually, just as everything else at the winery is done, by hand.

There was a time when Chiarito turned his hand to another avocation than that of master of the vineyard and winery. For a while he shared his family's generations-old pasta-making techniques with a class.

Participants learned two handmade pasta shapes, orecchiette and ferrettini. Orecchiette is a common pasta shape in Puglia and is often served with sautéed bitter greens, chili flakes, and olive oil. The name means "little ears" because the pasta is shaped like a small disc with a hollow center. The hollow in the center is perfect for catching sauce in each mouthful. Ferrettini is another family recipe. The tubular-shaped pasta is formed around a thin wire, so the pasta is nicknamed "the little iron." I remember hearing stories from my grandmother about Ferrettini being made on a shaft of wheat instead of wire. Ferrettini is not available from commercial pasta makers and making it is a lost art in the culinary world. Class participants learned to prepare the pasta dough recipe, form the shapes, sauté a simple sauce and savor a memorable Sunday lunch at the winery matched with Chiarito Vineyard estate wines.

I am always open to learning, and had a great experience when I took a cooking class with an Italian chef visiting California in 2006. Even though my Italian was pretty bad, I invited him and his wife for dinner. After that, my Nero d'Avola was on the wine list at his restaurant in Sicily.

And so the world turns when an American wine made from a Sicilian varietal returned home.

"I do believe in climate change. In 2008 thirty days of frost hit the vineyard. I lost half my crop. There was too much rain in the springs of 2010 and 2011, and again I lost half my production. It was the most vulnerable I ever felt. We had a decent year in 2012, but I can't work this hard and not earn any money. Then my father died and I couldn't see going on without him at my side." Sadly, Chiarito closed the winery and looks forward to starting a new chapter in his life.

## Sonoma

Sonoma County is located on California's northern coast and is the largest of nine San Francisco Bay Area counties. The Pacific Ocean and several rivers create a maritime influence over the region's extensive vineyards. Sonoma abuts Napa Valley, but the personalities of the two wine regions are quite different. Sonoma is a more bucolic, home-spun farming environment. Napa Valley, on the other hand, takes pride in its more elaborate lifestyle, with fancy wineries, mega-mansions, and world-class restaurants.

Archeological evidence, including rock drawings dating between 8000 and 5000 B.C., indicates several native tribes inhabited the Sonoma coast. Sonoma is said to derive its name from Chucuines o Sonomas, another local tribe. American students learn about Spanish conquistadors who worked their way into the New World from South America to parts of North America, including its western coast. In 1823, they arrived in California and moved up the coast to the Sonoma area, where Padre Jose Altimira founded the Mission of San Francisco Solano and planted several thousand grape vines. Cuttings from the mission's vineyards were propagated, and thirty years later, wine grapes played a role in the region's agriculture. Wine production was relatively successful in the region until Prohibition. The law's repeal revived wine consumption and brought a simultaneous growth in grape production. Sonoma is generally agricultural, with 75 percent of the region devoted to grapes and the rest to cattle raising and cheese making. Sonoma's hospitable environments have a variety of terroirs and are excellent for both cool- and warm-climate grapes— Chardonnay, Cabernet Sauvignon, Pinot noir, Merlot, and Zinfandel.

# GUY DAVIS
## DAVIS FAMILY VINEYARDS

Winemaking wasn't on the career map for Guy Davis back when he was a college student in Seattle. School occupied his days, but at night he worked the late shift at a French restaurant. The best part of the long day came with a free dinner and a bottle of wine at midnight he shared with the restaurant's chef.

*Each new wine was an* ah ha! *moment that pointed me in a new direction. At nineteen, I realized the importance of food and wine in life. My delight in the simplicity of sharing bread and wine evolved without my chasing the idea. The occasion didn't have to be expensive or formal. The connection with wine just welled up in me. I appreciated the idea of wine as a historic beverage. I enjoyed the idea that life was more fun after people discovered grape juice became a new beverage. Life got even better over centuries when humans learned to progress from ordinary wine to good wine to elegant wine.*

Davis entered the wine world through the business end, using his degree in economics to get a job as marketing director for Kendall-Jackson Vineyard Estates in Sonoma.

*I left the company to partner with a friend in Passport Wine Company. We connected connoisseurs and collectors with American and European boutique wineries. I developed a wine palate after tasting three to four hundred wines a month. Then my road took a different turn when I moved to producing wine. In order to expand my knowledge about wine production, I donated my time to work harvest in both hemispheres between 1989 and 1996.*

*Wineries in certain California terroirs like Sonoma are as suitable for Pinot noir as France's Burgundy region. In my neighborhood, there are a lot of distinctive, complex, and unique wines produced from different clones and vines of different ages. Soils have deposits of volcanic ash from Mt. St. Helena. There are areas with pockets of fog, and places that are warmer, as is the case when the Russian River heads south and then turns west to empty in the Pacific.*

*Joseph Swann's pioneer work with the varietal encouraged me to think about Russian River and Sonoma's potential to produce a wine I loved. Swann's property is on the Russian River where it turns north, while Tom Dellinger's acreage on the end of Laguna Ridge is different again and gets complexity from being located in a cool pocket where the grapes hang a long time on the vine.*

Davis checked around and came to believe he could produce world-class Pinot noir in Sonoma.

"I like the opportunity to share ideas with other professionals. We taste together and bounce ideas off each other. It's a huge exchange of information. I bow to the locals about weather when I see huge rainclouds at harvest and want to pick. Hand harvesting is impossible when the fields are muddy.

"My vineyard was originally an old abandoned property planted with Zinfandel vines since 1896. It was a perfect east-facing, hillside site protected from the wind with a 2.5-acre block of viable, gnarly, misshapen Zinfandel vines, each with one arm. I packed them with organic compost and, in return, they gave me 70 cases of wine. Zin from hundred-plus-year-old vines as a bonus." Davis replanted an old Carignan portion of the vineyard with Chardonnay and two small blocks of Syrah. "Our first vintage in 1997 had 200 cases of Napa Valley Cabernet auvignon from the Stagecoach and Llewellen vineyards, each vineyard providing different flavor components." Davis talks fondly of his ancient vines as though they are Eveready batteries with potential to last forever.

Davis articulates the steps it takes to make excellent wine.

*Winemaking is based on a series of decisions from the first days in the field until the wine is bottled. Large companies make formula-based wines. They use recipes to achieve their specific house style, which makes the expression of*

# MUSHROOM CONSOMMÉ

1 onion, diced
3 shallots, diced
2 cloves of garlic,
  chopped
Enough fresh and
  dried mushrooms
  to fill a large pot
3 tbsp butter
3 tbsp olive oil
½ cup Sherry
12–16 oz chicken or
  beef stock (or half
  and half) per
  person
Salt and pepper
  (truffle salt if you
  have the money)

Use an assortment of sliced mushrooms: Crimini, porcini, shitake, and chanterelles or a similar mixture of dried mushrooms. The mushrooms will reduce to one third the amount. If using dried, soak them overnight first and add the liquid to the stock.

Heat 3 tbsp butter and 3 tbsp olive oil. Add the diced onion, shallot, and garlic and sauté on low until translucent. Raise the temperature to medium and add the mushrooms. Once you have them at a full sauté, turn down the heat slightly and begin to sweat and simmer the mushrooms, stirring fairly often until soft and brown. Deglaze the pan and add the stock. Raise the heat to medium high and stir as they come up to a full sizzle to get small brown bits in the bottom of the pan without burning or sticking. Add the sherry and stir rapidly, getting all those goodies from the bottom of the pan. Slightly cool. Simmer until the alcohol has evaporated. Add your stock—12–16 oz per person, plus 8 oz of water per person.

Reduce liquid by one third, simmer on low, and cover. Continue to simmer to blend the flavors. Reheat and adjust seasoning. Pour the soup slowly through a large, fine-mesh strainer over a large pot or bowl. Spoon the rest of the mushrooms into the strainer with a large spoon and press them with the back of that spoon to squeeze all the liquid from the mushrooms. This recipe can be made a day in advance.

Serve the consommé in mugs or small bowls. Drink without spoons. Make sure the Pinot is flowing and enjoy. Additional suggestions: Let the mushrooms cool down to room temperature, seal, and refrigerate them. Use them in an omelet at breakfast. Brush thick slices of good crusty bread with olive oil on both sides.

*Mushroom consommé with full, wonderful aromas and flavors pairs magically with Pinot noir. Mushrooms are one of the ultimate pairings for Pinot noir because a nuance of the earth is a varietal character that runs through all great Pinot noirs. In some wines the earthy trait is a faint background aroma and flavor, and in others it is a main characteristic of the Pinot noir grape.*

a vintage insignificant. For example, these companies do a lot of manipulation, like adding tartaric acid to increase acidity. In contrast, we're the real thing, a complete soil-to-vine-to-bottle family, producing artisanal, hand-crafted quality wines. I'm proud to be an artisan who wears all the hats and do all the jobs that require transitioning from season to season. As the wine-maker, I make decisions to highlight the qualities of a site, like exposure to sunlight. I decide on trellising and pruning. My hands-on approach gives each varietal the opportunity to achieve the true expression of the terroir of a certain place in a particular year. My job is a loop, encompassing the life of a farmer who learns the personality of the site, unlike some colleagues with fifteen vineyards who never visit them until harvest. I manage each vine and every barrel. The great challenge in winemaking is to get all the factors in balance. As conductor of the operation, balance is my central focus from midwinter, when we set the crop load, through each season until harvest.

Patience is the biggest challenge when Mother Nature and weather make each vintage unpredictable. Every year is different, and each year nothing is at the same point during a vintage. Forty things don't necessarily line up at the same time. Our results vary from vintage to vintage. The most important decision is when to pick. At harvest, all the ripeness factors must be in equilibrium. It's when we strive to get all the ripeness factors in balance. Workdays in the vineyard are extremely long during harvest. I crunch on grape seeds and look for the taste of toasted almonds. I rub grape skin against the roof of my mouth to taste astringency and spit into my hand to check for color. I make mental comparisons with past vintages. Still, it's unclear how a wine will turn out until crush. It's possible to throw grape clusters into a bucket and make wine. It's great to say we pick at 24 brix, 6 grams per liter for acidity, but that's not all. I can sample at 24 brix and the juice could be too astringent. In a cool season, I can't wait to let the tannins soften and settle down. Pinot noir skins are thin, so three days of heat can jump the level to 26 brix, which produces too much alcohol. You need to look at all those factors to get the balance and physiological components right. It's the great challenge about winemaking. There are perfect vintages, like 2009, when we had a ball with the Pinot. Even the worst, like 1998, was challenging and exciting. Sometimes it's the most fun, especially when, six months later, you're surprised and in love with the wine.

The trend is for lots of New World vintners to want to achieve bigger, bolder wines. Trends always exist, but the pendulum swings way out, back and forth from one direction to another. I believe the center provides the perfect balance.

*Fashion is a good example. The basic black dress is always classic. I don't chase trends, like heavily malolactic and oaked chardonnays or the new inclination for wines that see no oak. Global techniques don't have any place on my property, so I use traditional, tried-and-true methods that fit my vineyard.*

*I do small trials in the vineyard on three rows over two to three years, choosing soils with a positive effect on grapes. I want to see what could be a perfect fit. The vineyard is completely organic and half biodynamic. There are more than twelve techniques to be certified biodynamic, but they're not all suited to me. We use cow horns filled with our own compost. The calcium in the cow horns adds to the compost and makes it easier for a plant to uptake the ingredients it needs for growth. I don't want a piece of paper for certification merely to impress consumers.*

Davis prefers native to manufactured yeasts.

*Native yeasts deliver a more natural taste. I'm careful not to introduce anything artificial that would alter the specific personality of my particular site. Some wineries introduce too many tricks. Wine is becoming homogenized because yeast strains reduce the effect of terroir. Manufactured yeasts can increase the floral profile and make the wine a little prettier, but they mask aromas and take away from the complexity in the wine.*

*I don't go to the extreme of making wine without barrels. Oak is an important ingredient, like salt in cooking, but it requires good judgment. A cook needs to know just how much salt is necessary. I make sure taste comes from the vineyard, not from wood. I choose tight-grained Allée and Tranchée barrels from cold forests in France. We do 70 percent in the barrels for richness and creaminess and 30 percent in stainless steel for purity, and clean, crisp natural acidity. I look for richness, complexity, and the pretty side of each varietal.*

Davis spent several months a year working below the Equator, jetting to New Zealand when work in Sonoma was finished. "It's a throwback to my early days harvesting Malbec in Argentina. I met an incredible group who produced a beautiful, balanced Malbec I attributed to a coastal climate until I learned about the effect of elevation of the vineyards and the snow pack of the Andes on the vines. It's exciting to work two seasons rather than one. An artist can work year round and constantly refine the work. That's not true about wine. Each season comes to a finite end. So my work in both hemispheres doubles the pleasure. Each place brings me a different experience and I to it."

Davis Family produces 4,500 cases of wine.

*I wouldn't mind growing to 6,000 with different varietals. But I don't want to change my business model of single-vineyard, estate-designated wines from Horseshoe Bend and blends from blocks called Soul Patch in the Russian River region. I'm experimenting with white wine from a Marsanne/Roussanne/Viognier blend. I occasionally make Port that is only sold in the tasting room.*

*Over the years, a winemaker's aims change. Sometime in the future, I'd like to switch from working in South America to making wine in South Africa. But at home, I maintain my stylistic goals. My connection to the land has deepened. I see this piece of earth as a living thing whose health I am responsible for forever. My goal is to learn how to make better wine. Now I'm making plans further into the future because I want my sons to participate in the winery. We're not rich, but we have a rich life.*

# New York State

## *Finger Lakes*

Cayuga, Mohawk, Oneida, Onondaga, and Seneca Indian tribes believed the Great Spirit's fingerprints created the five great Finger Lakes and the eleven smaller ones. Geologists tell us that a series of glaciers gouged valleys; the five long, deep lakes; and a number of smaller ones. The promise of the New World attracted an influx of European settlers, who slowly changed the topography of the area, clearing land for agriculture and commerce. After the Revolutionary War, veterans received grants from an immense tract, including land around the Finger Lake region. The country's first commercial winery started in the region in 1829, using native American Labrusco and Concord grapes. The hardy, sweet, and fruity Labrusco is more resistant to diseases like phylloxera. Consumers are more familiar with Concord grapes as the ingredient in grape jellies and juice. Neither varietal has a reputation for making fine wine. Winemakers in the region have developed fine wines from *Vitis vinifera* varietals that fare well in cold climates.

Most vineyards in the region are planted near lakes that moderate the region's harsh climate. Only hardy vines survive the challenge of winters that dip well below freezing, midwinter thaws, rain, ice, and hail storms. Today New York State's 200-odd wineries rank fourth in the country's production behind California, Oregon, and Washington State. The Finger Lakes AVA, with its 2.3 million acres, is the leading producer of wine in New York State.

# PETER B. SALTONSTALL

## KING FERRY WINERY AND TRELEAVEN WINES

King Ferry Winery, owned and operated by Peter and Tacie Saltonstall since 1984, is one of twenty wineries around Cayuga Lake in the Finger Lakes region. Pete, the grandson of Leverett Saltonstall, former governor of Massachusetts and a U.S. senator, grew up on a farm run by his father, an agronomy professor at Cornell's agricultural school. It was he who bought 700 acres of local farmland.

*My father raised beef and wheat, barley, oats, and red clover seeds for neighboring farmers. Most of the family land was sold when my father passed away, except for Treleaven Farm, a small 150-acre parcel. I wasn't excited by the seed business. I followed my brother, who owned a parachuting resort in Pope Valley, one of California's wine-growing regions.*

*I returned home to Ithaca to start a construction business without realizing I was bitten by the wine bug in California. My friendship with owners of a local restaurant became a turning point in my life. The restaurant's cellar was filled with excellent red and white Burgundies. Tasting all those great wines made me wonder if I could replicate those great wines on our farm. We had the right soil types and proximity to a large lake—two key factors for producing the high-quality vinifera vines.*

Saltonstall looked into the idea of opening his own winery as he saw the development of the New York State wine industry.

*I wanted to re-create my memories of pleasant wines. Tacie agreed it was an exciting possibility. We went into the business after a revelatory trip to Burgundy, some basic research, and conversations with local New York vintners.*

Out went the seed business and in went 30 acres in Riesling and Chardonnay. King Ferry Winery, Inc. became our official business name and the producer of Treleaven wines. Originally, the winery and vineyard were designed as separate businesses, but a later reorganization joined the two entities. We honor our family history with Treleaven on the label of our premium wines. Our value-priced wines are sold under King Ferry labels. Along with our 100 tons of grapes from our vineyards, we buy grapes from several growers on Seneca Lake.

Riesling and other hardy varietals thrive in the Finger Lakes region. King Ferry Winery is halfway up the east side of Cayuga Lake, where glaciers created a conglomeration of soil types. The lake, 42 miles long and 400 feet deep, has a profound influence on wineries within half a mile of its shores. Numerous lakes, including Cayuga, provide a maritime-like influence that tempers the climate and helps us and the other twenty-two wineries that are directly on Cayuga's shores. The water warms up in summer and doesn't freeze in the winter, although a mile from its shores it can drop to 10° below zero. Soil maps of the area are like whacky jigsaw puzzles, with different soils of heavy clay, bedrock, shale, slate, and loam. Vines get our attention when the temperature reaches zero because of potential bud damage. In previous seasons, Mother Nature slammed us with severe bud and vine damage. It wasn't a lot of fun when we had to replant, especially Chardonnay. It's a constant challenge to discover which varietals could tolerate the tough conditions to produce quality wines. It's a struggle late in the season to get good ripening in some places around the region. Sometimes in October, frost can shut down the vines, but near the lakes we can avoid frost. It gives us an extra two or three weeks of ripening time.

Cold weather and the ensuing bud damage are continuing issues and the most harrowing experiences we've had. The spring of 2012 scared many vineyard owners. The warmest March on record pushed an early bud break, accompanied by freezing temperatures. In our vineyard this will probably mean that our Chardonnay production will be cut in half. Such is grape growing in the Finger Lakes. We hope a year like that is an anomaly.

Some vineyards have put up $25,000 wind machines. A vegetable oil can be sprayed to retard bud break. Our approach is to have the vines balanced and healthy going into dormancy. There really isn't a lot to do if the buds break and then you have a hard freeze of temperatures of 28°F and below. A hard freeze is a lot different from a frost.

Like many small winery owners, Saltonstall wears lots of hats and is pulled in many directions. The very capable enologist Lindsay Stevens works side by side with him and is in charge of year-to-year consistency. Saltonstall says,

*I've learned a lot over twenty years. My personal contribution is the care and attention to detail I bring to the process. I believe it's why our wines are the region's benchmark. We can't compete in quantity or price with bigger wineries, but our aim is to produce very good wines. Lindsay and I made some changes, not so much in technology, but in technique. We tweak all the time, trying harder in the vineyard and the winery. We bleed the Pinot noir juice after crush to get more concentration of fruit and to maximize mouth feel.*

*I love to work with barrel fermentation. Our Reserve Chardonnays spends time in newer French and Hungarian barrels that let the fruit speak. Treleaven Chardonnay is our signature wine, created in the Burgundian style with hand-harvested grapes, reduced yields, barrel fermentation, aging on the lees in oak casks, and full malolactic fermentation to develop complexity and character. This wine is the high-end big brother to value-priced King Ferry Chardonnay.*

*Riesling is a simpler wine to make. It doesn't need oak, but it requires cool fermentation. We experiment with different yeasts to see which work better in cool temperatures. Lindsay and I have formal tastings to see what goes into the blend from 150 barrels. We want our wines to be complex, balancing fruit, oak, and other characteristics. We involve all our staff in our blending trials because it's important that everyone in the winery understand where we are going with the wines. It's especially true for our sales staff. Ultimately, Tacie signs off on our main release, less heavily oaked Chardonnay, since it's her wine of preference. She even drinks it in restaurants when we go out to dinner, although we have it at home every night. She makes it clear she's involved in its final blending decision or all hell breaks loose.*

*King Ferry Winery shuns mass production, mechanized cultivation and harvesting, sacrificing quantity to achieve quality fruit with intense varietal character. Every step in our winemaking is personally attended to—from approval of each bottle in each vintage for both King Ferry Winery and Treleaven labels. We're working on a sustainability program with Cornell University, but we can't go completely organic. We forgo herbicides and use more compost. Our house is in the center of the vineyard, and I don't want to poison my family, especially since Tacie had breast cancer. Striving for better wines means swallowing hard to buy $1,000 oak barrels.*

## TRELEAVEN SWEET AND SPICY
## FALL VEGETARIAN SURPRISE

*It's a surprise because people will like squash and Brussels sprouts*

1 large sweet potato, sliced into 1-inch chunks
3 cups of halved Brussels sprouts
1 roasted red bell pepper, sliced into strips
2 cups acorn squash cut in 2-inch slices
¼ cup maple syrup
2 tbsp roasted garlic
2 tbsp butter
4 tbsp sweet chili paste—preferably Mae Ploy brand
½ cup Treleaven Reserve Chardonnay
1 tsp nutmeg
2 tbsp Thai seasoning
2 tsp salt
1 tbsp coarsely ground black pepper

In a large pot, melt butter, then sauté the garlic with the sweet potatoes on medium high heat for about 5 minutes. Add the Brussels sprouts and cook for another 5 minutes. Add squash, black pepper, salt, Thai seasoning, and nutmeg. Continue to cook for 5 minutes or until the squash, potatoes, and Brussels sprouts start to soften and brown. Leave the ingredients in the pot and add the Chardonnay to lightly deglaze the sauce. Add maple syrup, roasted red bell pepper, and chili paste; then simmer on medium low for 5 minutes, or until the vegetables are glazed.

SERVES 4.

*Treleaven Gewurztraminer 2011 is fun, because this wine will emphasize the spicy and savory qualities of the vegetarian surprise. Our semidry Treleaven Riesling 2011 is our most popular wine and, in general, our most diverse food-pairing wine. The semidry and fruit qualities of the Riesling are round and soft and can almost cool down the mouth when matched with spicier foods. Its really great acidity cuts through sweeter or saltier food.*

Wineries in Burgundy can limit themselves to three or four wines, but our customers want more choices. King Ferry Winery has a portfolio of a 10,000 cases of seventeen different wines from 27 acres of vines nearby in the Cayuga Lake Appellation. It's a challenge to be all things to all people. It's our cross to bear. We are sensitive to market demand, so we add something new every year. Two hundred customers recently signed a petition for us to come up with a sweeter red. I answered with a wine labeled Mystère, 2,000 gallons of a semidry red with 6 percent residual sugar and light tannins. The wine isn't cloyingly sweet and pairs well with pizza, hamburgers, and picnic food.

Other customers demanded a third Chardonnay, unoaked, with bright acids and without buttery characteristics. It's called Silver Lining. Our 4,000 cases of Rieslings are made in two styles: one third dry and two thirds semidry. Pinot was our only red and was so troublesome I needed a more stable red in our portfolio. So we now bottle red viniferas: a barrel-aged Cabernet Franc and a Pinot noir.

I used to buy Merlot from my mentors and pals, Eric Fry, winemaker and Sam McCollough, vineyard manager at Lenz Winery on Long Island's North Fork. Lenz sold me 10 acres of ripe Merlot, since Merlot doesn't grow well in the Finger Lakes region. The deal required a round trip to the North Shore of Long Island, loading up fruit and returning with a truckload the next night. It was a manic trip. The Long Island Expressway wore me down, even when I drove in the middle of the night. As much as I liked the Long Island Merlot, it became too expensive and I just couldn't get the price for the wine that I needed in our Upstate market. We switched from Merlot to Cabernet Franc, a decision driven by economics and the varietal's winter hardiness. We are relying on our own Cabernet Franc grapes to make a wonderful varietal wine along with our Pinot noir. My vineyard manager, Thom Bechtold has been working very hard to get these vines balanced, and we think the resulting Cabernet Franc is exceptional.

Vidal blanc is an extremely hardy and high-yielding hybrid grape, not a vinifera. The juice exhibits a lively acidity balanced with high sugar content. It's mostly used to produce semi-dry and sweet wines, and we blend it with the winery's blush wine, Saumon. Gewürztraminer is another grape that flourishes in the Finger Lakes region. We start with fruit that is so ripe that its aroma and flavor characteristics jump out of the glass. It is so well balanced you can drink three or four glasses at a go. Every other year King Ferry produces a late-harvest dessert wine. It's a style of Ice Wine that is made with grapes picked and then frozen in a nearby commercial freezer facility. We can't honestly call it Ice Wine because dead-ripe grapes aren't frozen on the vine. The commercial process involves a huge block of frozen juice pressed over twenty-four hours. Pressing yields only half the juice but with twice the sugar content of a wine with 18 percent residual sugar. It's a delicate procedure because the ice can tear the nylon bag that holds the juice during the press cycle. Sometimes it means we re-inoculate the juice with special yeasts. The yeasts that are put into this very unfriendly atmosphere need to be happy. The resulting 400 gallons of wine is bottled in splits.

Cornell University in nearby Ithaca inaugurated an undergraduate enology and viticulture program. Students at the school's winery work with grapes from the school's long-established vineyards. "King Ferry is one of the contributing wineries to the program. Two interns worked in our vineyards last year."

Asked what the future holds for King Ferry and Finger Lakes wines, Saltonstall says,

*I'm hoping for economic stability for dozens of wineries across the state. As is the case with many wineries, the recession affected our wholesale business more than our retail sales. Liquor stores and restaurants pared down their inventories and were reluctant to add new wines. We're looking for a niche in an ocean of wine and want buyers to think of us instead of buying Chilean wines because our wines are getting better and better with a combination of age and experience. We get permission from the State Liquor Authority and the Department of New York State Agriculture and Markets to sell wine by the bottle and do tastings at farmers' markets. There's been an improvement in our wholesale sales as the economy improves. There's a pretty rigorous application process to get into the system of fifty-four markets that "grownyc" runs. We sell at farmers' markets in Ithaca and Syracuse, as well as year-round in New York City at Lincoln Center, Union Square, and Brooklyn's Grand Army Plaza. The city is crucial for us. A chef who buys lettuce might buy our wine for the restaurant. We're pursuing greenmarkets in New York City, particularly in Manhattan. We will be working nine markets in the city this year and we received a New Jersey Wholesale license and permit to ship directly to consumers. My son Leverett works four greenmarkets in the Big Apple, and I'm sometimes the cheap help. I enjoy inquisitive customers who take my serious invitation to come to the winery and then arrive. The experience of educating consumers and restaurants about our wine and the Finger Lakes region is good for my soul.*

## Long Island

Dutch and English settlers in the seventeenth century battled over land rights in Lange Eylant. The English were victorious and anglified the

Dutch name. Even today, signposts proudly indicate towns named after long-departed Indian, Dutch, and English inhabitants. Many battles fought on Long Island during the Revolutionary War stained the land with English and American blood. As Manhattan moved north and its population grew, farms shipped food across the East River to the city. Post–World War II city dwellers seeking cleaner air moved to suburbs built by real estate entrepreneurs, and large swathes of farms were covered with houses and schools. The city's proximity made the suburbs a draw for workers who commuted by subway, railroad, highways, tunnels, and bridges.

Farmlands and beaches are light-years away from the city's frenzy. An hour's drive takes visitors to the beginning of the easternmost tip of the island, where it divides into two forks. Imaginative minds peering at a map claim it resembles a giant lobster claw.

The two forks have schizophrenic personalities. The South Shore is a summer playground of beaches, expensive homes, and upscale restaurants. It swarms with day-trippers and fashionable residents from Memorial Day to Labor Day. The bucolic North Shore's picturesque towns, some with histories going back to pre-Revolutionary days, and farm stands chock full of fresh-picked produce and flowers dot the landscape. Long Island potato farms have made way for grapes since Louisa and Alex Hargreave developed the island's first successful winery in 1973, setting the stage for a new industry. Farsighted vintners and investors who felt success was in the wind followed the pioneering couple. At the beginning, serious wine drinkers laughed at the thought of thousands of grapevines growing on sandy soil once dedicated to potatoes, hardly the most ideal terroir for grape. Wine snobs considered good Long Island wines an oxymoron, but the wines have come a long way and their reputation is changing. The Long Island wine region, two to three hours drive from New York City, plays a significant role in New York State's wine production, and its accessibility draws thousands of wine lovers along its wine trail. The wines can't quite compete with Bordeaux or Napa, but they are improving in quality each year.

# JOE MACARI JR.
## MACARI VINEYARD

It was a cloudy fall day on Long Island's North Shore. Grape leaves on the vines turned to purple and gold in the vineyard and the last of the berries hung low on the vines waiting to be harvested. Kelly Urbanik introduced us to her boss, Joe Macari. Macari said, "Jump in my van. I'll show you my property." He trundled us around his 440-acre vineyard and estate, speaking passionately about his belief in sustainable agriculture. The property, with a dramatic view overlooking Long Island Sound, ended precipitously at the edge of a cliff. Macari's plan to build a house on the site was squashed by his wife, who refused because the site was too remote.

In addition to grapes, Macari raises German Shepherds, poultry, bees, and cattle. His contented cattle huddle together, and nearby, turkeys and chickens peck at the ground. He and his team are devoted to principles of organic and biodynamic farming that include priming the mostly sandy loam soils. He charts farming activities according to the lunar calendar, taking into account the rhythmic influence of the sun, moon, and stars. He says,

*I noticed how flowers brighten their colors during a full moon, so I plant by phases of the moon, as past generations did. We hope to influence winemaking colleagues in the region to adopt greener farming principles to protect biodiversity, water quality, and the landscape. This respectful regard for the earth yields a farm that is environmentally balanced and sustainable, with increased plant and animal biodiversity that promotes the health, vitality, and nutritive value of plants.*

~ℓℓ~

# MACARI'S RICOTTA GNOCCHI

1 lb fresh whole-milk
  ricotta cheese
1 large egg
1 tbsp olive oil
¼ cup finely grated
  Parmesan cheese
Freshly grated
  nutmeg to taste
2 cups flour, sifted,
  plus extra for
  rolling dough

Add egg to ricotta cheese and oil and mix thoroughly. Add grated Parmesan cheese to mixture and sprinkle with nutmeg to taste. Add sifted flour a little at a time and continue to mix thoroughly until dough comes together. Dump onto generously floured surface and work with hands to bring together into a smooth ball. Add more flour as necessary until dough is smooth and no longer sticks to your hands. Cut off slices of dough like cutting a loaf of bread and roll into ropes thumb size thick, rolling from center out to each edge of the rope. Line one rope parallel to another and cut two at a time into 1-inch pieces. Roll each piece off the back of a fork to make imprints that will help hold the sauce.

Transfer gnocchi pieces to a lightly floured or nonstick baking sheet so they don't stick together and put in the freezer while making the rest of the batch. To save any gnocchi for future use, allow to freeze on the baking sheet before storing in a zip-lock bag, to prevent them from sticking together.

When ready to cook, bring a large stockpot of generously salted water to a boil. Add gnocchi to boiling water and gently stir once with a wooden spoon to create movement and prevent gnocchi from sticking to the bottom. As gnocchi rise to the top, a sign they are done cooking, scoop them out with a mesh strainer or a bamboo wire skimmer, shaking off excess water and immediately place in serving bowl. Scoop some sauce on top of each layer of gnocchi as they are placed in the bowl. This will eliminate the need to stir them with sauce in the end and risk damaging or smashing the pasta. Generously grate Parmesan over the top and serve.

SERVES 4.

*Pair with Macari Vineyards Sauvignon blanc. The light, bright fruit flavors are a perfect match for the gnocchi.*

My plan recognizes a plant's natural ability to maintain and boost healthy soil and plant growth. While many farmers use chemicals to boost quantity and aspect of their fruit, our commitment is to reduce the use of substances harmful to human and ecological health. We compost and use little or no pesticides. Herbicides have been banned from the vineyard for years, although under certain conditions, it is necessary to use fungicides. An elaborate composting program uses naturally occurring plant and animal materials combined in certain seasons. Our cattle donate somewhere between 100 and 200 horns filled with cow manure from our herd and horse manure from local farms for our biodynamic program. Each fall, the horns are filled with manure and deposited in nearby woods until spring. Then the horns are dug up, the contents are stirred into water, and the compound is spread around the soil to enliven it. Skins, pits, and stems from grapes, as well as fish, kelp, and seashells stimulate soil life. I buy 30,300 pounds of waste fish from a Brooklyn fish wholesaler that we turn into compost, along with tractor-trailer loads of kelp, deposited on the soil twenty-two shots at a time. Nettle teas are applied to vine leaves to enhance their ability to receive light. Soils once deadened with arsenic and chemicals are now vital and alive. There is now a life force on this farm together with a connection to earthly and cosmic forces. I'm building this place for life and for my children.

# KELLY URBANIK
## MACARI VINEYARD

Kelly Urbanik grew up in St. Helena, California, the heart of Napa Valley's wine region. When she was young, her grandfather's homemade wine spiked her interest in wine and led her to the enology program at U.C. Davis. "College was too close to home, so after graduation I flew to Burgundy in time for harvest. My favorite memory is digging out a tank after fermentation. We emptied the wooden casks with buckets. The smell of finished wine clicked and confirmed my future." Urbanik returned to California with practical winemaking skills and snagged a job at Bouchaine Vineyards in Napa Valley. Soon after, she graduated to assistant winemaker, helping with the winery's production of Pinot noir and Chardonnay, two cool weather crops that flourish in the Carneros region. She also had a hand in working with custom-crushed Syrah and Sauvignon blanc.

The idea of working in other wine regions exerted a pull. She headed for the North Fork of Long Island and signed on for a two-year commitment with Bedell Cellars that lasted four and a half years.

*The day after I left Bedell the phone rang and Joe Macari offered me a job at his winery. There's a huge difference between fruit on Long Island and California, especially the way grapes ripen. Every winemaker wants to find a sense of place in the wines. We have particular factors that make our wines very distinctive, impeccably balanced, elegant, and great with food. Some of our vines are twenty-one to thirty years old. A profound maritime influence of the Atlantic Ocean and surrounding bays affects the vineyards and unquestionably shapes the wines. Our sandy soils drain excessive water better than heavy* soils, a saving grace when there is a lot of heavy rainfall. In California the weather is more constant. I prefer Long Island's change of seasons to California's generally milder climate. I love the drama of spring, when everything explodes into life after a winter of snow and cold weather. A blanket of snow is fantastic. Fall is my favorite season because harvest is always exciting. There is so much to do you can't relax for a second. The changes make even unplanned events fun. The weather on the east coast is totally unpredictable from season to season and from year to year. No growing season or harvest is remotely like another. The growing season is shorter and sunshine can be inconsistent, making each vintage unique.

The grapes keep you constantly on your toes. It's like the Top Chef competition. You deal in a short amount of time with what you are given. I control what nature hands me with new techniques and with my gut feelings about how to deal with the fruit. I don't have a set recipe. I only do what my heart tells me to do when I judge how the fruit looks and tastes. I believe there is a lot of artistry in winemaking and admit to having my own opinions about picking and blending.

Aroma and flavor components in wine are said to come from the soil. However, aromas can be accentuated by differences in fermenting temperatures, types of yeast, and fermenting vessels of stainless steel and oak. We don't look for high alcohol at Macari. We taste fruit in the vineyard and harvest to check for balance and harmony, when acids, tannins, and sugars mesh together. Although it's difficult to define balance, I know what's balanced for me and what will give me the style I want in a wine.

We pick at different sugar levels for each varietal. Ripe flavors on Long Island come in at a lower sugar level, usually between 23 and 25 degrees brix. We pick at 19 degrees brix for our sparkling wines. In California, sugars can rise to 30 degrees brix sometimes before the fruit tastes ripe and when acids are lost because of respiration. Out here, the grapes rarely get to 30 degrees brix. In 2010, we were almost on a par with California because of an exceedingly hot summer. Generally, there is a higher amount of acid vis-à-vis sugar, and that creates a good balance because of less heat. We don't take a heavy hand with extraction or oak. Our Merlots have raspberry flavors and the whites have good acidity.

Long Island winemakers experiment with a wide selection of individual varietals and blends at a range of price points.

Macari has a full range of wines, including a small production of Syrah and a new production of Malbec. Varietals are bottled individually or in blends

## URBANIK'S THAI GREEN CURRY CHICKEN

### CURRY

1–1.5 lb (about 0.7 kg)
boneless chicken
thigh or breast,
cut into chunks
1 can coconut milk
4 kaffir lime leaves
(can be purchased
frozen at most
Asian food stores),
OR substitute 1 tsp
grated lime zest
1 red bell pepper,
seeded and cut
into chunks
1 zucchini, sliced
lengthwise several
times, then cut into
chunks
Generous handful
fresh basil
2 tbsp coconut oil or
other vegetable oil

Warm a wok or large frying pan over medium-high heat. Add the oil and swirl around, then add the green curry paste.

Stir-fry briefly to release the fragrance (30 seconds to 1 minute), then add ¾ of the coconut milk, reserving 2–3 tbsp per serving portion for later. Add the chicken, stirring to incorporate. When the curry sauce comes to a boil, reduce heat to medium or medium-low, until it simmers.

Cover and allow to simmer 3–5 more minutes or until chicken is cooked through. Stir occasionally.

Add the red bell pepper, zucchini, and strips of lime leaf or lime zest, stirring well to incorporate. Simmer another 2–3 minutes, or until vegetables are softened but still firm and colorful.

Adjust the salt, adding 1–2 tbsp fish sauce if not salty enough. If you'd prefer a sweeter curry, add a little more sugar. If too salty, add a squeeze of lime or lemon juice. If too spicy, add more coconut milk. Note that this curry should be a balance of salty, spicy, sweet, and sour, plus bitter from the fresh basil garnish.

Serve this curry in bowls with Thai jasmine rice on the side. Top each portion with fresh basil, then drizzle over 2–3 tbsp coconut milk. ENJOY!

SERVES 2 TO 3.

*Serve with Macari Vineyards' early wine Chardonnay. The flavors of the wine are a splendid match for the exotic flavors of the curry.*

---

depending on the year. We produce about 12,000–15,000 cases or 144,000—180,000 bottles per year. We bottle everything we grow, and have a second, lower-priced entry level labeled Collina. We have a Collina Merlot and a Collina Chardonnay.

In 2009, bad weather throughout the summer made harvest tough. Normally we're done picking at the beginning of November, but the fruit never really ripened. So we didn't finish harvesting until Thanksgiving. On the other hand, 2010 was an incredible vintage of a quality we've never seen out here. We had an early bud break and a long growing season with plenty of heat and

## GREEN CURRY PASTE

4 small green Thai chilies, OR substitute 1 to 2 jalapeno peppers
¼ cup shallot OR purple onion, diced
4 cloves garlic, minced
1 thumb-size piece galangal OR ginger, grated
1 stalk fresh minced lemongrass OR 3 tbsp frozen or bottled prepared lemongrass
½ tsp ground coriander
½ tsp ground cumin
¾–1 tsp shrimp paste
1 (loose) cup fresh coriander/cilantro leaves and stems, chopped
½ tsp ground white pepper (can be purchased at some supermarkets, OR at Asian food stores)
3 tbsp fish sauce
1 tsp brown sugar
2 tbsp lime juice

Place all the green curry paste ingredients together in a food processor and process to a paste. If necessary, add a few tbsp of the coconut milk to help blend ingredients. Set aside. Prepare the lime leaves by tearing the leaf away from either side of the stem. Discard the central stem. Then, using scissors. Cut leaves into thin strips. Set aside.

sunshine. Disease pressure was incredibly low and we had the luxury of picking whenever we wanted, without having to worry about weather being a factor in harvesting decisions. The fruit had incredible ripeness and concentration, resulting in beautiful and refined wines. It was a very exciting vintage.

Sauvignon blanc, with its lovely minerality; Merlot; and Malbec are the most popular varietals for Macari and, like all our other wines, represent the terroir of the Macari property. I'm proud of the wines that I produce hand in hand with the Macari family.

## North Carolina

When the explorer Giovanni de Verrazzano explored the east coast of America in 1524, he took note of a prolific white, bronze, or lightly pink grape. Sixty years later, two captains from Sir Walter Raleigh's fleet landed their ships at Roanoke Island on the Outer Banks and sent back messages about a land filled with grapes growing so abundantly the vines covered trees and shrubs. The Scuppernong grape derives its name from an Indian term for the nearby Scuppernong River. In 1585, English Governor Ralph Lane confirmed that the area's wild grapes exceeded the best grapes from Spain and France. Colonists in the seventeenth and eighteenth centuries propagated the vines, whose grapes yielded sweet wines.

Grapevines are usually blessed with a few decades of long life, but the productive mother vine has continued to bear fruit and donate cuttings on Roanoke Island for more than four centuries. The gnarly trunk of the beloved iconic vine is 2 feet thick. Wooden trellises support the tremendous weight of branches reaching across close to an acre. The varietal, an offshoot of the Muscadine grape, thrives in the hot, sandy condition of the state. More than twenty variations of bronze, red and purple-black Scuppernong grapes are now cultivated for both red and white dry and sweet wines.

North Carolina was the leader in the country's fledgling wine industry, a fact verified by Thomas Jefferson, a noted wine collector. The state's first commercial winery was established in 1835 and flourished until it was impacted by the Civil War and Prohibition. Even when Prohibition was repealed, rivalry from other wine-producing states negatively affected North Carolina's industry. Today one hundred wineries flourish around the state, making it the seventh largest American producer. Local vintners focus on wines from the old favorite Scuppernong grapes and European vinifera varietals. The industry is back on the road to success as grapevines replace agricultural products like soybeans and tobacco.

## SHARON FENCHAK
### BILTMORE ESTATE

Mega-wealthy George Vanderbilt's country getaway, Biltmore, near Ashville is a mind-boggling domain of 250 rooms amalgamating the architectural styles of three famous French chateaux built in the late 1880's. The magnificent property in North Carolina's mountains is a favorite tourist destination. The Biltmore Winery was established in 1971 to introduce a wide variety of wines to visitors. The winery is leading the way to the rebirth of wine production across the state. Every year the estate is a mecca, attracting 600,000 visitors who tour the house, grounds, and winery.

Sharon Fenchak's path to her career as a winemaker at the Vanderbilt Winery took a circuitous path. A small-town girl from Pennsylvania, she joined the military at nineteen against her parents' wishes. The Army sent her to Italy, where she fell in love with the country's joyous lifestyle. Italy might have that effect on every visitor, but Fenchak's experience expanded her horizons about wine and food. Her experience sent her in an unexpected direction. When she came home after two years, she registered in the Food and Science Program at Penn State University and went on to take a graduate degree in the wine program at the University of Georgia. She put her new degree to work at Chestnut Mountain Winery and Habersham Winery in Georgia. In 1999 she spotted an ad for a job at Biltmore Winery as assistant to Bernard Delille, who came to the United States from France in 1986 to join the Biltmore Wine Company. "It's very special to be a winemaker at Biltmore. The winery is part of the long history of winemaking in the U.S. and is an important contributor to North Carolina's role as a major wine-producing state in the Thirteen

Colonies. Delille and I work well together as a team, even though we have different thoughts and ideas. Becoming a team takes work, but Bernard and I value and respect each other's opinion. We know when to push each other's buttons," she says. In addition to wine production, Fenchak is involved with in-house research and development in winemaking and viticultural practices to continue Biltmore's tradition to be informed about the latest technologies.

*North Carolina is a difficult place for grape cultivation. Weather is our most difficult problem. An abundance of rain and humidity affects the development of good grapes. Our vineyard crew checks the sandy clay loam soil every season and makes adjustments to ensure the vines receive proper nutrients. Organic and biodynamic methods don't work too well in North Carolina. The heat in 2010 was severe and created a quick, early, fantastic ripening. In the early fall, hurricanes come off the coast often in the early fall. The soil is drenched and the grapes don't ripen properly. Fortunately, Denis Wynne, our excellent, experienced vineyard manager, provides us with acceptable grapes during the most difficult seasons. Undoubtedly, fewer pesticides are desirable, but in most cases, we use them when necessary. It's crucial to have a spray program that puts us on top of our particular weather problems.*

*As I find my way through the multitude of wines we produce at Biltmore, I learn each one has its own particular personality. Over time, I've gotten to know them all as well as the terroirs of all the vineyards. Every year we cross our fingers and hope for a good vintage with good grapes. I especially enjoy when the grapes are harvested in good shape because everything in the grape is expressed in wine. My goal is to produce wine that is true to the varietal character of the grape. I want our customers to taste in the bottle what we taste from all our vineyards. We bottle a combination of fifty still and sparkling wines at Biltmore. We harvest 200 to 300 tons of Chardonnay, Riesling, Viognier, Cabernet Sauvignon, Cabernet Franc, and Merlot from our estate vineyards. We also purchase grapes from other North Carolina farmers. Once the fruit is picked, I monitor the fermentation daily in the cellar. The artistic side of winemaking comes with a number of factors. It is absolutely crucial to choose grapes and new varietals with late bud break coupled with an ability to ripen before fall frost in western North Carolina. Grapes with tight clusters and thin skins like Pinot noir grow poorly in our humid conditions. Cabernet Sauvignon and Cabernet Franc have thicker skins and their less-tight clusters*

# FENCHAK'S MUSTARD-GRILLED PORK TENDERLOIN WITH SWEET CORN GRITS AND BEAN CASSOULET

## FOR THE PORK

3 each pork
  tenderloin
2 sprigs fresh
  rosemary
2 sprigs fresh thyme
3 tbsp Dijon mustard
Kosher salt and
  pepper to taste

## FOR THE GRITS

10 ears Corn
¾ cup chicken broth
3 tbsp butter
2 tbsp sugar
Kosher salt and
  pepper to taste

## FOR THE CASSOULET

1 shallot (minced)
2 tbsp garlic (minced)
3 slices of bacon
  (chopped)
3 oz chorizo
1 cup peas
½ cup oven roasted
  tomatoes (diced)
2 cups green beans
  (halved)
2 cups yellow wax
  beans (halved)
10 oz chicken broth
4 tbsp butter
Kosher salt and
  pepper to taste

For the pork, preheat oven to 375°F. Begin by removing the herbs from the stems and finely chop. Rub the mustard over the pork thoroughly and add the herbs. Season with salt and pepper and grill to an internal temperature of 145°F, about 15 minutes. Let rest for 10 minutes. Slice and serve.

For the grits, grate the corn on a hand grater into a heavy-bottom pot. Add the broth, butter, and sugar and cook over low heat for approximately 40 minutes. Season with salt and pepper.

For the cassoulet, in a sauté pan sweat the shallots, garlic, chorizo, and bacon for 4 minutes. Add the peas, tomatoes, and both beans. Cook for 2 minutes. Add the chicken broth and cook for 2 minutes. Add the butter and season to finish.

SERVES 6–8.

*Pair with Biltmore® Reserve North Carolina Chardonnay.*

*allow airflow through the cluster. Once the grapes are harvested, it's impor-*
*tant to decide what path to take. Options about yeasts, fast or slow fermenta-*
*tion in stainless steel, and choice between French or American barrels allow*
*some creativity. Blending is the most artistic and creative part of the process,*
*when decisions are made to use 1 percent of this and 5 percent of that.*

*Fermentation is the part of the job that always fascinates me. It's the pro-*
*cess of adding yeast to the juice that converts the available sugar into alcohol*
*and carbon dioxide. An easy fermentation is fantastic. Temperature control is*
*the best tool in modern winemaking, together with the availability of new*
*types of yeasts. We don't want to manipulate the wines, so we generally use*
*traditional yeasts. However, yeasts vary with the temperature during fermen-*
*tation. It's crucial to deal with both slow and fast fermentations. Occasion-*
*ally, fermentation gets stuck when juice lacks certain nutrients, so we pur-*
*chase yeasts that are compatible for particular grapes each harvest. Wild*
*yeasts are often more unpredictable, so we use yeasts that allow us more con-*
*trol. We get some from Scott Laboratories because the company isolated yeasts*
*with characteristics well matched with particular grapes each harvest. Some-*
*times we have one or two fermentations that act like misbehaving children*
*who need extra attention. It's important to take care of difficult fermentation*
*issues early. Once fermentation is over, it becomes more difficult to make*
*changes in the wine. All this is the scientific part of winemaking.*

*I've changed over the years. I'm more patient with wine. I always wanted to*
*rush in and fix a problem, but I learned to slow down because wine is so dy-*
*namic. It's not necessary to jump on the wine or add too many adjustments*
*right away. Now I wait for wine to talk to me, rather than my telling it what to*
*do. Working at a big facility with so many scenarios has taught me to handle*
*many different problems. This exposure gave me the skill to turn a difficult*
*situation into an acceptable outcome. I look forward to the next challenge,*
*knowing the exposure gives me the confidence to handle it.*

*We're gaining a reputation for producing quality wine. Biltmore wines can*
*be purchased in over twenty states and we're on our way to becoming a national*
*brand. Some loyal customers return to buy the estate's award-winning wines.*
*Some visitors have never been to a winery and like to start with sweeter wines.*
*Sweet wines definitely have their place, although they're generally best for des-*
*sert. Our best seller is a white blend called Century, a blend of Muscat Canelli,*
*Riesling, and Gewurztraminer. Our transitional red, also called Century, is*
*made in the Italian style from Sangiovese and Merlot. Century Rosé is a dry*
*pink made from Syrah grapes. Pas de Deux is our fun, méthode champenoise*

*sparkling wine made from Muscat Canelli. Pas de Deux is a result of my memories of Italy, where I enjoyed a sparkling Moscato. Its hot pink label and cap make the package easy to recognize.*

Fenchak and DeLille also make wine from grapes from California and Washington State. They visit all the vineyards on both coasts as harvest approaches. Biltmore Winery rents space to barrel, ferment, and bottle California grapes under their total control. The West Coast wines are bottled under the labels of Antler Hill and Biltmore Reserve. "Our production totals slightly under two million bottles at a wide range of price points and with a wide variety of varietals crafted in a number of different styles. Our production is designed to suit our visitors."

Fenchak works out with weights and cardio so that she can indulge in good food and wine. Her own choice of wine is based on her mood and a wine's region rather than label or varietal. "I appreciate any good wine with the right food and the right company. But my first choice is always Biltmore."

# Oregon

Once only inhabited by Native Americans, Spanish explorers and missionaries led the way to the northwest area of America, describing its riches and drawing a mix of fur traders, American pioneers, and European immigrants. President Thomas Jefferson sent Lewis and Clark to map the territory, which encouraged settlers to cross the country on the Oregon Trail, a difficult route. They found deep forests, a dramatic ocean shoreline, and a favorable climate for agriculture and fruit orchards. Transcontinental railroads expedited the growth of the lumber industry and the concomitant metropolitan cities. Wine production got off to a start in the state in the 1840's, with commercial production beginning in the middle of the next century. The state has more than three wineries in several AVA regions specializing in cool-varietal grapes —Pinot noir, Pinot gris, and Chardonnay. Warm days, cool nights, and maritime influences from the Pacific Ocean and rivers impact on vineyards. Frequent rainfalls in spring at bud break and harvest present problems but don't deter determined winemakers.

Burgundy and Oregon have a long-standing connection of mutual assistance and rivalry. Oregonian winemakers spent time in Burgundy learning to match varietals with their cool-weather terroir. Oregon's wines from fifteen appellations and several subappellations often garner accolades in competitive tastings against French Burgundies. Oregon wine garners compliments from Pinot noir fans who once turned their noses up at anything but Burgundian Pinots. Small operations produce a few thousand cases, compared with hi-tech wineries making a wide variety of styles.

Oregon is a leader in the United States dedicated to developing high standards for the wine industry. A new program called LIVE—Low Impact Viticulture and Enology—promotes earth-friendly viticulture and winemaking. Strict state regulations require 90 percent of a specific grape varietal before the name appears on a label. Ten years after the passage of the state bill, the federal government raised the labeling standard to 75 percent.

# SHEILA NICHOLAS
## ANAM CARA CELLARS

Whenever we speak over the phone, I can conjure up Sheila Nicholas's ready smile and sense of humor. Decades ago, I met Sheila through her job in public relations at Sterling Vineyards when I was invited to the winery's viticultural seminar as a wine journalist. At the time, she and her husband Nick were part of Napa's lifestyle. Nick's pizzeria was a hot draw to local vintners. Many winemakers often traded their cult cabs for a large combination pie. But pizza was only a means to an end for Nick. "My husband dreamed of owning a high-end steak house and becoming filthy rich," Nicholas says. The couple was seduced into thinking winemaking was easy.

*Nick grew up on a ranch in southern California. I always wanted land to grow things, so it wasn't surprising I was a willing partner in our new venture. We said if other people can do it, we could too. It seemed like a good idea to pick up and go when our two kids were in middle school. Our funds were finite, certainly not enough to drop a couple of hundred thousand dollars for 1 acre of land in Napa. Oregon attracted us with its lifestyle, clean air, and great food. It's the same reason people come here from all over the world to make Pinot noir. There was another plus. We knew a few people who had already settled here as winemakers.*

*We each flew to Oregon on alternate weekends and never saw the same properties together. We could've rented a small corner of a winery and an extra fermentation tank. But that was a major problem. It isn't easy for newcomers to the area to buy fruit from good vineyards. Worst of all, there's no continuity from vintage to vintage. Our own vineyard with our own fruit was important for total control.*

## NICHOLAS'S SALMON IN RED WINE

1 bottle Pinot noir (not from Oregon, which is too good to simmer away. It can be one that's stale, open for days or unloved.)
Approximately 20 white peppercorns
One fresh filet of wild salmon side
Sel gris

Pour Pinot noir into sturdy, shallow pan and sprinkle with peppercorns. Simmer on hot burner for approximately 2 hours—watch constantly to make sure it doesn't boil over or burn the pan. Enjoy the aroma! Remove from heat when ⅓ inch of the liquid remains in pan. Cool uncovered for approximately an hour. Place salmon, skin side down, in a well-buttered, nonmetallic baking dish. Strain peppercorns when Pinot noir reduction is cool. Brush the wine marinade evenly over the flesh side of the salmon. Cover with foil. Bake at 400° for about 20 minutes. Remove foil, rebaste, and check for doneness. Return to oven if necessary. Sprinkle with sel gris and serve with sautéed English cucumbers and brown rice.

SERVES 2 TO 4.

*Pinot noir is obviously a perfect match.*

Luckily, a new property came on the market during one of Nicholas's visits to the Chehalem Mountains, a 20-mile-long AVA region within the Willamette Valley AVA in Oregon. "I stood still and realized the land called to me. I heard it say it needed a vineyard. We did the math, did the homework, and bit the bullet, even though it was a big, unloved, dilapidated mess. It was an overgrown orchard of filbert, plum, and walnut trees with a hundred-year-old house that we lived in until we built our new house. Buying it was a gut decision." Her Scottish roots provided the property name: Anan Cara, the Celtic term for "soul friend."

*We hacked our way through 70 acres of a single road. We cleared 30 acres and dug soil pits. We recognized its 350- to 700-foot elevation was perfect for a vineyard. Southeast-facing slopes took in whatever sun was available in Oregon. Best of all, the Willamette Valley has the perfect a cool climate for Pinot noir. It's on the fifty-ninth parallel, the same as Burgundy's. Oregon has longer days, although Burgundy has a longer season.*

I like to think I'm the winemaker, although I don't know much about chemistry. I have the passion and want to learn everything about making wine. I taste tendrils on the vines in spring. Once, on a whim, I wondered what it would be like to taste drops of water from a vine's bark after pruning when water was pushing up from the earth. Translating the taste from the soil is an indescribably gorgeous experience.

Learning a vineyard is intuitive. We hired a consultant who works for a winemaking facility with all the bells and whistles where we make our wine, but we rack, clean, and schlep. It means taking care and appreciating what we have. We divide our responsibilities. Nicholas rides the tractor and tends the vineyard where we planted 28 acres of Pinot noir and single blocks of Gewurtztraminer and Riesling. The vines were planted in two stages in 2001 with year-old vines. We continue to work carefully and work hard to figure out which clone responds to which barrel, and to learn which part of the vineyard has potential for a reserve.

We went through a baptism of fire the first year and made a lot of mistakes. It sounds like a pun, but it's been a hard row to hoe. Then we had a few heart-rending frights in the earlier years. Fermentation got away from us, but we got our first vintage out in 2004. It was a picture-perfect summer in 2007 until rain came in three huge waves. We thought the Ark was on its way. In 2008, it poured over Labor Day when our grapes were barely in véraison—the onset of ripening. Even so, we pulled out the most incredible vintage after the weather cleared during an amazing six weeks. Everything came in perfectly in the end, although the sugars came in first, and the flavors took their time.

We produce Pinot noir, an off-dry Riesling, dry and dessert Gewürztraminers, and a Chardonnay. Our special productions include two Pinot noirs of approximately fifty cases each named for our children: Heather's Vineyard from ten rows of a single clone and the Mark series. Occasionally we produce a rosé. We continue to live on the edge. It's impossible to predict what will happen. The cost of farming is consistently high. One night we sat on our porch after our first vintage in 2003 and figured it cost us $836.12 per bottle.

Nick and I have been married for thirty-odd years. We're lucky. Our wonderful community means we have two or three friends who are always there for us. It's been an incredible journey. Our vineyard has already received some awards. Our Riesling consistently ranks among the top in Oregon by Northwest Palate magazine. Nicholas Estate Pinot noir has garnered Double Gold Medal Oregon Wine Awards.

# CHILE

C HILE DOESN'T COME immediately to mind as a country with a long history of winemaking. Yet the South American country, bound by the Pacific Ocean to the west and the Andes Mountains to the east, is not a newcomer to the wine industry. Spanish conquistadors and missionaries planted European vines in Chile in the sixteenth century. By the mid-seventeenth century, Chilean winemakers planted enough grapes to compete with Spain. Spanish rulers prohibited Chile from exporting wine, but distance between the two countries made the edict impossible to enforce. By the eighteenth century, Chile was producing generally poor-quality wines. As time went on, wealthy Chilean landowners visited France and brought back French vines and expert vintners who were looking for new territories after phylloxera decimated France's vineyards. Chile was the perfect fit for adventuresome vintners. By the late twentieth century, word spread about the excellent terroirs: A strong maritime influence, morning fog, and a wide range of day and night temperatures together with loam, sand, clay, and gravelly soils with poor organic compounds. The terroir presented a picture judged to be an excellent choice to produce better wines. Foreign investment and an influx of talented winemakers slowly changed the industry. Modern equipment like stainless steel tanks and imported oak barrels replaced many traditional methods of viniculture. Varietals like Chardonnay, Sauvignon blanc, Pinot noir, and Syrah develop interesting characteristics in a variety of terroirs. Today Chilean wines combine quality with affordability, making them popular choices across the international market.

"Flying winemakers" like Grant Phelps put Chile in a position to compete in the world market by introducing new vineyard practices and contemporary winemaking techniques. He settled in as winemaker at Casas del Bosque in the Casablanca Valley about 45 miles from Santiago and 20 miles from Valparaiso, the main port from which wine is exported. The family-owned boutique winery was established in 1993 with the goal of producing limited-edition, cool-climate wines. Initially, all wines were 100 percent estate grown. The winery's vineyard is planted with Sauvignon blanc, Chardonnay, Pinot noir, Syrah, and Riesling. Recent additions of Carménère and Cabernet Sauvignon from the Rapel and Maipo regions were added to Casas del Bosque's portfolio. Today Casas del Bosque is recognized for producing highly regarded Sauvignon blanc with newer productions of Pinot noir and Syrah. The winery's total annual production reaches around 90,000 cases. Sixty percent of its wines are exported.

# Casablanca Valley

## GRANT PHELPS
CASAS DEL BOSQUE

Grant Phelps hosted a wine tasting of Casas del Bosque Estate wines at Puro Chile, a wine center in the heart of Manhattan's Soho district. One wall of the handsome space showcased the country's vast array of reasonably priced wines and gourmet products. By the time we met, Phelps seemed talked out, but he revived when the tasting ended and the crowd left. The winemaker, who has the appearance of a hip rock star, is the fastest talker I've ever interviewed. His conversation is peppered with unique personal observations and an occasional salty expression. Phelps is originally from New Zealand, where he received a degree in winemaking in 1995, followed by a master's degree in Pinot noir. "My interest was in Pinot noir, so I headed for two great areas famous for that wine. I went to Oregon, but I got bored. I went to Burgundy but found its winemaking techniques weren't relevant to new Pinots that are a different style and very terroir driven." The young winemaker needed to find a challenge and found it in the Casablanca region, which has a climate similar to Carneros in Napa, perfect for cool-climate grapes.

In the 1980's, the idea of flying winemakers took hold. Everyday wine sold in English supermarkets was affordable and accessible, but the Brits wanted better inexpensive wines. English brokerage companies sent winemakers to make wine in different regions around the world. The companies form agreements with countries, determine a price, and send off a winemaker.

I signed a contract, got on a plane, and became a Flying Winemaker. One of my first jobs upgraded wines for Sainsbury, the famous English supermarket chain.

I worked for three different British firms. I was able to choose where I wanted to work. I picked Ibiza, Hungary, and Cyprus. I made 100,000 liters of AC Chardonnay in the Loire, where I found winemaking to be very rudimentary. I wanted to get the vintners to give up their tradition of picking by date even when grapes were green. In Rumania, I made Chardonnay, often for private labels. I worked in Hungary, Australia, and California for Golden State Vintners. I enjoyed working in two hemispheres, sharing information with local winemakers and dealing with growers and new varieties. It was a compressed way of getting a lot of experience. Consultants can drive style with no idea about the vineyards and only a few decisions along the way. I encountered a few problems and tasted a lot of inferior wines. Most of them weren't clean, nor were they terroir driven. The winemakers were very insular and worked the way their grandfathers did. Local rules and regulations hamstrung them. I think it's why Europe got left behind.

Then I tasted Chilean wine in 1997, when the wines were beginning to enter the market. Most of them were entry-level wines—jammy, overextracted, oxidized, or green. But they sparked my curiosity. I would have picked Chile if it was on the contract list because I wanted to return to my cool-climate roots. I headed for Casablanca Valley. At the time it was one of Chile's relatively new wine regions. It started late in the game, although Chile has been producing wine for 400 years. Located on the west coast of the country along the Pacific Ocean, Casas del Bosque was a beachfront resort until the 1980's. There are some places where grapes shouldn't be planted because nature isn't working with you. But Casablanca Valley and the Casas del Bosque property are perfect for Pinot noir and Sauvignon blanc, two varietals that do great in cool climates. Other areas along the coast are being developed for wine, but the conditions in Casablanca, its long-established vines, and its reputation remain untroubled by the competition.

The vineyards were planted in the mid-1980's on three to four geologically old, unique soil types. There were no glaciers or new soils deposited by rivers. Instead, there is a massive bed of granite and a thin layer of clay from broken granite. The Humboldt Current exerts a powerful maritime influence along the Chilean coast, coming from the Antarctic. Morning fog drifting off the ocean deposits a saline characteristic on the vines, while afternoon breezes fill

## PHELPS'S SCALLOP TARTAR

*The recipe is adapted from Alvaro Larraguibel, the chef at Casas del Bosque's Restaurante Tanino.*

| | |
|---|---|
| 1 tsp Dijon mustard<br>Olive oil, salt, and<br>pepper to taste | Cook scallops in boiling water for 2 minutes, drain, and add them in a bowl together with the rest of the ingredients. Marinate for 2 hours. Serve cold with toast.<br><br>SERVES 4.<br><br>*Pair with a Chilean clean, crisp, citrusy Sauvignon blanc like Casas del Bosque.* |

*the valley with cooling mist. Enough afternoon sunshine burns through to allow grapes to ripen.*

*Casas del Bosque is a family winery. The owner's goal is to make good wine with the taste of the soil and the land he loves. He rides his horse every day to feel the ground under his feet. Our 20,000 cases of Sauvignon blanc make it our most important varietal, although we bottle Chardonnay, Riesling, Pinot noir, Syrah, and Merlot grown on 224 hectares. We offer a variety of styles, including 2010 Pequeñas Sauvignon blanc, 2009 Pequeñas Pinot noir, 2010 Reserva Sauvignon blanc, 2010 Reserva Chardonnay, 2010 Reserva Cabernet Sauvignon Rapel, 2007 Gran Estate Selection, and a 2008 Gran Bosque.*

*In keeping with the estate's philosophy of achieving high-quality wines, clusters are thinned on 100 percent of our vineyards to achieve the desired yield for each variety, and the best clusters are selected to meet our high demands. All our vineyards use a modern drip irrigation system from water coming from subterranean wells. Each block in the vineyard, depending on the variety, soil, and climate, gets a different treatment. Red wines are stressed with little water to get the highest concentrations of flavors and aromas. Weed control is managed with the smallest amount of chemicals. Wind generators and heaters work together to control severe frosts. The estate takes pride in wines that come from their own vineyards, except for Cabernet Sauvignon and Carménère, which we buy from the Rapel Valley. Many of those vines are thirty-five years old or older.*

If I wanted to make Marlborough-style Sauvignon blanc, I would've stayed in New Zealand. Those wines have a different profile with herbaceous, "cat's pee," and gooseberry flavors. They have high acidity and require chapitalization. People love New Zealand Sauvignon blancs, but now they suffer from a sameness that makes them boring. They're very attractive to people who don't know much about wine because they project a kind of security blanket effect. Instead, Casas del Bosque Sauvignon blanc flavors are very fresh, very citrusy rather than herbaceous and vegetal.

The way I make wine is my personal backlash against globalization in winemaking. I'm opposed to formulaic wines. I want to make wines that taste like they come from our vineyards. Wine from multiple vineyards can't speak of terroir. Control comes directly from the vineyard and the way I get the grapes to grow. That way I don't have to do a lot of manipulation. A good winemaker doesn't intervene too much, except to determine style with a bit of tweaking that translates into what goes into the bottle. Every decision I make from myriad choices affects the quality of the wine. It's like choices in cooking —how to cut carrots, how much salt and pepper. I want a natural synergy between food and wine. A winemaker who can't cook can't make good wine.

The first major decision to be made is when to pick. I'm looking for flavors in the grapes. I spend three hours a day at harvest, especially for Sauvignon blanc. That grape can change its character from day to day. We used to harvest by hand, but a lot of our labor force went south to work in construction after the earthquake. We machine-pick at night, when temperatures are low to retard fermentation. This method is actually more environmentally friendly because it leaves less of a carbon footprint.

I experiment with three or four blends and try them with food at home. When it works with food, it's the blend I know I should go for. I try to make a wine so that an individual can drink a whole bottle, but that's impossible when wine is overoaked or unbalanced. A winemaker needs to ask whether to try for a rating of 95 or to create a wine that will sell without pissing anyone off. I have a vision for my wine, but I don't want people to say this is a Grant Phelps wine. Our wines have come a long way in fourteen years.

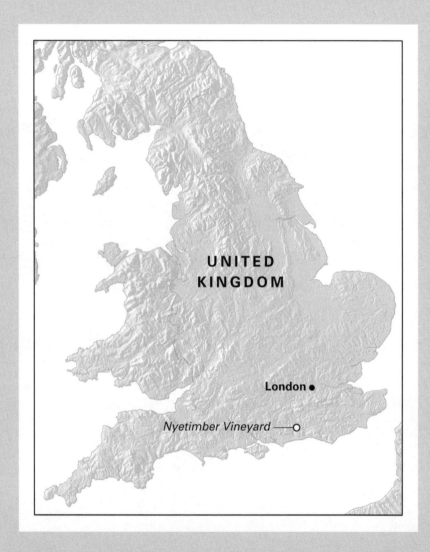

UNITED
KINGDOM

London ●

*Nyetimber Vineyard* ──○

# ENGLAND

Early on, inhabitants of what ultimately meshed into the British Isles unlocked the secret of making wine, beer, and ale. The inhabitants of the sceptered isle, as Shakespeare called it, have always relied on the three staple beverages. It is surprising to note that winemaking is undergoing a renaissance, since English winemaking skills disappeared into the mists of time. Many issues—including wars, invasions, and a cool, rainy climate—were responsible for the decline in local winemaking, but those same issues should have led to the decline in French winemaking, whose history and weather are remarkably similar to those of Britain.

Archeological digs uncovered a long history of wine paraphernalia that proves wine was made on English shores before the Romans invaded and planted grapes. The slow conversion of the population to Christianity begun by St. Augustine in the sixth century led to the growth of monasteries where vines planted by monks supplied the church with sacramental wine. Invasion by various tribes halted winemaking until 1066, when the French cohorts of William the Conqueror crossed the Channel, settled in England, and reintroduced winemaking. The Conqueror insisted on a census called the Domesday Book that compiled the value of his new territory for tax purposes, including tallies on vineyards. The dissolution of the monasteries during the reign of Henry VIII resulted in reduced production of wine. Centuries later, plant diseases and labor shortages caused by two world wars wreaked havoc on vestiges of the industry. Wine production across the British Isles fizzled.

Until recent decades, English wine and food had equally dismal reputations. By the 1950's a few adventuresome souls found Britain's climate suitable for sturdy, cool-weather white grapes. Around 400 wineries scattered around the country specialize primarily in white wines. England's vintners experimented with wine styles and varietals like Seyval blanc, Müller-Thurgau, and Bacchus. The great success wine story is sparkling wine. Nyetimber and other English bubblies bested some of the best French Champagnes at international blind tastings. A buy-local campaign, low prices, and developing high quality are creating a market for English wines. Optimistic winemakers are looking to expand sales internationally.

# CHERIE SPRIGGS
## NYETIMBER VINEYARD

Canadians Cherie Spriggs and her husband Brad Greatrix are the winemaking team at Nyetimber Vineyard. The Canadian couple met when they studied biochemistry in Vancouver. "You'd think as a Canadian I'd be a hockey player, but my interest in wine was sparked by Brad's parents' lovely tradition. On Friday nights the family turned off the television and caught up with each other over dinner and wine. I learned to drink wine without being a wine geek," says Spriggs.

Brad had a job in Switzerland that gave them an opportunity to visit Burgundy. Something clicked in that wine region for Spriggs. "Wouldn't it be funny to get a Ph.D. in winemaking?" she asked. After they returned to Canada, they both signed up for a master's degree in a wine research program at a top-level wine institute in Vancouver. They quickly realized the program was too heavy on science for their needs. Instead they wanted to learn about production and went to the University of Adelaide in Australia. Their next decision was to work for top-quality wineries in different parts of the world. "We always thought we'd make wine in Canada and in fact turned down two opportunities. Brad's language skills landed him a job at Chateau Margaux in Bordeaux."

Spriggs's English father gifted the couple with a bottle of Nyetimber sparkling wine. "It wasn't perfect, but it had a lovely texture, delicacy, and femininity. The memory of the wine stayed in my mind." Coincidentally, the couple spotted a help-wanted ad for two winemakers at Nyetimber.

*We were young and willing to take the risk. They interviewed us over the phone and we were hired for a six-month trial. From our standpoint, it felt like the right fit. We liked the idea of making a specific wine. I think every winemaker needs some degree of specialization. A winemaker responds naturally to some varieties. I know Pinot noir, but I'm not that good at Cabernet Sauvignon.*

*From the winery's beginning in the 1980's, when the first Nyetimber vineyard was planted, the owner's goal was to make premium sparkling wine able to compete with Champagne. It wasn't an impossible dream because the winery's location in West Sussex in southeastern England sits on chalky bedrock with sandy soil identical to that of the Champagne region. Nyetimber's 350-acre vineyard is the largest in the UK. Its soil is perfect for the three traditional grapes in the classic blend of French sparklers.*

*Prior to our arrival, Nyetimber made a classic nonvintage Cuvée blend and a Blanc de blanc from 100 percent Chardonnay every year. Now we make mostly Brut with a small percent of Demi-sec. We set our wines apart from our peers with expertise in the vineyard coupled with skilled winemaking. We trellis and prune our vines like the French. We're trying a number of different innovations in the vineyard and the winery.*

*Britain benefits from a long growing season. Its mild climate gives us plenty of sugars without high heat. The terroir is particularly beneficial for sparkling wine because we don't want high alcohol. As to climate ... after all, it's England, and rains can fall at inopportune times. Remember how it always rains during Wimbledon? Those same spring rains cause serious problems at flowering. Rain also gives us problems with botrytis. It's necessary to manage the vineyard to avoid botrytis with an open canopy that allows air to circulate. Otherwise, yields can plummet shockingly low. Weather and horrendous rain take choosing a date for harvest out of our hands. We try to avoid disasters caused by weather, planning ahead to pick during October, when it generally drizzles.*

*Our job is to respect terroir. We look for delicacy in the wine as well as in the characteristics of tannins. Other winemakers might want to pump over to introduce oxygen into the juice, whereas we think the technique covers up the flavors from the vineyard. We have one small vineyard section of Chardonnay with unusual white flower characteristics. Why they are there is a mystery, but every year we can taste the vineyard's atypical fruit and floral characteristics. If I pumped over it or chucked the juice from that vineyard in a barrel, those characteristics would be lost. Our wines generally don't go into barrel. We don't want oak's overt characteristics to override the characteristics of the vineyard.*

## SPRIGGS'S SUMMER BREAD PUDDING

*This dessert can be made with store-bought or wild strawberries and/or a mixture of berries, such as raspberries, blueberries, strawberries, and red currants.*

2 pints strawberries, hulled, quartered
2 pints blueberries
2 pints blackberries
2 pints raspberries
1 cup sugar (or to taste, depending on the sweetness of the berries)
1 tbsp vanilla
1 lb brioche, challah, or excellent-quality white bread with crusts removed
Unsalted butter at room temperature

Butter a 9–10-inch spring form pan or a deep serving dish and set on a rimmed baking sheet. Combine the berries, 1 cup sugar, and vanilla; simmer, stirring until the sugar is dissolved and the berries are softened and mixed. Drizzle ½ cup of the berry juice onto one layer of bread in the buttered spring form pan. Add a portion of the berries. Continue to alternate layers of bread, juice, and berries.

Cover with plastic wrap. Weigh the pudding down with a plate. Chill for at least 1 hour or up to 2 days. Remove plate and plastic wrap. If using a spring form pan, invert the pudding onto a serving platter or spoon into individual portions.

*Nyetimber Demi-sec is the perfect wine for a summer pudding because of the sweetness of the wine, which balances the sweetness in the dish. This means the wine won't taste too acidic and the sweet fruits and the fruits won't taste too sickly sweet. Also, the Demi-sec has a lovely lemon citrus flavor that complements the berries very nicely. Add in the lightness on the palate that the bubbles bring and you have a drink that is extremely refreshing and suited to the warm days of summer.*

Our concern for stewardship of the soil means reducing the amount of agrochemicals. Our vineyards aren't organic, so we use a pesticide if needed. We can't take the risk of losing the whole crop. We're doing an organic trial for better yield rather than for reasons of taste. At the end of the day, we run a business. Generally, we produce 500,000 bottles, but yield varies from year to year. In 2012, there will be a dramatic reduction to 100,000 to 200,000 bottles because of bad weather.

Harvest is the most stressful time of the year, but at the same time, nothing is more fun. Sometimes the most nerve-wracking thing can be the best. We hire a number of like-minded workers who are willing to work through lunch *and dinner during grueling twelve-hour days while smiling most of the time. If rain dilutes the juice, we get rid of water in white wine by pressing grapes in whole bunches and discarding the first 200 to 300 liters of juice. Individual sections of each vineyard are picked and processed in separate batches. It allows us to capture the individual characteristics of our vineyard.*

*Nyetimber is the only English producer of premium sparkling wine made exclusively from estate-grown fruit. Our approach has been to build on the tradition of champagne, but enhancing this with technology where we could achieve a clear quality improvement. We invested in the very best Coquard presses capable of exerting the gentlest of pressing pressure, ensuring the optimum balance of concentration and character in the grape juice. The grapes are pressed and stored in separate stainless steel tanks. This absolutely crucial step gives us as much control and flexibility as possible at blending. Our wines then undergo the same secondary in bottle fermentation as Champagne, spending as much time as they need on lees. In many cases this is greater than three years, developing the complexity, elegance, and freshness that we strive for.*

*Blending is right up there with the part of the job I find pleasurable. It's tough, but good fun. Watching the progress of wine go through several stages is difficult, but I enjoy evaluating wine as it evolves on the lees. We age on lees longer to get delicate bubbles and texture. Knowing when to say a wine is ready is really hard because during frequent tastings, the acidity and the bubbles tire my palate quickly. During secondary fermentation, the wine is completely dry without any sugar. At disgorgement, we add a dosage of sugar into the wine to get it to the sweetness level we want.*

*From the company's perspective, I'm the head winemaker and Brad is the associate winemaker. Greg and I are often asked if we work comfortably in tandem. We come to the job with our own strengths. I hold the title of "Boss" at home and in the winery, but I never want to be in the position of making autocratic decisions. All our decisions are made together and we choose a decision that makes the least impact on the wine. We're frank with each other and can call each other out. A good winemaker needs a sense of humility, not one who brags, "I'm great." If I worked with another winemaker, it would lead to a lot of negotiating and politicking. If I would tell them what to do, it would be a problem because we all react differently to the juice. But Greg and I have worked and tasted together so long we really understand each other. Sometimes I struggle to find the exact word to describe what it is I'm tasting. Brad describes better than I do. Tasting together gives us a better platform to see the whole picture. My palate has a certain spectrum so we take into account each* other's tasting capabilities when we taste. My general observation is that a woman's palate can pick up certain unpleasant, funky smells, like garlic and rotten eggs that can show up in wine.

Nyetimber wines are highly respected and have won many awards. Our product competes very well against the top Grand Marque Champagnes. The first time we won, they said it was luck. The second time made the point. When the crop doesn't turn out well, we sell a significant portion to competitors to keep our standards up. We're starting to publicize ourselves, looking to expand into a larger at-home market, since many English don't know about us. It's also on our agenda to expand our market beyond the UK borders. Our labels were recently redesigned to bring them up to date.

Our Dutch owner fell in love with wine at eighteen. He's not from a wine family, but he had a dream to own a winery. He's a huge Anglophile who saw the potential in English wine and made an enormous commitment in money and work. We're seeing the English wine industry grow. More people are confidently investing time and money. Some come into the business because they think the lifestyle is attractive. They don't realize it takes a lot of hard work.

# FRANCE

ROMAN CONQUERORS were responsible for the spread of viticulture to France, but it's more important to jump ahead to 1152 A.D., when Eleanor of Aquitaine married the English king, Henry Plantagenet. Her vast property included the land around Bordeaux and its wines. Clarets, pale-colored reds from Bordeaux, became an instant success in England. The tradition of admiration for French wine was passed to their son, Richard the Lionhearted. Claret, anglicized from the French, was purportedly served warm and mixed with spices and herbs. The famous marriage dissolved, but the English devotion to dry red Claret endures.

The impact of Christianity and the growth of monasteries pushed the development for sacramental wines. Eventually, a successful merchant class took control of all aspects of winemaking and selling. The first recorded comparative tasting of eighty European wines in 1224 A.D. included some from Bordeaux. They failed to win, but honors came later.

## Bordeaux

Admirers of Bordeaux consider it the Mt. Everest of the red wine world. But there is more to Bordeaux than wine. The bourgeois city built by wealthy wine merchants in the eighteenth and nineteenth centuries is undergoing a renaissance, replete with excellent restaurants, museums, a concert hall, and art exhibitions. Bordeaux on a wine bottle label commands attention. Many wine lovers and critics consider Bordeaux to be the benchmark for red wine, so enviable that what is known as the classic Bordeaux blend is emulated in many wine regions around the globe. The region maintains its renowned position in spite of some ups and downs in production.

It is easy to lump Bordeaux wines together into one entity, as though the region has identical terroir throughout. But the truth is that quality can be spotty. The total area of Bordeaux is small, but the number of wineries created an array of labels from all its appellations and subappellations. History and appellation regulations govern what local winemakers are allowed to grow. Merlot, Cabernet Sauvignon, Cabernet Franc, and Petit Verdot with occasional plantings of Malbec are the major varieties comprising the famous Bordeaux blend of red wines. Each Bordeaux winemaker plants particular sites based on different proportions of Cabernet Sauvignon, Merlot, Cabernet Franc, and Petit Verdot, the major varietals of the region. Today in Bordeaux approximately 10,000 producers and 13,000 grape growers produce millions of bottles every year. Blending is the hallmark of Bordeaux wines. In some appellations, Cabernet is the dominant grape in one area and Merlot plays the principal role in others.

A winemaker's training and skill determine a blend by incorporating different proportions of the traditional grapes, depending on appellation requirements and house style. Bordeaux wines require wine lovers to take time and have patience in order to decipher the complicated system of wine regulations, terroirs, blending of the four major varietals, and individual style of particular chateaux in the fifty-seven appellations of Bordeaux. In the past, wines from the region required a long time in the bottle before they were ready to drink. New vinification techniques are making the wines more accessible sooner.

It was difficult, even for the French, to have sorted out the dizzying array of Bordeaux labels, appellations, and subappellations. Emperor Napoleon III ordered a classification system for Bordeaux wines during the Exposition Universelle of 1855, held in Paris to demonstrate the arts, technology, and scientific achievements of France's Second Empire. The project was meant to rival England's earlier Crystal Palace exhibition in

1851, when the Bordeaux Wine Official Classification established ranks called *crus* as a way of sorting through the vast number of Bordeaux labels. The chateaux rank in importance from first to fifth growths. Quality and price were the major determinants for classification. Five premier crus are Lafite Rothschild, Latour, Haut-Brion, Cheval Blanc, and the later addition of Mouton Rothschild. Critics insist the immutable system is outdated and fails to provide an accurate guide, since vineyards have changed in size and ownership over the years. Reclassification would upset the prices of downgraded chateaux, so for the time being, pressure from owners ensures the system remains set in stone. Margaux is one of the most prestigious of the appellations. It is the only one to contain all the range of wines classified in 1855 from First Great Cru Classé to the Fifth, as well as Crus Bourgeois and Crus Artisans Chateaux.

Unstable weather conditions, destructive plant pests, wars, disastrous frosts, and economic depressions caused serious fluctuations in production. However, winemakers found that disasters were the impetus for opportunities to replant and invest in modern equipment and new clones. Winemakers learned to control some of the variables after centuries of experimentation to plant a grape variety best able to thrive in a mix of soils composed of limestone, clay, gravel, sand, and minerals. Bordeaux's terroir includes maritime influences from the Atlantic Ocean, the Gironde estuary, and two rivers. History and appellation regulations govern what local winemakers are allowed to grow. Blending is the hallmark of Bordeaux wines.

Until the twentieth century, when wineries from the United States and other New World producers entered the picture, the region's unrivaled status went unchallenged except for wines from its eminent French rival, Burgundy. Noteworthy Bordeaux reds continue to compete for a position at the top of the wine world's hierarchy.

# Margaux

## PHILIPPE DELFAUT
### CHÂTEAU KIRWAN

Prestigious chateaux, whose names reso-nate loudly with Bordeaux lovers, dot the commune of Margaux. The chateaux are glorious remnants of centuries before the French Revolution, when the nobil-ity and rich bourgeois lived the high life.

It is a short 15-mile ride from Bor-deaux to Château Kirwan. The grand estate harks back to 1740, when Mark Kirwan, an Irishman from Galway, ac-quired Domaine Ganet and Domaine de la Salle. The two plots were amalgamated into a unique single vine-yard. In 1925, the Schÿler family, with a history of eight generations as négotiants, bought the chateau and winery. "Today the fourth generation of the family works to put the cake together. Our family tradition, vine-yards, and history are our added value. Our wines have steadily improved since the family hired Philippe Delfaut as general manager and wine-maker. He was working at the prestigious Palmer estate. Our winemaker and a combination of twenty-five soils in our 90 acres separate our wines from those of our neighbors," says Sophie Schÿler Thierry. Schÿler Thierry travels the world and deals with négotiants, marketing, promotion, and communication. Her sister, Nathalie Schÿler, is in charge of wine tourism and oversees the grand renovated visitors' center and new barrel cellar. Brother Yann Schÿler runs the family shipping business.

Winemaker Philippe Delfaut says,

*At one time, Bordeaux wines sold based on reputation. It is difficult to sell so-so wines, especially when we had some disastrous vintages. Small estates need to* produce excellent wine, especially as quality rises around the world. We had to make some drastic changes and turned to new technologies and methods, looking for big improvements across the industry. When profits rose in the 1970's, we went through some big changes. New barrels brought about the first revolution to the classified growths. In the 1980's a second revolution took place. Stainless steel fermentation gave us more control and the ability to warm up or cool down the fermenting juice and to develop better color extraction. It was a major improvement that helped make good wine in difficult years by adjusting temperatures. A third revolution occurred in the 1990's with improvements in the vineyards, including canopy management. We prune in June, leaving one bunch on each vine, enabling the remaining grapes to develop maximum flavors.

We separate our chateau in style and reputation from others throughout the Médoc because our aim is to respect the origin of our terroir. History and viticulture govern what we can grow. Wines from the Margaux appellation of the Médoc are generally medium-bodied, refined wines generated from soil made up of clay, sand, and gravel. We think of wines from Margaux as feminine. Château Kirwan's wines and the music of Mozart have the same characteristics of elegance, finesse, and perfect balance. Other estates choose a more standard and technical wine process to work. It's simply two different approaches to winemaking. My personal philosophy is to work more by intuition, innovation, and experience. Transforming juice into wine requires more feeling than technology. My job is to guarantee the sense of terroir in Kirwan's wine. I start from scratch with the land and work toward wine in the bottle. I have a stylistic goal and reach it with whatever nature gives me. I prefer the term wine-helping to winemaking, which I think refers too much to operating through a technical, scientific approach.

The human aspect of winemaking plays the most important role. I am the decision maker. Wine is a living product and therefore each year requires new decisions that can't be determined in advance. I guide Kirwan's entire process to produce fresh, complex, and balanced wines. Like most properties in the Médoc, traditional grapes are the backbone of our blends. Cabernet Sauvignon is the dominant grape at Kirwan and accounts for 45 percent of a vintage; Merlot, 30 percent; and Cabernet Franc, 15 percent. Petit Verdot, particularly present in the Grand Vin Château Kirwan in the last vintages, makes up 10 percent.

My worst fear is a natural accident that is impossible to control. The vagaries of weather in Bordeaux make winemaking as difficult as walking a tightrope.

## SOPHIE SCHŸLER THIERRY'S VEAL STEW

*This is a classic recipe, a true match with Château Kirwan that my mother made for many entertaining opportunities at the Château.*

2 lb of veal shoulder
1 lb pork sausage
4 shallots finely chopped
1 minced garlic clove
Several sprigs of parsley
1 tbsp olive oil
Juice of 1 lemon
Salt and pepper

Turn the oven to 350°F. Grease an ovenproof pan with olive oil. Place the veal slice flat in the pan. Blend the pork sausage, shallots, parsley, garlic, salt, and pepper. Cover the veal with the 2–3 inches of the mixture. Pour some olive oil over the mixture. Add water when necessary, a few times during cooking to create a nice gravy. Bake 30–40 minutes. Before serving, add the lemon to the gravy. Adjust seasoning. Serve with buttered potatoes sprinkled with finely chopped parsley or spinach puree.

SERVES 8.

*Pair with any of our delicious Château Kirwan wines.*

Soil is a given, but weather conditions in Bordeaux are always tricky, unlike Napa, where sunshine is generally consistent. Occasional hail in spring batters the vines. Summer droughts slow or halt maturation. Rain at harvest dilutes the juice. Destructive plant pests and fungus, like phylloxera and botrytis, are always on the horizon. Yet our gravel-over-clay subsoil has water reserves that nourish the vines until maturity. When there is a big rainfall, the water lays on the clay. Because too much water drowns the vines' roots, neighboring wineries built drains in every vineyard that deposit excess water into a pond on the Kirwan property. Water shortages in a dry spell are too much for areas of fine, gravelly soil that slows or even halts maturation. Each year we wish for a dry and warm, rather than a hot, season, a season that alternates between cool nights and sunny days in order to develop perfectly matured berries and seeds. In 2008, April brought a frost that hurt the early buds. May was warm, with heavy thundershowers. The vines grew rapidly, with a threat of mildew. This required cutting back on foliage to orient the leaves and get a better spread. In 2009, we had a beach chair vintage. Spring of 2010 got off to a rough start. Hail pounded the vineyard in May, causing significant damage. Chaos occurred in 2011, when summer came before spring.

~~~

# DELFAUT'S LAMPREY À LA BORDEAUX

2½ lb eel or any firm
   white fish
3 lb leeks, white parts
   only, cut into
   3-inch pieces
6 small onions,
   chopped
6 minced shallots,
   chopped
6 cloves of minced
   garlic, chopped
10 oz diced ham
1 bouquet garni
5 oz olive oil and
   peanut oil
2 cloves
1 bottle of good red
   wine like a Côtes
   de Bourg, a Loire
   red, Beaujolais, or
   Ch. Kirwan
¼ cup Cognac or
   Armagnac
1 tbsp powdered
   sugar
Salt and pepper
1 tbsp flour

Holding the eel by the head, make an incision in the tail and collect its blood. Scald the eel in boiling water and remove the spine. Cut off the head and tail. Cut the eel into pieces and marinate 3–4 hours in the wine. Then flambé it in the cognac. Fry it in a mixture of olive oil and peanut oil in a thick-bottomed pan with shallots, spring onions, cloves, and diced ham. When they are at the boil, add the crushed garlic and flour, stir, and add the wine marinade. Remove the bouquet garni.

Simmer gently for an hour. Sauté the white parts of the leeks and put them in the sauce. Brown the pieces of lamprey. Then flambé, adding alcohol to the pan. Continue cooking on low heat for another hour. Add sugar, flour, and the blood of the lamprey to thicken the sauce. Add salt and pepper to taste. Remove the cloves. Simmer 10 minutes.

SERVES SIX.

*Pair with Château Kirwan 1996, a mature vintage, both rich and delicate, offering a marvelous bouquet perfectly balanced with the richness of the lamprey or fish.*

*We had dry and scorched grapes caused by two blistering days in late June. The grapes were sorted and eliminated. Under these circumstances we can lose approximately 25 percent of the crop. We control many of these factors through analysis and constant tastings.*

*Odds are that, not so long ago, grapes in our region were picked far too early at less than peak perfection. Kirwan made distinct changes in vineyard management and harvest in the last four years. My objective is to pick grapes on each parcel at their ultimate maturity, tasting them on a daily basis. Petit Verdot, which never seems to cooperate with the others, has to be picked quickly because bees like them so much that they suck the juice right through*

~~~

*the skin. The bees, in their own way, tell us the grapes are ripe by showing how easily they pierce the fine skins. What a lovely sign of the vineyard's biodiversity! It is essential to be patient and wait for ripeness without reaching overmaturity. Once the fruit is overripe, it no longer expresses the authenticity of our terroir. Harvesting by hand through several passes in the vineyard is essential. Individually picked ripe berries are brought to the crusher by conveyor belt, where experienced workers sort the fruit on a vibrating table. It's very labor intensive to remove grapes that don't meet our standards.*

*Vinification takes place with more precision according to the specificity of the soils and to the type of grape within the same parcel. It is a gentle, daily monitored procedure in order not to damage the fruit, with emphasis on balance rather than only on extraction. The juice coming from the press accounts for the major portion of our Château Kirwan Grand Vin. Macerations last three to four weeks under soft temperatures. Malolactic and alcoholic fermentation happen simultaneously in the vats. Then the wines are sent into barrels by grape variety and by parcel. A challenge for precision has been important at Kirwan for the last four vintages. Only time will help me to get to know the terroir better.*

Delfaut is free to assemble the best grapes in the right proportion for each vintage of Kirwan's 8,000 to 10,000 cases.

*Blending is the keystone of Bordeaux wines, and the assemblage of different proportions of wines differs from year to year. We say assemblage is the birth of a vintage. It's very risky to make the blending. It's like putting colors together in a painting. We need to keep in mind the estate's style and the style of the appellation to produce consistent wine that also incorporates a vintage's character. I make a sample barrel tasting for one month and correct it under the guidance of a team that includes the estate's technicians and consultant enologists, Jacques Boissenot and his son Eric. Boissenot's experience with the history of all the estates in Margaux is helpful. Consultants like Boissenot bring essential knowledge of our property together with an overview of the appellation, vintage after vintage. The new teamwork undoubtedly obtains better results for the quality of our first label, Grand Vin de Kirwan, which represents two thirds of the property.*

*Only our best vats for aging are selected for our first and second labels. The Grand Vin has more body, complexity, and length of finish. This wine needs to age at least a decade to reach its peak maturity. Charmes de Kirwan, our sec-*

ond label, comes from the rest of the vineyard. This wine has more fruit, more suppleness, and less body. It is more accessible sooner than Grand Vin.

International taste and consumer palates change every decade or so. Winemakers are affected by a globalization of taste. Consumers now prefer younger, more aromatic, and fruitier wines. Bordeaux is in the game also, but on the other side, our wines show their terroir and personality. Alcohol levels have increased overall in the last decade because of global warming, reaching a level of 13 percent for Cabernet Sauvignon and 14 to 15 percent for Merlot in 2009 and 2010. A high degree of alcohol is not necessarily a problem, as our grapes naturally reach good acidity that gives us excellent structure, balance, and freshness.

As part of the complicated négotiant system, Bordeaux wines are tasted by around 5,000 professionals and négotiants during En Primeur week. They swarm to Bordeaux each year anywhere from late March to early April to taste all the classified wines. Less than two months later, each chateau announces a price to their customary négotiants, who secure their allocation from the estate. In turn, the négotiants offer their allocations to their various importers and wholesalers around the world. Our sales in China are strong, a positive sign as wine sales in that country are growing. Bordeaux accounts for almost half of the wine imports in China, and we see a great potential in this huge market. Wine sales are exploding on both the low and the high ends of the market, but I am confident that all segments of Bordeaux wines, including the Grands Crus Classés, will grow in the future.

In the end, I believe wine has the quality to please and to help us forget the problems of daily life in the same way that a fantastic meal elevates the spirit.

# ALEXANDER VAN BEEK

### CHÂTEAU DU TERTRE, CHÂTEAU GISCOURS, AND CAIAROSSA

The Dutch have had a long interest in Bordeaux wineries, so it is not surprising that a Dutchman, Eric Albada Jelgersma, expressed his love for the Margaux region by purchasing Château Giscours in 1995. In 1997 he took the next step and bought Château du Tertre's neoclassical chateau and a unique, single 50-hectare vineyard site. Giscours is close to the Garonne River, and its soil has a maritime river influence. Giscours is ranked a third growth in the classification system established by Napoleon III. Records show Château du Tertre's land was under vine cultivation in 1143, when its wines were already highly regarded. *Tertre* means "hillock" or "knoll," an apt designation for an estate on the highest point in the Margaux district of Bordeaux. Du Tertre, ranked as a Fifth Growth in 1855, also has a maritime influence from the Gironde River. The property passed through the hands of several owners over the centuries. Wars, phylloxera, and economic problems held du Tertre back from reaching its potential until recently.

Alexander Van Beek came to France in 1995 from the Netherlands and worked the harvest alongside students, local pickers, and Polish workers who cross Europe every year for harvest. As winemaker at the two estates, he says,

*Working in two wineries is like working with two children you love. Winemaking techniques move forward here in a controlled, measured way. The new owner combined modern and traditional techniques to the vineyard and winemaking facility. Jelgersma never deterred from his commitment to the*

*elegance of the appellation. The concept of elegance is holy to him and to me as well. Our wines must maintain hallmarks of elegance that come from our terroir. We can't afford to put our labels on bad or mediocre wine. Instead we must show the richness of each vintage. The style of wine must correspond to the personality of terroir. This is part of the wealth of our area. There was a time when some winemakers in Bordeaux went through a period of developing a style of heavy extraction that shook up the Right Bank and spread to the Left Bank. It was wine that saturated the palate. The overkill made a technical wine without the personality of terroir. It led to more tannins and bitterness, a detriment to our beautiful wines. It took a while to realize that overextracting reduced the natural elegance of Bordeaux wines and caused us to lose the identity of our terroir.*

*Jelgersma insisted on improving quality in the vineyards. We want contact with terroir that creates better fruit and developed a contemporary interpretation of vinification. Château du Tertre needed to find the right direction for its spectacular single block of vineyard planted in soil with large gravelly stones that hold and transfer daytime heat to the vines. It is planted in 40 percent Cabernet Sauvignon, 35 percent Merlot, 20 percent Cabernet Franc, and 5 percent Petit Verdot. Our forty-five-year-old vines continue to produce great fruit, and we work hard tilling the soil with plows. We hired Jacques Boissenot, one of the world's great viticulturists, to revitalize our properties. He consults for several of our region's most estimable estates. We monitor the vineyards carefully and changed the trellising, allowing photosynthesis to work better to create more mature fruit. We pulled up many of our vines and replanted 130,000 new vines. New vines need at least ten years before their root structure gets the true quality of the terroir. Our wines have gradually evolved in quality since we adapted new technologies.*

*Unstable weather in our region can create havoc. There's a risk in waiting to pick if the fruit is ripe and the weather changes for the worse. Good planning and organization pay off. Mother Nature rarely grants the region sunny summers and rain-free harvests, but a winemaker's hand can wrest feminine, supple, and graceful wines with elegant, fruity aromas together with sufficient natural tannins to ensure aging potential. Fifteen to twenty years ago, it wasn't possible to take the risks. Now our vines are well tended and better cropped, and even with heavy clusters, air circulates and saves the grapes from rot. The job starts again on the last day of harvest with preparation of the soil and pruning of the vines.*

At our two chateaux we are the opposite of industrial producers whose winemakers never step into the vineyard to check the fruit. Winemakers who deal in quantity produce bland wines without specific terroir character. Think of Kraft cheese-makers who never see a cow. Good wine requires contact with the vintner. A winemaker is the concertmaster who pulls together disparate elements from difficult conditions of poor soil and seasonal vagaries of weather to make a symphony in the bottle. It is why wines vary from one winemaker to another and from season to season. Each vintage requires different choices and decisions. Every year we ask questions about how to do it better without extreme change. It's better to work with knowledge about the personality of every parcel of our vineyards. Time helps us know the potential of individual plots and how richness in wine develops slowly. Clarity of purpose adds to our vision. We are meticulous, always looking for finesse, elegance, richness, and femininity in our wines.

While each house style is related to its terroir, it is the assemblage, or blending, that is a major part of each wine's personality. Blending gives us the opportunity to create better wines. The style of great wine must correspond to what the terroir offers. If we think of our wines as women, Giscours is mysterious and intellectual with a beautiful body and more personality than du Tertre. The wines of du Tertre have the same beautiful body as Giscours, only sexier.

At du Tertre, each plot is vinified separately in traditional large wooden vats, a convention used in great Bordeaux wine estates. Too much vinification leads to generalization in winemaking and can be like a woman with too much make-up. The wine spends up to eighteen months in 50 percent new oak barrels each year to add distinctive qualities to the wine. French oak is an essential step because its tannins provide an additional layer of complexity to wine. The wine goes through a malolactic secondary fermentation that changes its malic acids into softer lactic acids. Different batches are tasted frequently until the final blending. We rack with a traditional candle to detect the change from cloudy to clear wine. Lastly, we fine with egg white to clarify the wine. There is one more blending before bottling at the chateau and then the wine rests quietly in our cellars for the long process of aging. Aging offers some interesting surprises and pleasures. We still barrel-age our wines, but not as long as in past vintages. Wines are bottled at the chateau and then the process of bottle aging begins. In the past, Bordeaux wines required long aging until they were ready to drink. All vintages made after the 1980's are

# VAN BEEK'S LIÈVRE À LA ROYALE— HARE À LA ROYALE

*This recipe matches with the opening of the hunting season and the beginning of harvest.*

1 large hare (about 6–7 lb) or rabbit
2½ cups pork fillets, cut into small squares
Several slices bacon, cut into small pieces
2–3 slices white bread, crusts removed and diced
2 garlic cloves
Small bunch of savory herbs, finely chopped
1 large goose liver
1 large truffle chopped (about 50 g), with skin pared into shavings
4 eggs
6 oz Marc de Bourgogne (a brandy distilled from Bourgogne grape residue or good brandy)
½ tsp powdered garlic
Sea salt and freshly ground black pepper
10–12 boletus mushrooms

The day before cooking, reserve the rabbit's liver, heart, and blood. Debone the hare, being careful not to poke any holes in the flesh.

Add the bones, carrots, onions, shallots, bouquet garni, sea salt, and wine together in a bowl. Cover with cling wrap and set in the refrigerator to marinate for at least 2 hours. The day before, mince the hare heart and liver. Combine this in a bowl with the pork fillet and bacon pieces. Moisten the bread with the Marc de Bourgogne or other brandy and add this to the meat mixture. Stir in the truffle shavings, chopped herbs, powdered garlic, and seasonings. Mix thoroughly. Beat the eggs and add to the mixture, stirring to combine. Cover with cling wrap and set aside in the refrigerator for at least 18 hours, so that the flavors meld together. The following day, remove the hare from the marinade and lay on a chopping block. Separate the hind legs, so that you can lay them parallel to the ribcage. Season liberally with salt and freshly ground black pepper. Take the goose liver and separate the lobes from the sinews and blood vessels (run these through a mincer). Slice the liver into strips.

Flatten the hare out, then spread a layer of the chilled stuffing mix on top, followed by some goose liver strips and chopped truffle. Top with another layer of stuffing. Roll the hare up lengthways and place on grease-free paper rubbed with oil. Roll this into a sausage shape and secure with thread. Place the hare roll in a roasting tin with goose fat, transfer to an oven preheated to 350°F, and cook for about 30 minutes, turning occasionally, or until browned all over. Now remove the bones from the marinade and drain the garnish ingredients from the wine. Reserve the wine. When the hare roll is rolled, remove the paper. Secure the hare with string, then place back in the roasting dish with the bones and vegetables. Add the bouquet garni, boletus mushrooms, and sea salt, then return to the oven and cook for 30 minutes.

FOR THE
AROMATIC
GARNISH

3 carrots, diced
2 onions, diced
4 shallots, diced
Bouquet garni
Coarse sea salt to
    taste
3–4 bottles of good
    red wine
1 lb small white
    mushrooms—
    reserve and fry
    12 caps for a
    garnish.
16 small croutons
    (cut in heart
    shapes)
15 small cream
    potatoes, halved
    and turned to
    shape

Pour in red wine, enough to cover. Place on the stovetop and cook at a light boil for about 20 minutes, topping the red wine as needed. When done, remove from the heat and remove the hare. Prick the skin and set it aside on a wire rack to cool. For the final 40 minutes of cooking, heat goose fat in a roasting dish. Parboil the potatoes, drain, and roll in. Transfer to the oven and cook until nicely roasted. Strain the sauce into a pan, bring to a boil, and cook until it is reduced. Remove from the heat, add the minced liver trimmings and hare blood that was passed through a fine-meshed sieve. Return to the stovetop and cook gently until thickened. Do not boil, or the roll will separate.

To serve, cut the hare sausage into rounds. Place a round in the center of a soup plate and pour the sauce over it. Add the roasted potatoes. Garnish with the heart-shaped bread croutons and two fried mushroom caps.

*The finesse and elegance of Château Giscours perfectly pairs with the subtleties of the black truffle of Hare à la Royale.*

different from the old Bordeaux. Today vintages need three to five years of cellaring and will be good by the time they reach the market. Our wines are sold young, fresh and fruity, accessible and ready for consumption, with good aging potential. Our website recommends when the wines are ready to drink.

Négotiants who buy wine futures handle our wines. Each merchant has long-term relationships for allocations from particular chateaux. It's a very traditional, complicated system, but consumers have a big advantage because retailers can't mark up the price as much as exclusive importers and distributors.

Van Beek's duties include a recent addition to the Jelgersma portfolio in Italy. It is Caiarossa, an Italian estate located in a village called Riparbella, in the heart of the Val di Cecina on the Tuscan coast, a few kilometers north of the famous appellation of Bolgheri. Van Beek says,

*The soil contains large amounts of clay mixed with sand, chalk, gravel, and stones. The terroir is very heterogeneous. That's why we have so many different kinds of grapes. Total production includes three whites and seven reds made from eleven varietals. Most of the estate's production is red and divided in two labels.*

*Caiarossa's flagship wine is a blend of seven different red varietals Cabernet Franc, Sangiovese, Merlot, Cabernet Sauvignon, Petit Verdot, Syrah, and Alicante. Pergolaia is essentially Sangiovese blended with small additions of Merlot and Cabernet. We also produce four special wines. Two whites in very limited quantity: a dry labeled Caiarossa bianco made from 50 percent Chardonnay and 50 percent Viognier, and a late-harvest wine called Oro di Caiarossa made from 100 percent Petit Manseng. The terroir's different altitudes and exposures allow each varietal to reach a perfect maturity. Our Tuscan wines are all IGT Toscana, as we choose not to use the DOC.*

Van Beek manages to keep a hand in all three properties. He works with Dominique Genot at Caiarossa visiting the winery several times a year to taste the wine and to make sure everything goes according to his directions. Last I heard from Alexander in the winter of 2013 he was in Vietnam on a much-needed vacation far from thoughts of the winery business.

## Graves

Graves, an important appellation of Bordeaux, is situated on the left bank of the Garonne River. Graves derives its name from the gravel and stone deposited by glaciers during the Ice Age. Romans are credited with being first to introduce grapes to the area. Church records mention an estate owned by Pope Clement V. The reputation of Graves wines was already established in 1382. Château Haut-Brion has maintained its position at the apex of a worldwide reputation for estimable wines since the seventeenth century. Fifteen other chateaux from Pessac-Léognan follow close behind. Paradoxically, Graves is the youngest appellation in Bordeaux. It was excluded from the Bordeaux Classification of 1855. In 1987 Pessac Léognan, Sauternes, and Barsac in Graves were given their own appellation status.

Plantings of Cabernet Sauvignon, Merlot, Petit Verdot, and Cabernet Franc, along with lesser amounts of Malbec and Carménère, dominate the vineyards of Graves Pessac Léognan. Sauvignon blanc and Semillon are exclusively used in varying amounts for its white wines. Its wines, both red and white, are justifiably known as some of the world's finest.

## OLIVIER BERNARD
### DOMAINE DE CHEVALIER

Sophie Schÿler Thierry from Château Kirwan first introduced me to dapper Olivier Bernard at a Bordeaux tasting in New York City. Winemakers from the region present their latest vintage at the annual event. At 1 o'clock vintners wait for the onslaught of hundreds of wine professionals, journalists, and consumers who crowd up to tables covered with bottles. Palpable excitement grew as tasters spent hours sniffing and slurping the latest vintage. A year later, at our second meeting, he graciously left his wife in charge of pouring samples of Domaine de Chevalier. Fellow vintners congratulated Bernard on his recent election as president of the Union of Grands Crus de Bordeaux. The UGC develops wine-tasting programs to promote the reputation of the region's wines in France and around the world. He is also a member of two other Bordeaux wine associations and manager of Financière Bernard, his family's successful négotiant company. Bernard and several investors recently acquired a stake in the Château Guiraud in Sauternes. The adage "Give a busy man more to do and it gets done" apparently applies to Bernard.

"I was twenty-three in 1983 when our family bought Domaine de Chevalier, one of the most respected wine estates in Pessac Léognan," says Bernard. "At the time, I spent five years working together with the former owner. He became my second father. I traveled to Italy, Germany, Portugal, and other wine regions to understand different philosophies of winemaking. It helped me to develop my own philosophy." Bernard laid out his simple philosophy.

*I try to do things as naturally as possible, constantly seeking a balanced approach that encompasses modern methods within the framework of the Domaine de Chevalier's venerable history. I really believe one's past helps you to know where to go. I also believe too many people in our business represent themselves in the wine.*

*Bordeaux is quite flat, so 20 meters in terms of altitude is important because if you are high, water drains off. If a property is close to the Gironde River, the drainage is even better. The main part of our property has poor to good drainage. The red wine vineyards of our classified Grand Cru estate have 42 hectares of vines. In our first year of ownership, we replanted the oldest part of the property, where the vines were an average of twenty-five years old. In those days the vineyards were 65 percent Cabernet Sauvignon, 30 percent Merlot, and 5 percent Cabernet Franc. We aren't committed to this proportion, so we can play with percentages in our blends. Today we have basically the same proportions except for a change of lesser percent of Cabernet Franc and an increase in the percent of Petit Verdot. Petit Verdot is more aromatic, although if it's used too much, it sometimes has aromas resembling a little animal. The red wine vineyards are south of the 45th parallel, reaching the limit for red grapes, but red grapeskins protect the berries from the sun.*

Chevalier's whites come from five hectares that are planted in 70 percent Sauvignon blanc and 30 percent Semillon.

*The white wine plots lie on the 45th parallel, compared with more northern vineyards of France's Chablis and Alsace regions. Grapes for white wines ripen earlier than those for red. If the weather in the vineyards is too warm, juice from white grapes loses freshness and the expression of the fruit. The challenge is to create a white wine that keeps its freshness and acidity for decades. Slightly cool evenings enhance acidity and aromatic expression in our white wines. Under the right circumstances, we can achieve the best flavor profile for our white wines: powerful, fresh, bright, and complex with mineral accents. My 1,500 to 2,000 cases of whites keep getting better every year. A vertical tasting of the last thirty vintages showed the white wine's unmistakable personality and ability to age year after year. That's a remarkable achievement for white wine.*

*Terroir is by far the most important factor. Many vintners talk about terroir, but few can tell why it's important or where they are going with the idea.*

*Good wine can't come from anywhere in the world. Wine can be made any-where, but great wine needs another dimension. Great wine needs the right grapes, soil, and vineyard. Ninety percent of our wine is made by great fruit. The rest is blah-blah.*

*A winemaker must respect the fruit to develop the sensibilities of fine ex-pression from fragile fruit. Our philosophy is to make wine from grapes that have the capacity to express the mosaic of our soils. The soils are constant, yet every year is different and so the results are never the same. I make wine in the vineyard. I know each vine and each vineyard. It takes constant work to see how grapes develop. Too many vintners make wine in the cellar. Wine is not done by vinification. Vinification is merely the way to reveal the fruit, to give it expression. The real structure of wine comes from the fruit. From my point of view, the human factor must stay behind the wine. Man is only a facilitator. I like to say I am the liquid in which the photograph is developed. I didn't take the photograph, but I reveal it. There is less to do when the photo is perfect, and the same is true for winemaking.*

It's not so easy to be in front, but when you believe in something, you follow your road. Bernard knows that even with his winery's great terroir and a long history of winemaking, he must attend to countless factors.

*Our vineyards are planted north and south so that the vines get maximum morning sun from the east and maximum afternoon sun from the west. If there is too much fruit, we cut bunches back 20 to 40 percent to allow the remaining berries to ripen. By the end of July, we can predict the condition of the vintage and make decisions about how to work with it. We must always follow the fruit. By the end of August, we definitely know what sort of vintage we'll have.*

*The fruit must be very good to have a good vintage. When the vintage is difficult, you need to make sure the outcome will be as good as possible. Some years required more effort because it was hard to get good fruit. In 2008, we had to work very hard in the vineyard during the summer to make sure the grapes were healthy and without rot before harvest. We cut back closely bunched grapes and leaves to avoid humidity. We definitely don't want botrytis during vinification. We need long hours of warmth for reds during vinifica-tion to extract tannins. We believe the 2012 Domaine de Chevalier is a vintage born under a lucky star. After one of the coldest winters of the past thirty years, spring was very wet and replenished water supplies that otherwise*

## BERNARD'S LEG OF LAMB COOKED
## FOR SEVEN HOURS

1 leg of lamb for
  8 people
3–4 carrots
3 onions
10 shallots
1 garlic
1 lb baby Porcini
  mushrooms
1 bouquet garni
8 oz Cognac
½ bottle of white
  wine
4 cups of good beef
  broth or lamb
  stock
4 slices of diced
  bacon
½ stick of unsalted
  butter
Salt and pepper

Have the butcher bone the leg. Season with salt and pepper. Dice all the vegetables. Bake the lamb with its bone in the oven at 350°F for 30 minutes. Remove the lamb and put the vegetables in the pan and return to the oven for 15 minutes. Return the lamb to the pan with the vegetables, bouquet garni, and diced bacon. Deglaze with white wine and Cognac. Add the lamb stock. Cover the dish and bake at 275°F for 7 hours. Baste occasionally.

Remove the lamb. Add the diced cold butter to the pan juices, whisking constantly. Pour over the lamb when ready to serve. Serve with vegetables.

*Pair with a red Domaine de Chevalier.*

might have been deficient. While abundant rainfall meant that flowering was spread out over time, this nevertheless ensured good vine growth. Summer was rather timid and cool in July, but early August brought sunny weather and an important big gap between daytime and nighttime temperatures.

I like power built on structure with well-integrated tannins. I am always looking for subtlety, elegance, complexity, and finesse. Big is not a quality we look for at our winery, even though there's been a push in that direction throughout the winemaking world in the last twenty years. My alcohol levels are never 15 or 16 percent; rather, we aim for 13 or 14 percent, especially if the acidity is good.

As is true in all vineyards across the world, vintners look for an optimum moment to harvest.

Harvest is the most important part of the vintage. It's the final step after six months of waiting. I'm in the vineyards every morning by 8 during vendage. I *spend a lot of time with my workers because to attain quality, all the details must be stated clearly. It's the details that make the difference, so I must convince my workers to follow my instructions. In about twenty minutes I explain what I need with the right words and demonstrations. If grapes are picked green, there is low extraction. Fruit must be harvested in small baskets. It takes several passes, exclusively in the cool of the morning, to pick bunches at peak ripeness. At the winery, twenty-five people work on the sorting table because careful sorting gives us a chance to express more complexity in the wine. Juice from different parts of the property is placed in many small vats. Each vat has its own philosophy and personality. Tastings of the freshly picked fruit and new wine, together with laboratory analyses, can reveal if our hopes are fully justified.*

Bernard exudes a sense of confidence and a certain charm, like his wines. He claims he is lucky to have celebrated many wonderful moments in his life.

*In May of 2009, a German friend suggested we organize a four-century tasting of Bordeaux wines at Domaine de Chevalier. We started with a 1791 Lafitte Rothschild and finished with wines from 2001. I am pleased to announce the recent addition of two second labels to Domaine de Chevalier—L'Esprit de Chevalier 2010 white, a blend of 70 percent Sauvignon blanc and 30 percent Semillon, and L'Esprit de Chevalier 2009 red, a blend of 65 percent Cabernet Sauvignon and 35 percent Merlot. The second wines come to maturity earlier than our grand crus and can be enjoyed younger. L'Esprit de Chevalier reds and whites are complex, well balanced, well structured, and elegant wines, true to Chevalier's image while representing outstanding value.*

## Sauternes

The Sauternes region is remarkably distinct from the red wine areas of Bordeaux. Winemakers there are devoted to crafting some of the world's most delectable sweet wines that derive their name from the region. Château d'Yquem is perhaps the most highly recognized label from among many excellent producers of sweet white Bordeaux. The golden-hued wines share enticing flavors and bouquet that come from an alliance of diverse soil types and a special microclimate. Long ago, winemakers learned how to manage and maximize use from diseased berries infected by a fungus, *Botrytis cinerea*. Botrytis is generally not a farmer's friend. It is a danger to crops, causing gray rot on fruit like strawberries and some vegetables. Grapes, particularly Semillon, are a frequent target. Sauvignon blanc and Muscadelle make up two thirds of the three varietals in the Sauternes appellation. Unlike most other farmers who dread the onslaught of pests with potential to wreak havoc on a crop, grape growers and vintners in Sauternes eagerly wait for the first signs of blight. It is why, each fall, winemakers hold their breaths and hope what they call Noble Rot appears to perform its magic.

No vintage of the region's celebrated unctuous, sweet wines is without attack from the fungus. Unfortunately, botrytis is temperamental, erratic, impossible to provoke, requiring the presence of a variety of special conditions to appear and do its job. Botrytis thrives in an atmosphere of humidity and fog that covers the vineyards from dusk to dawn during warm autumn evenings that comes off the nearby Ciron and Gironde rivers. The fungus invades the grapes and consumes their water content, causing them to shrivel. Happily, the event concentrates sugars and acids in the residual juice, developing the first step to distinctively flavored, highly aromatic wines. Anyone passing through a vineyard where clusters of spore-covered, shriveled grapes hang on the vines would refuse to accept the idea that such profound ugliness could be transformed into great wine.

Chance plays a role in every vineyard, but Sauternes may take the award as the most unpredictable. Yields are low because evaporation reduces the amount of juice in the grapes. Berries immune to infestation and those too green to ripen are rejected. Pickers pass through the vineyards several times between September and November, separating each berry individually. The ensuing production costs for fungus-infected wines is high.

Vinification is essentially the same as for dry white wines. Because of the high sugar content, winemakers stop fermentation when their desired balance between sugar and alcohol is reached. Fermentation in small oak barrels or vats for two to three years adds to the cost. The flavors, aromas, and ability to age for years make the wait and cost for Sauternes worthwhile.

In 1855, when Bordeaux wineries were ranked for the Exposition Universelle in Paris, the chateaux of Sauternes and Barsac were considered separately from the rest of the Bordeaux classifications and classified as Premier Cru Supérieur, Premiers Crus, and Deuxièmes Crus. Château d'Yquem is the only Sauternes winery classified as a Premier Cru Supérieur. Other wines from Sauternes and Barsac were ranked from first great growth to second growth. Cognoscenti know the value of high-quality sweet Sauternes, which are sadly underrated in the States. I would personally carry a banner to popularize them.

# XAVIER PLANTY
## CHÂTEAU GUIRARD

A Bordeaux winemaker I esteem introduced me to Xavier Planty, saying, "Don't say I said this, but his Sauternes is the best." I hustled over to meet the vintner and taste his wine

*Understanding the development of dry white or red wine is fairly simple. Explaining the vintage of Sauternes and the creation and quality of its wines is also quite simple if we understand the idea of Botrytis contamination. To make a great Sauternes we need four conditions. The first requirement is perfectly ripe, early-maturing grapes. We harvested our dry white Château Guiraud between July 11 and September 14, 2009. Then there must be an underlying presence of botrytis on the grapes. Our strategy is for the grapes to have a lot of botrytis just ready to develop when the grapes reach maturity. A little moisture from dew, fog and/or light rain, and warm nights of 12°C provide optimal conditions for the fungus to grow quickly. Sunny and hot weather are needed to concentrate flavors. We can never anticipate the last two conditions. We must carefully monitor the progress of the phenomenon for insight.*

*On September 29, everything changed. We started picking a very few berries touched by botrytis from September 14th until the 17th. It gave us a small amount of quality but nothing exceptional. I like to hit point zero of botrytis. In the vineyard nothing moved. We see the grapes are ripe, very palatable, the skin is freckled, but we lack the moisture to initiate noble rot. The botrytis is there, but does not break out.*

*Finally it started to rain on September 15th. More rain fell from September 18th to the 21st. Hot nights generated the botrytis, which developed quickly. Three quarters of the vineyards were contaminated in three days. The botrytis was evolving, but the concentration didn't generate a critical amount. We*

## PLANTY'S SCALLOPS CARPACCIO
## WITH LIME AND GINGER

| | |
|---|---|
| 1 lb scallops | Cut the scallops into slices and put them in a bowl. Mix |
| Juice of one lime | the lime juice, garlic, ginger, and lime zest and pour the |
| Lime zest | marinade over the scallops. Refrigerate for 2–3 hours. |
| 2–3 cloves of garlic, | Heat olive oil in a frying pan and add the scallops and |
| finely chopped | the marinade. Cook for 2 minutes. |
| 1 inch slice of fresh | |
| garlic, finely | *Enjoy with a young vintage of Château Guiraud Sauternes.* |
| chopped | *The sweetness and silky texture of scallops is a perfect* |
| 2 tbsp of olive oil | *match for the unctuousness and intensity of the wine.* |

*spent a week following the evolution. I resumed harvesting September 28th, but the concentration was slow in coming. The weather was wet, with fog lifting slowly during warm nights. On the morning of September 29th, the grapes were completely rotten. The fungus was very active. This sight in the morning worried us a little, but the afternoon was quite another thing. The grapes finally shriveled. The sun began to concentrate the grapes and block the botrytis. I decided to wait another two days. Meanwhile, we saw the grapes drying before our eyes. The concentration was accelerated and the grapes took on a brilliant purple tinge. We gained two degrees of potential alcohol between Tuesday afternoon and Wednesday evening. On Thursday, October 1st, ten days of madness began. We worked on Saturday and Sunday, and requisitioned two additional presses the following Monday. Every day gave us lots of wonderful quality and aromatics, as concentrated as one could wish for in a wonderful raw material. We concluded on the evening of October 15th with a wonderful harvest. The wines fermented remarkably well, the balance was perfect, with a very expressive aromatic complexity.*

# Burgundy

The area known as Burgundy was, like most of France, occupied early in its history by the Celts. Then the region came under the domination of the Romans. The population converted to Christianity between the ninth and thirteenth centuries and monasteries became extraordinarily powerful, adding art, sculpture, and winemaking to the region. In Medieval times thousands of monks in monastic communities prayed and farmed on huge swathes of land. Cluny and Cîteaux, two of Burgundy's richest, most powerful monasteries had huge fields of wheat and other agricultural products, including wine grapes. Monks made wine for sacramental purposes and for sale beyond the monastery's borders. Romanesque architecture gave way to Gothic design in abbeys and cathedrals.

The powerful dukes of Burgundy had a reputation for a lavish lifestyle, poisoning enemies, power struggles, treachery, dynastic marriages, and pageantry. They vied for power with French kings, influencing the royal court in matters of food, wine, and the arts. Treasures at the Cloisters Museum in New York and the Cluny Museum in Paris testify to the wealth and creativity of artists of the era. Charles the Bold in the middle fourteenth century decreed Pinot noir to be the region's leading varietal, replacing the Gamay grape, which fares better in Burgundy's southern areas.

Wines from Burgundy's several appellations and subdivisions maintain an estimable worldwide reputation for centuries. Burgundy's status as one of the world's most eminent wine regions is surprising because of the region's small size and production of less than 10 percent of France's total output. Some wine lovers describe Burgundy's Pinots as overall delicious with food-friendly flavors. Pinots range from light and elegant to fruit-filled rich, depending on the terroir and winemaker's skills. Burgundy also has a long heritage of estimable Chardonnays, considered to be one of the world's best white wines. The region's reputation overcomes poor vintages of wines with undesirable off-tastes and aromas. While soil plays an important roll in every vineyard, a particular mosaic of hundreds of soil types crosses the narrow corridor of this wine region southeast of Paris. Variations in soil vary dramatically from one Burgundian vineyard to the next, sometimes within one vineyard.

Burgundy is subdivided into small, highly regulated small estates called *clos*. Many properties were split up after the French Revolution, then reduced further by French laws of inheritance. Almost 85 percent of more than 4,000 properties have between 14 and 20 acres. Traditionally, labels carry the name of the vineyard or the village where the wine is produced. Négotiants buy, blend, and bottle wines from less-well-known vineyards. The bottlers and shippers of the wines are vital.

# ETIENNE DE MONTILLE
## DOMAINE DE MONTILLE

I met Etienne de Montille one night at a tasting in a restaurant in Westhampton Beach on New York's Long Island. De Montille claims the history of his region goes back goes back to the time when Gallic tribes planted vines, even before Romans entered the picture.

"My family's heritage is a drop in the historic bucket. The de Montille family owned land and vineyards in Burgundy for a mere 400 years," he says. If one believed in the Lamarckian theory of the inheritance of acquired characteristics, it could be said winemaking is in his genetic makeup.

In 1947 Hubert de Montille, Etienne's father, inherited 2.5 hectares and began to accumulate vineyards in the best areas throughout the region, including a hectare of the prestigious Chardonnay property Puligny Montrachet Cru les Caillerets. He slowly accumulated other important vineyard sites, for a total of 17 hectares planted in Pinot noir and Chardonnay, and was known for wines of a more austere quality. At the time, Etienne was working full-time in Paris, returning to the winery on weekends and during harvest each year until he took over from his father in the late 1990's.

*I realized excellent wine needed more devotion to the vineyard during the growing cycle. The cold northerly climate in Burgundy is inhospitable for most grape varietals. Even Pinot struggles. Pinot noir is a fragile, difficult grape with a limited amount of tannins. Its thin skin can burst and spread rot. If there is difficulty in extraction, the wine is weak.*

*In 2001 I returned full-time to Volnay, one of the great towns in Burgundy, to work as consulting winemaker at Puligny Montrachet and several other* properties. *I take ideas from my father, but I try to bring my own style and palate to the wines. It wasn't a smooth transition from my father to me, because it is difficult for two people to make one wine. My philosophy is to respect what has already been done, to consider all the accumulated knowledge that has gone before. I would be pretentious to come up with extraordinary, revolutionary ideas.*

*My style is based on the things I love about my father's wines—elegance, balance, finesse, and authenticity of place. I want to get rid of qualities of harshness and austerity, factors I don't like. My personal attitude concerning Pinot noir aims for concentration and purity of fruit with a minimal use of new oak to develop a less austere, silkier wine, while retaining ability to age. I bring accessibility to young wines through better extraction and ripeness, trying to maintain low alcohol levels.*

*Our family recently purchased a fantastic, well-known vineyard, fortunate for us because it is rare for good vineyards to come on the market. Bad properties come on the market a lot, but it takes a mix of luck and hard work to buy an excellent one. The subsoil is as important as what lies above it, and location is key. Pinot noir can be fickle and undependable, but its reputation overcomes even poor vintages. A vintner's skill and personal goals coupled with the province's northern climate and variations in weather and soils create quality differences from one vintage to the next. That's why it isn't only humans who decide. Nature decides as well.*

*My sister Alix concentrates on the vinification of the white wines and I handle the reds.*

Together they have built up a highly respected and well-sought-after collection of Pinots and Chardonnays.

*Our idea is to respect tradition. Burgundian Pinot noir is the benchmark for other winemakers throughout the world because its tradition and qualities are worthy of emulation. Everyone who wants to make Pinot comes to Burgundy to study our methods. There is always room to improve. I devote what I have in my brain to understanding how vines function. My actions are driven by accumulated experience. Changes in the wine are questionable if we switch from oak to stainless steel because it is cleaner and easier to use.*

Yet he agrees some technological changes have been useful, including the way grapes are pressed.

# DE MONTILLE'S POT AU FEU,
## OR BURGUNDIAN BEEF STEW

1 large onion, diced
6 large leeks, white
   and pale green
   parts only, cut into
   2-inch pieces
6 celery ribs, cut into
   2 inches
6 carrots, peeled and
   cut into 2 inches
6 medium parsnips,
   peeled and cut into
   2-inch lengths
6 medium turnips,
   peeled and
   quartered
1 lb rutabagas,
   peeled and cut into
   eighths
3 lb beef rump roast
   or bottom round
small handful of
   parsley sprigs
4–5 thyme sprigs
2 bay leaves
1 tsp whole black
   peppercorns
Kosher salt
2 quarts water or
   beef stock
½ bottle red wine
1½ lb small potatoes,
   cubed

In a large pot, combine the onion and half of the leeks, celery, and carrots. Set the rump roast on top of the vegetables. Wrap the parsley, thyme, and bay leaves in a piece of moistened cheesecloth and tie into a bundle. Add the bundle to the pot along with the peppercorns and 1 tbsp kosher salt. Add the water. stock and wine. Bring to a boil, then reduce the heat to low, partially cover and simmer, skimming occasionally, until the rump roast is very tender, about 2½ hours.

Transfer the roast to a large bowl and cover. Strain the broth and return it to the pot. Boil over high heat until reduced and skim off the fat.

Add the remaining leeks, celery and carrots to the broth along with the parsnips, turnips, and rutabagas. Cover and simmer over low heat until the vegetables are just tender, 30 minutes. Add the potatoes. Cover and simmer until the potatoes are tender, 40 minutes.

Slice the rump roast across the grain. Add to the pot and reheat. Season to taste. Serve with horseradish or whole-grain mustard.

*Pinot noir is the absolute match for the stew.*

---

*Alix and I instituted organic and biodynamic practices out of environmental concerns and a desire to return to something more simple. We use a gentle, more efficient pneumatic press that is especially helpful during difficult harvests like the '47 and '03 vintages. In '47 we expected to double what we eventually got. Much of the juice turned to vinegar because we had no means to control heat during fermentation. Once the fermentation stopped, it was*

*difficult to restart it. The wine was not suitable to market. Alix and I insti-*
*tuted organic and biodynamic practices out of environmental concerns and a*
*desire to return to something more simple. We use a gentle, more efficient*
*pneumatic press that is especially helpful during difficult harvests like we ex-*
*periences in In '03, in a difficult harvest, we switched to more advanced fer-*
*mentation techniques. Thanks to technology and temperature control devices*
*in the fermentation room, we had more cuvées. The problems we have with*
*Chardonnay are basically the same as those with Pinot. There is more to do to*
*conserve white wine, especially because of premature oxidation. It's been an*
*issue for the last ten years. We comply with Burgundy's strict quality con-*
*trols, and at our properties we maintain standards twice as high as local laws*
*require.*

*It's true the grapes don't jump into the bottle by themselves, but are depen-*
*dent on a winemaker. If you give a Stradivarius to someone who can't play it,*
*who would attend the concert? On the other hand, a maestro can play a bad*
*violin, and it could be an interesting concert. The same is true for wine. A*
*creative winemaker can make interesting wine from poor grapes, but superla-*
*tive wine is the result of great grapes. Our fun rosé is made from grapes from*
*one vineyard that has difficult ripening. It would be hard to make an appro-*
*priate red, but it makes a great rosé. It's important to give the best treatment*
*to the best grapes to maximize the potential of both the fruit and the wine-*
*maker in order to take everything to another level. For us, the potential lies in*
*the soil. Our vineyards are 95 percent organic together with 5 percent homeo-*
*pathic ingredients sprayed at low concentrations.*

De Montille mentioned his relationship to Israeli consumers. In one
of those six-degrees-of-separation moments, I mentioned Zelma Long,
a wine maker in Napa Valley and South Africa who also consults in
Israel.

*Zelma took care of me when I took a sabbatical in California. I go to Israel a*
*lot. I've seen the sophistication of Israelis change dramatically over the last*
*few years. The quality of food has vastly improved, along with their interest in*
*wine. We sell our wines, especially in Tel Aviv, and there are some major col-*
*lectors in the country.*

*Alix and I started a négotiant business, Deux Montilles Soeur et Frère. We*
*haven't been affected by the recession. What we lose in the U.S. we make up in*
*Japan and China. They are on the way to becoming big markets.*

De Montille sums up with this idea. "If you want to be good, you must stretch yourself. Not necessarily to reach the top level, but to have a sense of self-reward. Every job can be wonderful with passion and dedication. I would have loved to be a pianist, a pilot, or an architect. But my passion lies in winemaking." When asked what he does for fun, de Montille says, "I drink wine when I'm not making it."

# ITALY

ONLY A FEW COUNTRIES can boast Italy's 4,000-year-old wine-making legacy. Ancient Greeks called its neighbor across the Adriatic Sea "Enotria," the land of the vine. Italy's natural beauty and its reputation for food and wines drew countless invaders through the centuries. Eventually, the Romans turned the tables, turning from vanquished to conquerors. Romans spread their knowledge of viticulture as they subjugated Europe.

Fly over the country from the top of Italy's proverbial boot to see how much land is dedicated to agriculture and vineyards. Innumerable local varieties, unfamiliar place names, and myriad producers come from more than twenty major wine regions, each with its own subregions, character, and terroir. Italy is two thirds the size of California, but its annual wine production exceeds California's by a factor of nearly 2. Tradition plays a large role in Italian viticulture, especially with a dedication to 2,000 native varieties and many regional wine styles. The Italian classification system lists 300 DOC's and DOCG's. Add IGT's and the total rises to more than 500.

Italy's wine reputation declined over the years when winemakers favored quantity over quality. The country failed to keep pace with competitors in the world's wine industry. Italian wines have improved since the 1970's, when many vintners decided to play catch-up with New World competitors who grabbed larger shares of the market. Forward-thinking winemakers turned to modern technology and planted international varietals like Cabernet Sauvignon, Merlot, and Sauvignon blanc to blend with native grapes. Although there are strict regulations about varietals and blends in each Italian appellation, canny vintners circumvent them inventively. Italy is reaffirming its role as a great wine-producing country and now can claim to be the oldest new competitor in the world wine game. It's hard to sort out the extraordinary number of regions, producers, and labels, but it is exciting to explore the vast possibilities.

## *Friuli*

Within Friuli-Venezia Giulia, better known as Friuli, lies the small appellation of Romandolo in northeast Italy. Friuli is bordered by Austria to the north and states of the former Yugoslavia to the east, with the foothills of the Alps as its backdrop. It has a distinct personality and history as a crossroad of many cultures. Its wines are highly sought after, although it produces the smallest number of bottles of the Italian winemaking regions.

The timeline for its history and wines is vast. Around 1000 B.C., the Illyrians built fortified villages but were eventually pushed out by the Romans, who built roads and set up a social system. The invasion of barbarian tribes led to the fall of the Roman Empire, and the inhabitants of what was to become Friuli fled. The region became impoverished but its wines were always well regarded. Records indicate that wines from the region were served at the Vatican Council of 1409. In the eighteenth century, Charles of Hapsburg established the free ports of Trieste and Fiume, giving the Austrian Empire access to the Mediterranean Sea. World War II interrupted wine production, but some small winemakers in the region banded together in many local cooperatives for better marketing opportunities.

Friuli produces only 2 percent of Italy's production, but connoisseurs think they are comparable in quality to wine of Piedmont and Tuscany, two of the top Italian wine regions. Friuli-Venezia Giulia wines are mostly white, though some excellent reds are also available. The local wines are remarkable for the number of grape varieties that are used in their blends. In addition to the native grapes, different varieties have been introduced, including Chardonnay, Sauvignon blanc, and Muller-Thurgau. Add winemaking skills to the mix and the result is the creation of exceptional wines.

# GIOVANNI DRI
## IL RONCAT

The church bells of San Giovanni Battista ring twice a day over Giovanni Dri's vineyards. The estate is in northernmost corner of Italy, where the Alps protect the vines with relatively mild winters, but during pleasant summers, nighttime temperatures drop rapidly. Grapes prefer warm summer days and rapidly cooling nights, a combination best for concentrating flavors in grapes.

The variations in climate may seem perfect, but at the same time, Friuli is in an earthquake zone and has frequent rainfall, a damp climate, and difficult soil. Persistent winemakers like Dri overcome these conditions.

There was a period when wine was made mostly by cooperatives and customers came to visit the beautiful area and carried away wine. Giovanni Dri, one of the cooperative's members, began to improve his vineyards and produce a wine called Ramandolo commercially. Considered one of the region's top producers, Dri says his personality is perfectly suited to the area's difficult, steep slopes and rocky terrain. He overcomes difficulties of local terroir to produce fresh, fruity, delicate white wines and a smaller amount of reds. "I admit I am as difficult, temperamental, and obdurate as my vineyard's soil. I can be bad-tempered and obstinate. I'm stubborn enough to give a good fight to get what I need for the luscious wines I produce. On a more positive side, I am passionate, truthful, and ambitious to show my wines beyond my local borders." I met Dri twice at an Italian tasting at the Waldorf Astoria in New York City and my sense of the man was on target with the way he describes himself.

*My vineyard has an ideal microclimate for my wines. I'm in love with this tiny piece of unique land I've been farming for over forty years. Ours is the closest winery in Italy to the Alps. It has a continental microclimate, very different from other viticultural areas of Italy. The great gap between warm day and cold night temperatures is perfect for the red and white grapes that go into my dry reds and sweet whites, concentrating sugar, aromas, and acidity. The mountains behind us shelter the vineyard from extreme cold with a flow of air that prevents freezing. The proximity to the Alps and numerous rivers created soils composed of calcareous marl, sand, rocks, and pebbles. The stony soil breaks the extreme cold by holding in heat. The terroir, rich in minerals, brings out the maximum characteristics of our white Verduzzo grapes, a local grape with a long historical tradition. Verduzzo has so much character, so much tannin we vinify it as if it was a red grape. They are wonderful for sweet wines with naturally rich tannins and flavors. Their thick skins are resistant to rain, botrytis, and bad molds. They hang on the vine, ripening slowly, and drying naturally.*

Dri expresses deep love and reverence for nature. "I respect and love my vines. It's a very paternal feeling. They are like little children who I've taken care of since they were born. I watch over them, constantly checking during the growing season to make sure they aren't attacked by parasites and to make corrections as needed. The quality of our wines begins in the vine that we carefully tend by hand and that receive no chemicals or fertilizers, except for the first two years to give new vines a head start. After that, we farm organically, although we haven't received certification. I even go to work on Saturday and Sunday, and when normal people are on holiday."

Sweet wine goes through a complicated process that requires concentration of fruit with underlying acidity.

*Starting in July, we're already thinking about harvest. We must intervene to get maximum quality between the vine, leaves, and grapes. Too many leaves upset the correct equilibrium of the vine. Vines need to be on a diet ... to be healthy, but hungry. It hurts my heart to prune away bunches of grapes, but we know it's best to leave one or at the most two bunches on each arm of the vine. It's a very important step, or else the grapes won't mature properly with proper tannins. My experience is key to guaranteeing a sense of place of origin. I must see everything with my own eyes. I am always looking for perfection, for* the highest quality from my grapes. We can make mistakes, but if we pay attention, growing and harvesting with care automatically creates high quality. The hardest part of the job is to define the exact moment to achieve deep perfume and flavors. By September, the berries develop intense tannins, high aromas, concentration of sugars, and pleasing astringent flavors that create an outstanding sweet wine. I don't need equipment to tell me when to harvest. The leaves announce time to harvest when they turn from green to golden yellow to light red. I taste the grapes to check for a change in flavors. I taste the sweetness in the berries. It's the perfect time to pick when my mouth tastes honey. We harvest late in November, sometimes into December. The berries have long hang time on the vines, losing lots of water so they dry naturally. The grapes are handpicked, one by one from each bunch rather than by clusters, with several passes through the vineyard. Romandolo is vinified with techniques similar to those for red wine, only lacking its color.

Weather is a pitfall, particularly with potential rain around harvest. If the microclimate and soil weren't difficult enough to manage, in May 1976 a devastating earthquake destroyed the winery and part of the vineyard. It overwhelmed the region's agriculture. It's hard to say this, but fortunately, the event coincided with the time when modern technology began to take hold in our winemaking industry. We built a work shed of monastic simplicity made of stone, brick, wood, rock, and iron, materials able to withstand major shocks. When I bought new equipment, my father thought I was crazy to challenge the historic system. Even though I challenged some of his methods, I am at heart a traditionalist. We have no laboratory, although our facility is modern and has top equipment. We used to ferment wine in used oak barrels, but now juice ferments in stainless steel tanks. In 1984 I bought my first new French barrels. I believe there is no need to use sophisticated technology to achieve high-quality wines. My philosophy is to grow high-quality vines that produce high-quality wines. Then, if you work with care, you automatically get fantastic high quality.

Dri crafts three white wine styles. Romandolo DOCG, made from 100 percent Verduzzo grapes, is dried and fermented slowly in order to develop refined, not-too-sweet wine.

Our Romandolo white wine is fermented on the skins for a short time. The amount of sweetness and color that varies from pale to deep gold depends on the proportion of dried grapes. We achieve about 12 percent alcohol, the minimum demanded by local laws. Lower than 12 would be even better in my *opinion. Uve Deciembrine is made from vine-dried grapes harvested in December. Before it is bottled it sees one year of aging in oak to round off tannins for extra refinement. Picoli DOC is made with hand-harvested grapes in our traditional manner, developing elegance and trace aromas of apple, honey, almonds, herbs, wildflowers, stone fruit, and occasional nuances of tropical fruit. These sweet wines are excellent aperitifs, pairing well with strong cheeses, antipasti, and foie gras. They can't be compared to sweet Sauternes or ice-wine. Ours are simpler, with less aromatics, but more importantly, they offer consumers pleasure, freshness, and approachability with potential to age.*

Dri also makes a Sauvignon blanc DOC and four reds blended from Cabernet Sauvignon, Merlot, and varying amounts of local grapes: Schiopettino and Refresco. He compares his wines to a Viennese waltz, having a lot of emotion coupled with wonderful harmonies. He prefers to drink his own wines, but opens bottles produced by friends in the Veneto and reds from Piemonte. "I like to know the philosophies of other producers about how and what they achieve in the bottle. My curiosity extends to wines of other countries as well as to neighbors in Italy who grow our varietals in different terroirs. On holiday, I drink the native wines of the region I visit, like Austrian Gruner Veitliner. While in France, I prefer Champagne."

Dri works with his daughter Stefanie, who has a degree in winemaking. "I teach her which grape varieties are sometimes more difficult. We know nature doesn't grant you the same conditions every year. God and the weather are responsible for 80 percent of the process and winemakers account for the remaining 20 percent. We print *Romandolo* with pride on our labels. It immediately identifies the importance of our region and its terroir. I consider it a more important designation than the grape varietal. Our customers come from Udine and Trieste to buy our wines on weekends and to enjoy the scenery and excellent local cuisine. An old proverb says, 'A wine from Ramandolo is a taste of Friuli.'"

## Lombardy

Tourists are drawn to Milan and to Lombardy's cathedrals, palaces, and museums, as well as to the scenic beauty of Lake Garda, Lake Como, and smaller lakes dotting the foothills of the Alps. Lombardy is a fertile plain bounded by the southern Swiss Alps and the Po River. The region, with a sunny Alpine climate, is considered the heartland of northern Italy. Lombardy has played a role in European history for 2,000 years. Its fortunes waxed and waned because of foreign invasions, beginning with Celts who founded Milan in the seventh century B.C. The Romans occupied the city in the third century B.C. and called the city Mediolanum, or "Middle of the plain" in Latin, and it became a major outpost of the Roman Empire. Virgil, author of the *The Aeneid*, was born in Lombardy. Emperor Constantine declared Christianity the empire's official religion by issuing the famous Edict of Milan in 313 A.D. A succession of legions of conquering barbarians included Goths, Huns, and Longobards, or Lombards whose name stuck. King Charlemagne conquered the area, followed by French, Spanish, Austrian, and Moslem invaders. By the twelfth century, the Lombard League brought several city-states together to oppose the Holy Roman Emperor. Leonardo di Vinci, who noted the region's excellent wines, painted the Last Supper in Milan's Santa Maria delle Grazie church. Agriculture flourished since the Middle Ages, when Lombardy, Venice, and Tuscany were major economic centers in Europe.

One sixth of the Italian population lives in Lombardy's twelve provinces, making it Italy's second most densely populated region. Lombardians owe their high standard of living to a combination of agriculture and modern industry that began after World War II. Lombardy is one of Italy's smallest wine regions and is known for red wines crafted from Nebbiolo grapes and sparkling wines. Nebbiolo and other varieties grow on steep terraces that make the harvest an adventure. In some places, growers rig cables to carry grapes from vineyards on steep mountainsides.

# ANDREA PERI
## PERI BIGOGNO WINERY

"Lombardy, Italy's richest region, is a fertile land of dreams and culture, whose poets drank and praised wine. It includes several notable wine regions: Valtellina, Franciacorta, Lugana and Garda, and Oltrepò Pavese," says Andrea Peri, the charming, enthusiastic spokesman for Peri Bigogno Winery. The winery is located in northwest Italy. I slid into the last seat at a luncheon in New York City where Peri and other Italian winemakers showcased their wines. He went home to be married and we met again for dinner when he returned several months later with his wife.

Peri claims wine has been an important part of Italian life for centuries and quotes an older generation's expression—*il vino fa sangue,* "wine creates blood." The saying implies wine and good health go hand in hand. "Unfortunately, I think food and wine habits have changed somewhat because some modern dietitians insist wine creates fat. The saying became more important in our country in the 1950's, when everyone drank wine at dinner and lunch. The new attitude has created a decline in our per capita wine consumption. It makes one wonder about how changes in social habits will impact on the wine industry now and in the future."

Peri, a third-generation scion of a wine-producing family, speaks with great affection and pride about his paternal grandfather, who was captured by the Germans with other young men from his town in World War II. He spent time in a concentration camp and was rescued by his brother, who brought the emaciated and barely recognizable man home from Germany.

*My maternal grandfather, whose last name was Bigogno, successfully managed a small farm where he helped people market their products through the difficult 1930's. It was the time when Mussolini pushed every aspect of Italian production from industry and farming to the maximum. It affected key staples of the region's life and economy, including grapes, olives, fruits, and vegetables. This grandfather also created a successful manufacturing company, producing transformers. He was highly esteemed by his former employees, friends, wife, and relatives.*

*The Peri grandfather made some wine for family and friends, the first step to the family's current business. In 1946 he purchased a 23-acre chicken and grape farm in Castenedolo, a commune in Brescia. The house, surrounded by grapevines, used the cellar as a warehouse to store wine barrels and cheese. Our current wine cellar was originally part of a palace built in the fifteenth century. Both the Peri and Bignogno grandparents supported the decision to make wine and cooperated in building the business, which is why the winery bears both names.*

*Interestingly, my Bignogno grandfather was also a private flight instructor at a nearby airport. He had a daughter who married one of his flight trainees, or cadets. The cadet was my father. Thanks to our family's passion for flight, I am here. My father was born during World War II. By seventeen he was a national bicycling champion, and in 1960 was the first reservist for the Italian bicycling team in the Olympic Games in Rome. He had a thirty-five-year career with Roche Pharmaceuticals while maintaining his parallel interest in agriculture. He continued to work in our vineyards and make wine as the winery replaced the chickens.*

*I helped my father at the winery from the age of six, but I was slow to realize winemaking was my calling. When I came home after working for Dannon, my parents asked if I was sure about the change in my career path. At first I worked in administration with my mother. Then I helped my father in the vineyards and cellar. Now my father and I make wine together. My experience as winemaker is growing. My father's knowledge is very important to me. I also get technical preparation and advice from Alessandro, our enologist/ agronomist, whose father worked with my father since the winery's first years. To this day, decisions about planting, harvesting, fermentation, and other aspects of winemaking are made by my father, Alessandro, and me.*

Peri applies important personal and professional lessons he learned away from the family and is more than content with his important decision to return to the winery.

The three-year job I had after college with Dannon's European baby food and yogurt division in Paris, Milan, and Amsterdam made me realize how the marketing tools of an international company would be useful for our winery. My Dannon team marketed products with concern, as though it was for our children. I see this as a good parallel for the way we make and sell our wine. I am convinced wine marketing has similarities with the sale of other luxury goods, like perfume, make-up, and fashion. These are markets where wishes, dreams, and status symbols influence the customer, unfortunately sometimes more than the goods warrant. I know, without a doubt, the excellence of our wines is absolutely important because marketing cannot replace quality. I am more than content with my important decision to return to the winery

The experience, history, and tradition of the old farm and house play an important role in our wine production. Our winery is considered a small producer compared with large Italian companies. We don't compare in longevity with the Champagne region or Tuscany, but we explain our history to consumers in a positive way. In our earliest years, the goal was to produce good wine. That is not good enough today. The market has changed as consumers created a demand for better wine.

Wine is also linked to history, images, and marketing. Peri Winery is considered a small producer compared with large Italian companies, but we concentrate on wines with a strong image, competing with new companies that sprung up in our area without the same historical heritage or winemaking experience. I maintain the term quality is overused and too general, even though it's a goal my father and I work toward.

I could write a book about the amazing number of native grapes in Italy. Our local varietals include Marzemino, the source of 80 percent of our red wines. This grape was first described around the fourteenth century in the areas of the Veneto region, Lake Garda, and Brescia, where stone was quarried for the American White House. Music lovers hear it mentioned when Mozart's Don Giovanni asks for a glass of Marzemino before his deliverance to Hell. 'Versa il vino! Eccellente Marzemino!' Don Giovanni cries out. It is a quote many wineries in the neighborhood print on their label in a grand tradition.

Our vineyards are planted in clay and friable soil on gentle hills 10 kilometers from Lake Garda, which moderates our climate. We produce both single varietals and blended wines, some from grapes we buy from different families *whose vineyards we supervise and control. We also produce Merlot, Cabernet Sauvignon, and Barbera. Vineyard plantings of Marzemino are increasing according to plans of Alessandro, our agronomist, so we can achieve wines that are 100 percent of that varietal.*

Peri maintains the grape is an excellent alternative to Cabernet Sauvignon, Merlot, and Syrah.

*Gobbo Rosso was the first wine our company sold by the bottle in 1972. Gobbo is the Italian word for "hunchback," and we call it that because its vineyard stands on a hill with a bulge. The wine is a blend of 40 percent Cabernet Sauvignon, 40 percent Merlot, and 20 percent Marzemino that rests on the lees for a long time. Then it is aged in large oak barrels for at least thirty months before it is bottled. Schiava, which means "gentle," is another typical local grape popular in nearby Alto Adige used for light-bodied red wines. These light-to-medium wines have good fruit flavors and enough tannins and acid to make them food-friendly.*

*We used to make a white wine from Invernenga, a native white varietal grown in the world's largest urban vineyard in the area surrounding Brescia's castle. But my father tore out those vines in 1996, so today our whites are made from Chardonnay and Trebbiano. We want to raise the quantity of our white wines made from Gropello, another local grape.*

*Our sweet wine, Luna Nuova, is made from Moscato we have bought for thirty years from our neighbor. Harvested grapes spend all winter lying in open crates pockmarked with holes. Strong winds over the winter evaporate the water and reduce 1 kilo of grapes by 50 percent, concentrating perfumes, sugars, and flavors. The grapes are softly pressed and the juice ferments in stainless steel. The wine rests to get rid of tartaric acid and is bottled in spring, when it is full of fruity flavors. It's a great dessert wine, matched with strong cheese, like Gorgonzola. One must learn to love this special combination of tastes. But if this match doesn't please you pair it with fatty foods like foie gras.*

*The sparkling wine sector in Italy is in an uproar. There is a movement throughout Italy for winemakers to make a quality sparkling wine called Talento made from Chardonnay and/or Pinot white and/or Pinot black. Among the four appellations reserved for* metodo classico *sparkling wine (the same technique used in the Champagne region) two are located in Lombardy. More*

## PERI'S BEEF STEW

| | |
|---|---|
| 4 lb boneless beef chuck or top blade steaks<br>Extra virgin olive oil<br>2 stalks of celery<br>1 large onion<br>2 carrots<br>4 or 5 cloves<br>8 oz red wine<br>8 oz beef or vegetable broth<br>Sea salt to taste | Clean the vegetables and cut them in little pieces.<br>    Add olive oil to a large pan and fry the beef lightly on each side. Add the vegetables and continue frying, stirring occasionally. Add the wine, stir, and cook for 2 or 3 minutes. Add enough broth to cover the meat. Add salt and cook slowly, stirring occasionally. Add more broth when necessary. Set meat aside when very tender.<br>    Puree the vegetables. Return the meat to the pan and keep it warm while you prepare a nice polenta or mashed potatoes as a side dish.<br><br>*Pair with Borgo dell'Ora Marzemino, which has smooth tanins, freshness, and aromatic fruits.* |

or less, every Italian sparkling wine with bubbles is called Spumante, a word derived from spuma, meaning "bubbles" or "froth." Peri Winery markets 100,00 bottles of wine and 15,000 bottles of 100 percent Chardonnay-based Talento, proudly supporting the Talento Institute, whose role is to enhance this new category with events and special tasting sessions. Our first task is to add producers of Talento in other regions to the project, and then interest investors. The second stage is to educate consumers to the new term. We will do that by printing Talento on the front label, with a cogent explanation on the back label.

We changed our old wine profiles and our wines have improved in the last ten or fifteen years. The winery is making big changes in our production aimed at raising our quality. The winery instituted a number of more modern techniques, some of which I learned at Antinori Cellars, the famous Tuscan winery. We're moving part of our cellar underground to avoid pumping. Barrels are filled from above and then the wines ferment. We used barriques in the past, 50 percent old, the other half used after two or three years. We avoid chemicals and are more attentive to nature. Although Alessandro thinks biodynamics has no basis in fact, we use a variety of organic techniques to improve our soil's quality. We could double our quantity, since Marzemino is a high-yielding vine, but since we don't want to make an inferior product, we crop to reduce the harvest to 8,000 kilos per hectare in order to get better fruit. In other places in Italy vintners often produce wine from 14,000 kilos per hectare. I'm sure, in the end, that wouldn't make me happy. We want consumers to taste our individual, unique varieties closely linked to our territory. In my opinion, the winemaker must be convinced his wine is good.

The wine world is a complex puzzle, and many wineries don't understand the discreet factors that go beyond terroir, production techniques, and grape varieties. It's not enough to have a good product with pretty labels. It's important to sell wine with the story of the passion that goes into making it. Competition from South America and South Africa, with China looming on the horizon, forces us to be very clear about our product. For example, most consumers have a strong image of French wines, but Italian winemakers haven't presented the same clear picture. I hope young winemakers like me will face these problems of competitive products ... and, like me, will present the story of our excellent products.

Not only do I make wine, I work at reaching a vast number of wine lovers. At our winery, we plan tastings matched with special dishes at a local restaurant for press, wine experts, and consumers. I lead the sales direction and plan for future changes in our portfolio as we see where we should go. For example, we decided to bottle some red wine in a 375-ml bottle, half the size of a customary bottle, to take advantage of a business opportunity. Most of our wines are sold in Italy, but I'm working hard to introduce them abroad. I firmly believe Italian brands need more exposure because our market is static. Since competition is tight, we also focus on advertising, press relations, and public relations. Our logo was restyled and we have invested time on a website and a bi-monthly newsletter. We reach about 1,000 addresses by e-mail, which creates a closer relationship between the winery and our customers. A large number of visitors arrive at the winery, after learning about us through our website. We developed a VIP sponsorship and support events with important politicians and sports figures.

The Peris, *papa e figlio*, attend trade fairs to check on their competitors.

Tasting other wines is a positive learning experience that helps expand our expertise. Two weekends a year, we host an open house for journalists and the public. At these events, we don't necessarily concentrate on selling wine.

*Rather, we want to underscore our production by educating consumers about our tradition and our terroir. One event we hosted the theme "Sparkling wine and the New York City Marathon, 25 years later." Orlando Pizzolato, the Italian athlete, was presented with a bottle of a local sparkling wine as a special prize when he won the 1985 marathon. It's amazing how people react when they see a famous person holding a bottle of our Chardonnay. It's ridiculous, I know, but people are really crazy.*

## Sicily

The island of Sicily, separated from Italy's toe by the Straits of Messina, has more land under grape cultivation than any other Italian region. Wineries like Planeta Winery and Vineyards dot the perimeter of the island's nine provinces. Vintners tempt fate and plant vineyards on the slopes of Mt. Etna to garner distinctive aromas and flavors from the mountain's volcanic soil.

Sicily's favorable climate and turquoise waters lured Greeks, Romans, Goths, Vandals, Etruscans, and Moors to its shores. The island's highly regarded wines were mentioned in the history of the Punic Wars between Rome and Carthage in the first and second centuries B.C. Julius Caesar was reputed to have been a fan of Sicilian wines. One by one, conquerors disappeared from the wooded isle, leaving behind legacies: Greek and Roman temples, Etruscan ruins, mosaic pavements, medieval churches, and cloisters, some declared World Heritage sites. Olive oil and wine have dominated the island's agricultural production for eons.

Until fairly recently, the island produced mostly strong, sweet wines like Marsala. Winemaking has improved steadily over the last couple of decades with the adoption of modern technology. Sicilian wines have dark fruit flavors and good tannins from the local red grape, Nero d'Avola, the island's primary varietal. In recent decades, new plantings of Syrah, Cabernet Sauvignon, Chardonnay, Merlot, and Sauvignon blanc are blended with indigenous varieties. Sicilian winemakers are increasingly interested in developing fruity, fresh whites, reds and rosés plus the historic lush sweet wine Vin Santo.

Marsala is a major product of the region, a fortified dessert wine made with white or red grapes, ranging in taste from dry to sweet. An addition of grape spirits stops fermentation, leaving a desirable amount of sugar in the wine. Each Marsala producer blends grapes and ages the wine to maintain a distinctive house style.

## ALESSIO PLANETA
### PLANETA WINERY AND VINEYARDS

Alessio Planeta, the Planeta family winemaker, and I talked over lunch in New York.

*We have been plagued by foreign incursions for centuries, and finally phylloxera traveled from northern Europe to infiltrate Sicily's vineyards. Many reasons were responsible for the decline of the wine industry, beginning at the end of the nineteenth century, when three times the number of vineyards existed than do now. A lot of replanting took place around 1895, but the Sicilian wine industry shrank as other nations forged ahead with new technology and different varieties of grapes. Sicily, with excellent terroir for grape cultivation, is ranked first or second in Italy's total wine production, with whites generally outnumbering reds. Today there are approximately 500 wineries, although only thirty or forty play a significant role in the market. Winemakers are renewing their interest in local grapes with personality, often blending them with the five great international varietals: Cabernet Sauvignon, Merlot, Syrah, Chardonnay, and Sauvignon blanc.*

Planeta believes the family migrated to Sicily from Spain in the seventeenth century and settled in a farm at Ulmo in the western part of Sicily.

*Our farm's deep, chalky soil was planted with wheat, the island's major exported crop, plus citrus fruits, artichokes, and grapes. A small winery in the middle of the family's village originally generated wine from local grapes. Olive oil has flowed from an ancient press in the center of the Planeta's 100-hectare grove.*

*Over fifty years ago, Baron Planeta, my grandfather, an open-minded, influential landowner understood life was changing. He started a wine cooperative for large and small landowners that became very important in the region's economy. Sicilian winemaking hadn't changed for centuries. In the 1970's, local vintners traveled to Australia and Ethiopia, once an Italian colony, to learn new winemaking techniques. All of Italy was challenged and started to change production in the 1980's, after a huge scandal shook the wine industry. At the same time, consumers cut back on their wine consumption while becoming more discerning about the quality of a bottle's contents. The wine community, consumers, and those in the business are becoming very knowledgeable. When someone tries a good wine, they will never go back to a poor one.*

*My brother Santi, cousin Francesca, and I are Planeta's younger generation. We expanded the family's horizons in the 1980's, desiring to produce wine under our own label. Each partner in the trio brings something to the family table.*

Alessio, with degrees in agriculture and winemaking, is the winemaker.

*I needed experience and traveled a lot to other wine regions. I worked in Burgundy, traveled to the Rheingau in Germany, and visited Australia three times. I see other areas around the world that remind me of our soils and what they are capable of producing. I maintain friendships with a group of international winemakers. We stay in touch with each other and share our fabulous experiences. For example, on January 13, 2011, twenty-five friends and gourmets met at our winery at Menfi, where we served a huge lobster, a large pot of stew, artichokes, tortellini, and seventy bottles of wine from around the world. It was like a nonstop ten-to-twelve-hour rock festival.*

*Without a doubt, my first and second harvests were the most difficult. I hired a consultant, Carlo Corino, who is from the same generation as the well-known, tradition-defying Angelo Gaia and other winemakers of his stature. Corino was an old-style Piedmontese who dressed like an Australian, slouch hat and all. He embarked on a revolution in Italian wine based on his philosophy and soul. Men like Gaia and Corino brought about a different approach to winemaking with information about modern technology and vineyards planted with international grapes. We call Corino the Prince of Enology. I consider him my master. Then ten days before the harvest began in August*

*1995, Corino moved to Tuscany, working with us from a distance. It felt as if the owner of the football team retired five minutes before the beginning of the World Championship finals. Then my second harvest was complicated when I got married and my life suddenly changed. However, my agricultural experience and the fantastic Sicilian climate helped me.*

*I'm proud when I see my label on shelves and menus. It's my connection between what I do and the rest of the world. Francesca, Santi, and I are young, with clear ideas about our projects. We want to preserve old Sicilian winemaking traditions while looking to the future and keeping our minds open to new ideas. Our business has grown to six wineries located on Sicily's periphery. I travel around the island hoping to transform the place and its wines. It takes a long time to find the right place for a new farm. I've explored many new possibilities for new sites over the last five years. I imagine where particular grapes will flourish in a particular terroir. Intuition tells me what and where to plant. I start with the land and think about what will arrive in the bottle in maybe fifteen years. We influence other local producers, lighting a fire under them and putting others in the distance. At the end of the day, I want Planeta to represent all of Sicily.*

Planeta talks with great enthusiasm about his new ideas for the wineries.

*Our farm on Mt. Etna is one of our new projects. It was on our minds once we thought about its higher elevation—the highest except for wineries in Chile and Argentina—and its friable, fertile black soils created by volcanic ash. The Mt. Etna site has two distinct vineyards focused primarily on whites, with the addition of a small amount of red. One vineyard has a special climate of high 70's in the day and 42 degrees at night. The weather is perfect for our native Carricante grapes harvested in late autumn, when snow comes early. Our 100 percent Carricante wine derives its minerality and its green apple and wild honey flavors from the microclimate and sandy black lava soil of Mt. Etna.*

A recent plan for a sparkling wine made from 100 percent Carricante grapes holds great appeal for the Planeta team.

*There are only three or four Sicilian sparkling wines, all artisanal products. All I know about sparkling wine came from drinking it, so I hired a consultant*

## PLANETA'S ARANCINI RICE BALLS

**BREADING**

1 cup bread crumbs

**FILLING**

2 cups cooked and
   cooled risotto or
   short-grain rice
½ cup bread crumbs
½ cup finely grated
   Grana Padano
2 eggs, beaten
4 oz each of
   Emmenthal, Edam,
   and Fontina cut
   into small cubes
Vegetable oil for
   frying

In a medium bowl, combine the risotto, bread crumbs, Grana Padano, and eggs. With damp hands, form 2 tbsp of the rice mixture into 2-inch balls. Make a hole in the center of each ball and insert a cube of each of the three cheeses. Cover the hole and enclose the cheese. Roll the balls in the bread crumbs to coat. In a large heavy-bottomed saucepan, pour in enough oil to fill the pan about one third of the way. Heat the oil until hot. Fry the rice balls in batches, turning occasionally until brown. Drain oil with paper towels.

*Serve with La Segreta Bianco Planeta.*

---

from Alto Adige in northern Italy to help make it using the traditional champagne method from grapes from our Mt. Etna vineyard. The first bottling was a small release in March of 2011.

I'm generally less concerned with terroir, except to master it for what it will do for our indigenous grapes and international varietals. We have to deal with so many variables. Amounts of sun and rain change the flavor of the grapes. It's a misperception that Sicily is very hot. Sea breezes moderate the coast and hot days in the island's center. The island contains thousands of combinations of climates and soils. Years of careful research revealed the diversity of the soils. Every day when we open the winery doors, a change in temperature of the room influences the eventual result in the bottle. We have a library full of old books that influence our choices. I check history to see what to plant at different sites. Every year we make fewer mistakes, which is important because a mistake can hold us back for five years. Planeta produces 2 million bottles a year of several types of wines from its aggregated 963 acres.

*My intuition was correct about planting Nero d'Avola on our property in the southeast of the island near land owned by our paternal grandmother. It produces a rich, versatile dark red wine blended with 40 percent of our local peppery Frappato grape with soft tannins and complex aromas of strawberry, cherry, and figs. [A comment in* The New York Times *describes Planeta's Nero d'Avola as a sunny and joyful wine.] If my intuition turns out to be wrong, we can graft another varietal or create a less important second wine*

*Local reports say bees love our Corneta grapes. I introduced this Italian grape to Sicily. It is harvested very late and imparts remarkable aromas. We're also experimenting with other Italian varietals, together with historic Sicilian grapes. We produce a Rosé of Syrah. A fresh window opened for us with Pinot noir and Riesling. The Rhine area is the inspiration for one wine. Its style of minerality and acidity is close to the German version and we sell it in a brown Riesling bottle. Our iconic Chardonnay is commercially very successful and is one of the wines that put Sicily on the map. Our second white is a fusion of two Italian grapes.*

Along with a few other Sicilian wineries, Planeta is adding to its portfolios by reviving the island's tradition of sweet Vin Santo. The winery crafts five cases of Vin Santo from 100 percent Moscato bianco, with its distinctive flavor of jasmine tea. Planeta considers Moscato bianco to be the world's original grape.

*We use a traditional method. The grapes are harvested, laid on the ground, and covered with leaves to dry for forty days in the open air. It's made in our winery located in the southeastern tip of Sicily, "invisible" because it was built underground out of the family's environmental concerns, our sense of social responsibility, and a wish to preserve the purity of the region.*

*Working with my large Sicilian family is fantastic. A great family gives you values. Together we discuss our goals and decisions. It's the family business of Planeta that makes it Planeta. The family goes along with my ideas, although they first ask if the plan will lose money. When I say I'm sure it will be good, they say okay. When my plans work, it is like an orchestra that makes a beautiful sound. I love sharing results with our team, the group involved in the everyday life of our wineries. For example, together we consider which of our terroirs will give birth to particular wines. We always want every vineyard to bring out all the possibilities we see in the vines every day. I alone create a specific style for our wines. You can like them, or not. For me, the idea of a personal style means that the winemaker ultimately goes it alone. I don't know if I do it the easiest way, but it's the way I've worked my entire life. Working with another winemaker would be like painting a canvas and having another artist elbow you out. My philosophy is to make wines that tell, in my words, the history of each vineyard. Infinite details, like a harvest that takes a total of three months, require daily trips to wineries located in very isolated areas around the island's edges. Happily, I get to view the sea every morning. Those are two reasons why I live in my car.*

*When my workday is over, I spend time with my children, and maybe taste the wine from our first harvests. Every year, on August 15, we celebrate an old family tradition. About 100 family members and other guests go to the sea at Capparrino, where there is a gorgeous pristine beach near our mill. We fry our aunts' homemade arancine rice balls and wash them down with our chilled Rosé of Syrah.*

The family built a facility with fourteen guest rooms, a cooking school, and a restaurant that features family-style and special wine dinners at the La Foresteria winery. It is close to archeological ruins near Agrigento on Sicily's southern coast. Many of the rooms overlook vineyards planted with Fiano, the backbone of Planeta's elegant floral white wine Cometa. Guests at the inn have an opportunity to taste rare wines from Planeta's personal cellar. "During the Film Festival at Taormina in 2009, Robert de Niro had dinner at our restaurant and fell in love with our Santa Cecilia wine. He brought two bottles home to the States. It was a thrill because de Niro is my favorite actor. Industrialist Gianni Agnelli always had Santa Cecilia in his cellar and I heard Naomi Campbell drinks our Chardonnay."

Planeta is very active in charitable activities.

*Charity is part of our duty and culture. We also have a passion for contemporary art. Paintings of the island's landscape are part of a program called "A Journey Through Sicily," which takes place during the height of annual vintage and goes through the most captivating parts of the island, from Val di Noto in the southeast through Vittoria and the district of Ragusa, visiting all the Planeta vineyards, finishing at Menfi and Sambuca di Sicilia on Lago Arancio. As for the general public, if anyone wants to do a journey through Sicily as*

*Goethe did, come and taste our wines situated from west to east and south to north around our island.*


## Soave

Soave, a walled city with a medieval castle lies in the eastern part of the complicated mosaic of the Veneto region. The relatively small area lies in the foothills of the Italian Alps. Verona and and Venice, the Veneto's capital, are in close proximity. Millions of tourists arrive every year to enjoy the region's scenic lakes, tree-covered hills, ancient castles, and olive groves, coupled with its heritage of great food and wine.

Wines from the Veneto were famous before Romeo and Juliet fell in love in nearby Verona, even before the doges ruled neighboring Venice. "In fact, it is recorded that in 685 A.D. the king of Swabia, one of innumerable invaders who trampled through the region, penned an order for his followers to go to the land east of Verona and find the grapes that made great wine," Giovanni Ponchia says. Since those early days, there has been no break in the production of wine throughout the Veneto.

Way back in geological time, a tropical sea inundated the Soave area. Traces of saline sediments in the locale's alluvial plain find their way into its wines. Garganega, Soave's native grape, thrives in black basaltic soils made rich by frequent volcanic eruptions. New techniques in winemaking led to the development of more complex and fruity wines with ability to age. The vines are cropped for fewer, high-quality yields and the grapes are allowed to ripen fully. Once celebrated for elegant wines in historical documents and praised by literati, Soave wines declined in quality in the twentieth century, and wines were inexpensive, pallid, lacking pleasant aromas, flavorless, with few enticing aromas to the nose. In other words, they were simply boring. Many small producers in the region continue to make incredible strides to vastly improve the wines using a combination of ancient traditions embedded in modern technology. Old habits are changing and in their place has come a quest to introduce a resistant public to better Soaves that are slowly being restored to their rightful place in the wine world.

Wines labeled Soave DOC are meant to be drunk within a year or two after harvest. Soave DOCG may be released after the first of September of the year following the harvest, only after bottle aging of at least three months to emphasize its characteristic maturity and complexity. Wines aged a minimum of two years may be labeled Riserva. The ancient, beloved Recioto di Soave DOCG, made from dried grapes, is gaining a reputation as one of Italy's finest dessert wines, only one of forty-one *Denominazione di Origine Controllata e Garantita,* or DOCG, in the vast sea of Italian wines.

# GIOVANNI PONCHIA
## CONSORZIO TUTELA

Giovanni Ponchia is enologist for the Consorzio di Soave. He is a hometown *ragazzo* from the Veneto. Even though he grew up surrounded by the region's famous wines, his path to winemaking was circuitous. "When I was twenty, I was conscripted into the military and sent to nearby Friuli as a member of a specialized troop. We Italians claim the army separates boys from Mama's skirts. It's where we 'lose the smell under the nose,' the Italian expression for fussy. " When we spoke, he mentioned his fortyish brother was still at home.

*Every night, I came out of the barracks and tried different wines with strange names and labels. It turned out the time I spent in the army was okay. I had time to figure out what I wanted to do and it helped me find myself. I didn't want to follow my father's career. I studied law first and started work in the motorcycle industry. Then my uncle, a professor in enology at the University of Padua, one of Italy's best viticultural schools, was a major influence in my life. I took the test for the university, one of 150 applicants. The competition for twenty places was tough, but I was accepted . . . as number 19.*

After graduation, Ponchia worked for San Filippo Fanti di Montalcino in Tuscany, where the vineyards were planted with Sauvignon blanc, Chardonnay, Cabernet Franc, and Merlot.

*I was totally in charge of everything from vineyard supervision to winemaking. I worked completely alone from 8 A.M. to 7 P.M. without talking to a single soul. I was so lonely I went out every night to drink with the guys. I found a planting of red Rabosso Piave and fermented it in the Charmat process we call* the metodo italiano—*to make a delightful sparkling wine. This method gives us smaller, longer-lasting bubbles through a secondary fermentation in bulk tanks. It was a good experience and taught me a lot.*

*The job and the loneliness got to me. I worked for several other wineries until I found a position with the Soave Consorzio Tutela. Right now, my job focuses on designating Soave's crus in what I call a viticultural garden. We represent the four types of Soave. Many winemaking regions in Italy are dedicated to their own favorite grapes, but Garganega is our queen and the dominant varietal in Soave. I believe Garganega was brought from Greece as far back as 2500 years ago, taking its name from a derivation of a Greek word. Romans cultivated it as well. Garganega is cultivated in Sicily and in small amounts on the island of Murano off the coast of Venice.*

*Garganega, Soave's workhorse grape and the fifth most important varietal in Italy, is the backbone of our food-friendly wines, with character, fresh flavors, good acidity, and aromas. I believe the quality of our wines lies under our feet, and I consider the soil here perfect for our wines. If a winemaker doesn't understand the classic combination of soil, climate, and the effects of his hand, he can't make good wine. Garganega is a vigorous producer, and traces of qualities from volcanic soils that are found only here and on Mt. Etna find their way into its wines. Way back in geological time, a tropical sea inundated the Soave and left saline sediments in the locale's alluvial plain that also add character to the wines. The long growing season is ideal for Garganega cultivation.*

*Garganega can yield 30 to 40 tons per hectare, but the heavy load gives us wine without body or aroma. It was the reason for poor wines in the past. A limit of a maximum of 14 tons per hectare gives us richer structure and adds drinkability plus personality. We irrigate only two to three times a year, and then only during an emergency. Strangely, it usually rains two days after we irrigate. We've been investigating new kinds of trellising and clones. Our long growing season pushes harvest well into October. So we can apply the secret of the creation of great flavors. It is due to cutting back on grapes before harvest, leaving only the best bunches. After the best grapes are picked, the rest are left on the ground. Then we walk on a carpet of vines and grapes. All the wine is cold-fermented in stainless steel tanks together with selected yeasts from our area. After all of that, we pray. The result is our beautiful wines.*

*My job requires organizing Soave tastings for international journalists and foreign buyers. I also do research projects on Soave, specifically on the Garganega grape and its effects on our local wine production. Most of our*

## PONCHIA'S BICOLOR TAGLIOLINI WITH MUSSELS IN GRANA PADANO TRUFFLE SAUCE

2 lb cleaned mussels
⅔ cup of chicken broth or fish stock
3 oz Grana Padano
2 tbsp of sunflower or other neutral oil
3.5 oz truffles, sliced
1 leek, white part only, chopped
3 scallions, white part only, chopped
Salt/pepper
½ pkg. each of white and green tagliolini pasta cooked al dente

For the sauce, combine ⅔ cup of chicken broth or fish stock with Gran Padano and the oil. Blend very well. Gently panfry the mussels with leeks and scallions. Add the truffles. Toss over the two pastas and cover with the sauce. Add salt and pepper to taste. Serve immediately.

*Pair with Gini's Soave DOC Classico La Froscà. Crisp, with hints of exotic fruit, smoky minerality, and a good finish.*

wineries are micro-farms—single vineyards often smaller than 3 hectares. Many are small blocks scattered around throughout the zone and divided into Classico and non-Classico areas. Only three producers cultivate more than 25 hectares.

I'm a member of the tasting commission of the Consorzio. Another part of my job runs from April to October, when I talk with our 3,000 growers about potential varieties for our area. I consider each one of them as a son. I believe strongly that there cannot be wine without people. The face of a producer should be in his wine. I help them take a common approach to label fonts, images, and logos. We discuss what to do to preserve the vines from insects and fungi. I put together a forum for white wines produced in volcanic soils and had a comparison tasting of aged Soave wines to similar Italian products.

I'm really lucky because I get to taste 2,000 to 3,000 wines a year. I can remember eighty to ninety telephone numbers, but I don't make a point of remembering anything about the different wines other than if they're good, very good, incredible, or sensational. I don't do marketing. It's something I don't *want to do. When I'm not working, my hobbies are movies, hard rock, punk blues, and '80's music.*

Ponchia has played the electric bass since he was sixteen and produced a music album in 2006 that is distributed in Italy. He loves soccer, tennis, and basketball, and was an avid skateboarder until he broke his back twice. "I had to stop before I broke something else," the thirty-something-year-old said sadly.

*What I like to do is travel with friends on vacation, somewhere where we don't talk about wine. Talking about wine continually is monotonous. My preference is to go to the Greek Islands, where I forget who I am and what I do. It's where I empty my mind, and when I come back, I can restart completely.*

*I don't particularly like red wines. My passion is for white wines from volcanic soils, like those from Sicily's Mt. Etna. I collect more than I can drink of Eiswein and Trockenbeerenauslese from the Moselle. One day I will make wine, preferably on the fabulous volcanic Greek soils Greece.*

*It may take a while to get people to change their minds and accept a wine they tried before and found unappealing, especially with the seemingly unlimited number of choices. I am undeterred. I represent Soave. It is my mission to open people's eyes and hearts to our wines. The translation of soave is "gentle," but in my mind it also means beautiful, and consumers will learn it is the correct name for our beautiful wine. The final judgment will be in the glass. Soave's clean flavors and excellent alcohol level of 12.5 percent invite you to indulge in a second glass.*

## Tuscany

Tuscany boasts of an ongoing relationship between culture, food, and wines dating from the Etruscan period. The Etruscans, famous for their paintings and pottery, also cultivated wild vines growing on the hills of Tuscany. Tuscany's terroir is ideal for grape growing and has been designated as an appellation zone since the fourteenth century. Sangiovese, the region's historic grape, is blended with more currently popular international and indigenous grape varietals to create Chianti, Italy's most recognizable wine. Besides its famous dry red wines, Vin Santo, or Holy Wine, is a sweet wine made from dried grapes.

Only a few decades ago, Americans ordered Chianti as a feel-good, uncomplicated wine to pair with pizza and pasta. Rustic Chiantis, along with many other Italian wines, were cheap and mass-produced from inferior grapes. Wine regulations required a minimum of 30 percent cheap white grapes, particularly Trebbiano, even though the wine was red. Many were not only cheap but generally dull and lacking complexity. Chianti was sold in easily recognizable straw-covered bulbous green wine bottles called *fiascos*, whose name was often an apt description for its contents. It was the introductory wine for American college students who carried home the empty bottles and used them as candleholders.

In the mid-1970's and early '80's, forward-thinking Tuscan vintners looked at the amazing growth of high-quality wines from around the world and were inspired to make drastic changes in their winemaking techniques. The revolution to raise their standards and individualize their wines began with the introduction of modern technology. Yields were cut back and less desirable varietals were torn out. Some organic and biodynamic methods have been installed. Chianti evolved into more complicated wines expressing their terroir, able to be aged for five to six years, but good to drink within two years.

Super Tuscans were one of the new wines to emerge. Super Tuscans bypass the Vino Consorzio Chianti, an organization established by a group of wine producers in 1927 to ensure conformity with incredibly complicated rules and regulations about vineyard management, vinification, and aging. As a result, Super Tuscans don't receive certification from the Consorzio.

# SERGIO GARGARI
## PIEVE DE' PITTI

The 1970's were a boon for Italian investors looking for properties and careers in wine. Savvy buyers bought estates and old vineyards in many areas, including Chianti. "My father-in-law was in the leather business and made an investment in land as a place to entertain customers for hunting and relaxation," says Sergio Gargari.

*He had the good fortune to find a beautiful eighteenth-century villa with a large garden and park 40 kilometers from Pisa. In the beginning, I continued to work in family business, but in 2004 I decided to dedicate all my time to wine. When my son and daughter came of age, they chose wine over leather.*

*None of us knew anything about winemaking. We started in the vineyard with many experiments and hired an enologist–agronomist who planted local historic grapes on 16 hectares of vineyards on a hilly site. The vines are planted north to south on cordons to maximize the sunshine. Two full-time workers crop one to two bunches of grapes from canes on each vine in order to develop maximum flavors in the remaining grapes. Sangiovese dominates, together with Canaiolo, white and black Malvasia, Trebbiano, and Vermentino, as well as Merlot, Syrah, and Petit Verdot for blending. Our daughter Caterina calls the introduction of different varietals contamination of our Tuscan grapes.*

*Caterina became interested in producing wine and spent a lot of time following our enologist. Now she is a force at the winery, devoting herself to winemaking while continuing to teach architecture two days a week. In 2007 we hired another eminent enologist from Siena who is a specialist in Sangiovese. It was an important move to help us improve the quality of our wines.*

*Our soils are a mix of clay and sand containing smooth river stones and fossils. We are close to the sea, and water covered the land in ancient times.*

The sea has an important maritime influence on our vines, especially on the whites. The local climate has big swings: Winter is usually mild and damp but can bring heavy snowfalls. Variations in sunshine and temperatures occur during the growing season. For example, in 2011, harvest temperatures fell below average, with grapes maturing slowly at their own rate. Our vines are treated with organic material and we are working toward organic certification.

Gargari says drily, "I believe biodynamics is for rich people. I don't think the stars affect the outcome of grapes." He nods his head pensively and adds, "The moon … yes, because it changes the earth's activity."

In the past, the old-style Chianti blend included a small portion of white grapes. It's not a requirement any longer, although it is still allowed. Today there are new regulations that require 80 percent Sangiovese and 20 percent estate-grown red grapes to be called Chianti. Most of our wines are recognized as IGT, or Indicazione geografica tipica, a classification of high quality that doesn't meet the stricter requirements of DOC or DOCG. A wine labeled IGT cannot contain anything a winemaker wants, including wines from Greece sold as wine from Tuscany made by unscrupulous vintners. An appellation designation is important in Italy and ours is Pisiano. Our wines also receive the pink label, another certification of quality from the Chianti Chamber of Commerce.

Italian families make red wine for winter and white for summer consumption. Our family fights about making reds or whites. Caterina prefers reds and I like whites, so I insisted on dedicating a section of vineyard to white grapes. Caterina spent two weeks in France and southern Germany to learn the philosophy of white wine. In 2006 the winery produced its first bottle of Vermentino. We called it Aprilante because of the month it was bottled. The vineyard is still young, so 100 percent of the white wine didn't have enough body and needed a boost from white Malvasia. Malvasia lacks appealing body or flavor, so it doesn't change the Vermentino too much. In 2011 we had a late harvest and so we put together the white wines piece by piece, making 1,500 bottles in total. Because we consider the wine special, each bottle is numbered.

We decided to make a 100 percent Sangiovese Chianti Superiore DOCG labeled Cerretello. It takes its name from one of the estate's vineyards and is called Superiore because we take less than 700 kilos per hectare. The wine, made from 90 percent Sangiovese, together with Canaiolo and Black Malvasia grapes, represents the signature austere style and the rough flavor of Chianti. The juice is fermented for twelve days and the wine rests in concrete vats for six months to bring out tannic components and taste of terroir. Concrete is neutral, unlike oak barrels, and doesn't affect the flavor of the wine. After complete maturation, it is aged in the bottle until release.

Before the grapes change color at harvest, we cut back on foliage again. Some of the varietals are harvested in September; others, later in October. Retired men from the countryside come every year and know exactly what to do to pick the grapes. My wife is an English teacher with a source of young students who come to pick. She tells them to do a good job or jokes she will see them at the end of the year. She also handles events, public relations, and cooking courses.

The first harvest of Sangiovese is dedicated to our Appunto label. An Appunto is a vino ruffiano. Ruffiano is our term for a matchmaker, someone who organizes dates or discreet dinners between a man and a woman. Appunto is an IGT Red from Tuscany made from hand-selected Sangiovese and Merlot grapes from a thirty-year-old vineyard with a low density of plants per hectare that produces a limited amount of higher-quality juice with freshness of aromas and taste. We train the canes on double or single-arched cane in the traditional Tuscan style as well as with a newer cordon system.

We harvest grapes at optimum ripeness to capture the freshness of perfumes and taste. Wines for our Appunto label are immediately put into steel vats, where they remain for twelve to fifteen days. After the first alcoholic fermentation takes place the must rests in vats for five to six months. Then wine is bottled to retain its youthful characteristics. Our Appunto is appealing and easy to drink, a wine that eases relationships and makes you enjoy life.

Overripe Trebbiano grapes are the basis for our late-harvest IGT Tribiana. Destemmed grapes are pressed gently and the free-run juice is immediately cooled and set to rest in steel vats. Alcoholic fermentation starts in little oak barrels, where it develops perfumes and aromas. After five months in wood, the second malolactic fermentation takes place and the wine goes into concrete to a final stabilization before bottling.

Scopaiolo IGT, a deep Tuscan Red, is produced from Syrah grapes grown in a new vineyard. The direction of the vines and stony soil are responsible for the tasty, spicy qualities of the wine. At harvest, the best Trebbiano and San Colombano grapes lulled by the sunshine and sea breezes are selected for Pieve de' Pitti Vinsanto and dried on racks until December. The must is pressed by hand and stays in small chestnut and cherry casks to age for five years. Vinsanto has an intense bouquet of dried fruit, apricots, and tamarind with a dry finish and balance between sweetness, freshness, and flavorful notes.

Grapes for our Moro di Pava grow in a southeast vineyard, overlooking the valley of Pava. The wine is made from a careful double selection of Sangiovese grapes from old arched-trained vineyards with a low yield. Moro means "dark" and refers to the grapes' dark brown skin. The must macerates with skins and natural yeasts for twenty to twenty-two days at 30°C without adding tannins or enzymes. Afterward it goes into little French oak barrels for sixteen months.

Grappa is potent Italian brandy similar to French Cognac, distilled from pumice, the pressed skins and seeds of grapes. Grappa is usually 80 to 90 proof and changes its flavors, depending on the grape varietal or fruit, such as cherries.

Pieve de' Pitti Chianti Grappa is produced from the skins and seeds of the Sangiovese and Canaiolo grapes. Distillation takes place in an Alembic still, the classic method that produces a crystal-clear liquid. Our grappa has aromas of violets, raspberries, and red fruit.

Labels reflect a wine's personality. One Pieve de' Pitti label has a round circle representing the sun. Artists who are my wife's friends designed two other labels. One features Pinocchio on a Vespa because the motor scooter is a major product of our region. Another label sports an image of a bee. I especially like the bee symbol because of the way they cooperate as a group to locate the best flowers and fruit. Our family follows the ways of the bees. We check quality in the vineyard day by day up to the last moment to make sure the berries are perfect before we harvest the crop.

The fact that people don't appreciate the work that goes into a glass of wine is my pet peeve. Few customers, including wine buyers and merchants who visit ten to fifteen wineries a day, care about the story behind the wines. They only want to hear the price, when in reality they should have a story to tell their clients. It's a problem for wineries when there is probably 40 percent more wine than buyers. If I consider our costs, I can't sell the wine. We make our own calculations, but most of all we must understand how the market, rather than the producer, sets the price. As a result, we don't make a profit every year. A total of 60,000 bottles are produced at Pievi de' Pitti, 30 percent *exported to Europe and some to the U.S. My dream is to enter into a new market where quality is more appreciated than price. As an unknown company, we must offer better quality.*

Asked about his hobbies, Gargari smiled ruefully. "I take off two or three days a year to hunt for boar and deer. Otherwise, I work in the winery and in the garden or help with weddings at our beautiful property."

# FILIPPO ROCCHI
## CASTELVECCHIO

Three Rocchis—Filippo, Stefania, and their father, Carlos—make their wines, press olives, and run a holiday property at Castelvecchio, one of several small satellite towns 20 kilometers from Florence.

*Our grandfather bought the estate, once one of the most important historic estates in the region, in the 1960's as a hobby. He sold wine in bulk or in fiascos. The winery is built on the ruins of an old castle and its logo comes from the coat of arms over the door of a nearby twelfth-century Romanesque Chapel of San Lorenzo. Inside the church, the pavement covers the tombstones of the region's early ruling families. A giant old quercia, or oak tree, stands as a landmark in the middle of the vineyard.*

*When I talk of my interest in wine, my grandfather comes immediately to mind. If I close my eyes I can still see a man with a wide-brimmed straw hat who loved to roam through his vineyards and olive grove with his dog. He was absolutely indefatigable and seemed strict, but he had a huge smile whenever he saw his grandchildren. His eyes became playful and his voice soft as he told stories about things he had done long ago. He wanted us to keep his dreams and his warm memories close to our hearts. He left us his passion for Castelvecchio, for our land, and for wine. Our lives today are made up of thousands of ideas, small steps, great adventures, and most of all, endless emotions. Grazie, Grandfather!*

*Our father designed and fabricated silverware, but he realized his true interest lay in wine. He had little experience with the wine industry, but after my grandfather died, he decided to focus his full attention on the winery. He gave it three years to see if he, Stefania—a graduate in political science—and I loved the work. We all made the commitment. We realized winemaking* needs people who are totally invested in this particular way of life. We deal with so many aspects of the business, including marketing and a newsletter. My father still likes to chat with customers and sell wine in our wine cellar.

It was mostly for fun that I began to work at the winery with my father and Stefania. I immediately realized that the emotion you get from creating wine matters the most. The choice I undertook led me to a project that requires strong emotions, commitment, and sacrifice. It needs passion for work in the vineyard because it is the place where a winemaker's life and dreams take form. Over the years, experience taught me that the care we take in the vineyards is the basis of our success.

Since 2003, we have reinvested our lives and money to make excellent wine. Being a winemaker is very good for passion and the heart, but not for profit. Think of the immense investments it takes to make wine. For example, French oak barriques cost between 700 and 770 Euros each. And then we have to sell our wines in the face of global competition.

When the old vineyards needed replanting, we hired an excellent consultant to guide us. Castelvecchio, using only its own grapes, produces 100,000 bottles of wine, from Sangiovese, Canaiolo Nero, Trebbiano, and Malvasia del Chianti to Petit Verdot, Cabernet Sauvignon, and Merlot—a total of five reds, one white, a rosé, and a seductive Vin Santo. We planted Sangiovese for its power, together with two 5-acre blocks of Caniolo Nero, for its freshness and flowery characteristics. We planted 5 acres each of Cabernet Sauvignon, Merlot, and Petit Verdot because I love international varietals. Some become single varietal wines. Each grape adds intricacy, elegance, and roundness to our blends.

Every year, Rocchi complies with the Conzorzio and sends samples to the committee for analysis.

Ever since we moved from Florence and chose Castelvecchio's estate for wine-making, we have supported sustainable agriculture. Castelvecchio is 1,500 meters beyond the border of the Chianti Classico region, though its wines fall into the Chianti Colli Fiorentini classification. In a way, we are lucky to be excluded from the Chianti Classico region. It gives us more freedom to produce what we love without the tight restrictions imposed on the wineries within the borders that define the varieties that go into the Chianti Classico blend. We are not organic, but we avoid pesticides and other chemicals in the cultivation of both our vineyards and our olive groves because we participate in a European program to reduce chemicals in agriculture to protect the *environment. We don't write about it because we think it's become a meaning-less marketing tool.*

*We are interested in biodynamics and follow some of the rules, but not strictly. We have chosen this way of agriculture not to be fashionable. We use sulfites in the cellar and in the wine as a preservative. We dry-farm since no irrigation is needed at Castelvecchio. We are lucky the very good soil in our vineyards holds moisture. Even in the hottest summer our grapes do not suffer.*

*Every year is different. Sometimes we get the most incredible Sangiovese. When it's not good, we lower the quantity or sell some wine off as bulk. There are perilous decisions in each vineyard and for each kind of grape. The many steps of harvest are highly emotional and extremely exciting, from the first sampling of grapes to the correct moment of picking. The objective is to harvest perfectly sound bunches with perfect skins ready to express all their fruit, essence, and aromas in the vinification. Harvest begins after I use certain tests as clues to tell me when the grapes are ripe. The crucial moment of harvest occurs when the seeds have turned brown. I crush the skins in my hand and taste them to learn about color extraction. If they crunch when I chew them, I know it's the perfect moment to pick. It's an important step because color from extraction doesn't happen immediately. These are the characteristics needed to make an excellent wine. When it's the precise moment to harvest the grapes carefully, we send a team of local specialized workers and students to hand-pick the crop. The winery is only 2 miles away, so fresh grapes arrive there in a few minutes. The berries are gently pressed and separated from leaves and stems. Grape juice is transferred to stainless steel for temperature-controlled fermentation. After the first fermentation, the juice goes into cement tanks for malolactic fermentation. Temperature is crucial during the fermentation stage, when we press the juice over the must. Every choice about pressing and length of maceration makes a difference and therefore generates a lot of stress at the winery. The work continues intensely in the wine cellar where blending of different wines takes place. Blending is also another crucial step. It is the moment when our enologist Luca d'Attoma's talents and inspiration combine with our abilities and what we bring to the table. The wine is sent to rest in French oak barriques to reach the right balance before bottling. We must express our resolve before we move to the final maturation and fining stage. Once we fill all the requirements of the Conzorzio, we are able to buy the prestigious pink label we then put on the neck of the bottle as a guarantee of quality to the consumer. Every year our harvest gives us a new chance.*

ℓℓ

## DUCK STEW
### (RECIPE FROM BENEDETTA VITALI,
### LO ZIBIBBO RESTAURANT, FLORENCE)

1 duck
2 yellow onions
½ cup extra virgin
   olive oil
3 tbsp butter
1–2 glasses of white
   wine
3 bay leaves
1 small rosemary twig
10 juniper berries
1 finely minced garlic
   clove
2 peeled tomatoes
1 pinch of paprika
8 oz of broth or
   water

Chop the onions and garlic into small pieces and stir-fry in oil and butter in a big aluminum pan. Cover with water a couple of times. Cook the onion until translucent. Add the duck (plucked and cut into large chunks). Add bay leaves, rosemary, and juniper berries for at least 10 minutes. Stir often. Cook until the duck has a nice golden color and pour the wine over it. Let the liquid evaporate slowly until the duck begins to brown again. Add the tomatoes, garlic, and paprika. Pour the broth or salted water to cover. Cook at low heat for 45 minutes to an hour or until duck is tender.

*Serve with a delicious red wine like our Brecciolino.*

Wine and olive oil are integral parts of the Italian life. Castelvecchio produces olive oil from a grove of 3.200 trees, mostly Moraiolo and Frantoio, pruned annually by specially trained workers.

*My father, Carlo, takes care of every aspect of olive harvest from our grove. The land is worked and fertilized periodically. The olive harvest, done totally by hand, usually starts in the first week of November. Every evening after the olives are weighed, they are divided by quality and put into bins. The next day they are brought to our old mill, where my father controls the press. The crush takes place within twenty-four hours from the picking without heat or filtration so that the natural characteristics of the oil are not altered and remain completely genuine. After an hour or so, the oil is put to into stainless steel containers to settle. All these factors put together make for an extraordinary extra virgin olive oil with an intense green color, low acidity, and unique taste. It's why my father calls his oil the green gold of Castelvecchio.*

*I want my customers to understand my reliability, my personality, and my passion. I sell my ideas, my dedication, and my character through the styles of our eight wines, each with a different personality, each reflecting its particular terroir. I want them to see the character inside each bottle. I like to get other people involved in what I do and I hope that one day I will be able to create a wine capable of communicating the same sensations that this marvelous world of wine has given me. It probably is a dream, but I take it as an absolute challenge.*

## Veneto

Vine cultivation started in the Veneto in the sixth century A.D., long after Italians in the region learned to use an ancient Greek technique of grapes dried in the sun to concentrate sugars. The coveted sweet wines were the most costly in the world. During the Middle Ages, the Venetian Empire was a major commercial and shipping power, exploiting trade in many products, including wine. Wine continues to dominate much of the Veneto's production.

The region lies in the northeast corner of Italy, stretching between Venice, Padua, Vincenza, and Verona near Lake Garda to the foothills of the Italian Alps. The Veneto suffers from earthquakes, the last one in the spring of 2012. A number of wine-growing regions and subregions produce a large quantity of wines from a wide range of local grapes. Whites are made from Garganega, Soave's major grape, a component also of Spumante, our regional sparkler. Strict and often unclear regulations permit the addition of Verdicchio and Chardonnay in varying percentages to white wines. Regional reds include Valpolicella, Bardolino, and Amarone, the unique dry wine made from late harvested grapes and then dried in special drying rooms to avoid botrytis. The shriveled berries lose up to a third of their water during three to four months of drying. The wines are sometimes aged in neutral or new oak barrels to develop into more full-bodied wines. Recioto dessert wine, also called straw or raisin wines, is made from grapes dried on straw mats or racks to concentrate their flavors, sugars, and juice.

Valpolicella, its name derived from a mixture of Italian and Greek, means "valley of many cellars." Valpolicella is one of Italy's historic wines, made from a versatile grape that produces four wines of different characteristics and styles. The roster includes full-bodied red wines and sweet dessert wines. Most basic Valpolicellas are light-bodied, with moderate alcohol levels, often served lightly chilled.

The Veneto's vintners, like many of their Italian peers, mobilized their efforts, complementing their traditional techniques with modern methods. Italian wines overall have improved with the addition of Cabernet Sauvignon, Chardonnay, and Pinot varietals and better vineyard and cellar management practices.

## CRISTIAN RIDOLFI
### CASA VINICOLA BERTANI

Located in the Valpolicella Valpantena wine district in the province of Verona in the region of Veneto, Casa Vinicola Bertani's long, distinguished history dates back to the nineteenth century, when two Bertani brothers from a politically powerful family in the area around Verona founded their winery in 1857.

*The history of Italy is much like a chess game between France and Austria. Armies subdued parts of Italy from the early eighteenth to the mid-eighteenth century. When Austrians invaded northern Italy, the Bertani family decamped to Burgundy for four years, where they learned vine cultivation and commercial aspects of producing and selling wine. The brothers, prosperous wine merchants, returned to Italy in 1850 and invested in some of the finest of the region's vineyards. They chose a valley and planted their first vines of local grapes—Corvina, Rondinella, and Molinara—using advanced techniques they learned in France. Bertani's first product was called Secco Bertani. Today Secco Bertani is a unique wine with great personality that continues to be the flagship of the Bertani winery.*

*The people who chose a site and the specific grapes that match its microclimate and soil, in a sense, determine the terroir. Soaves and a wide range of other wines from the Bertani winery grow in limestone soils and volcanic soils in the flat area of the Soave appellation, whereas grapes for Valpolicella grow on hilly vineyards that lie in seven valleys. We produce 2 million bottles of wine each year, different wines from the same grapes because of our different terroirs and methods of harvest. Unlike many other local producers, Bertani oversees the entire winemaking cycle from vineyard to bottling.*

*Our reds are produced from 80 percent Corvina grapes and 20 percent Rondinella, varietals with a history that harks back to Roman times. A new* vineyard of 3,000 vines planted near the winery has low yield per hectare because of our trellising system and the way we crop in winter. It's important to know the territory very well, especially for vine cultivation. Issues about the quantity of sun exposure are crucial. The vineyard manager chooses the direction of the vineyard, and the trellising system determines the fundamental shape of vines. Harvesting time is critical. The grapes start to ripen from mid-September, when they turn yellow-green, but we wait until mid-October for the colors to turn yellow-orange. That's when the juice accumulates richer mineral, peach, and orange flavors. My viticulturist grandfather and my winemaker father picked in November, when the grapes dried out on the vines. In the old days, grapes very high in natural sugar became sweet wines that could age for a long time.

In the mid-1950's, the old technique of Amarone winemaking using local grapes was rediscovered. Longer aging techniques dramatically transformed the traditionally sweet or sparkling red wine into sumptuous Amarone, one of the country's most sought-after dry red wines. Amarone Bertani is produced in a very specific way, as it was done fifty years ago, and as a result we are considered one of the most respected producers of this regional wine. Our Amarone is made from carefully selected grapes from the finest vineyards. The ripe grapes are usually harvested in the first two weeks of October, when they have high acidity and soft tannins. Amarone is often produced in special drying chambers under controlled conditions typically for 120 days, but the time varies from producer to producer and the quality of the harvest. Grapes dry on straw mats to concentrate sugars and flavors, and the increased skin contact adds more tannins and color. This process, called appassimento, causes grapes to lose water. By January, after the grapes have dried, they are crushed and fermented from thirty to fifty days. After fermentation, the wine is aged in oak barriques. The final result is a very ripe, raisiny, full-bodied wine with very little acid. It's so difficult to make that there are years—'63, '65, '91, '92— we didn't produce any Amarone. Hail fell three times at crucial moments of the season in 2002. We lost most of the vintage, but in the last ten years, Amarone represents 10 percent of our total production.

We launched a new-style Recioto della Valpolicella. If fermentation of the grapes is stopped early, the resulting wine contains more residual sugar that produces a sweeter wine known as Recioto della Valpolicella. Unlike traditional Amarone, Recioto della Valpolicella can also be used to produce a sparkling wine.

Ripasso is another wine produced when the partially aged Valpolicella is left in contact with the Recioto Amarone lees. The lees still contain a lot of

# BERTANI'S CHOCOLATE MOUSSE TORTE

*A traditional, much-loved recipe from the Bertani family kitchens. This delicious chocolate dessert is often served as the scrumptious finale to a special occasion at Bertani's Villa Novare estate near Verona.*

8 tbsp butter
⅓ cup unsweetened cocoa powder
⅔ cup confectioners sugar
1 cup water
5 eggs separated
2 cups granulated sugar
1 cup flour
Whipped cream to garnish
Preheat oven to 350°F

In a saucepan, over a low heat, melt and blend together butter, cocoa powder, confectioners' sugar and water. When thoroughly blended, remove from heat and set aside. Proceed at once to next step.

In a mixing bowl, beat separated egg yolks, folding in granulated sugar, for about 10 minutes. Continue to beat while folding in melted chocolate mixture above and then stir in flour.

In a copper bowl, beat egg whites into a stiff meringue. Using a spatula, gently fold granulated sugar into the meringue mixture. Then gently combine meringue mixture with the chocolate mixture.

Thoroughly butter and coat with flour the inside of a 10-inch spring-form cake pan. Pour cake mixture into pan. Bake in preheated oven for approximately 45 minutes. Do not overcook. Properly baked, the outer edges of the cake should firm into a crust and the center should remain soft and mousse-like. Allow to cool. Serve with whipped cream.

*Serve with Bertani Amarone della Valpolicella Classico DOC.*

---

sugar and the Valpolicella undergoes a second fermentation. This will typically take place in the spring following the harvest. The resulting wine is more tannic with a deeper color, more alcohol, and more extract. The word Ripasso designates both the winemaking technique and the wine, and the term is usually found on a wine label.

It's not that one grape helps another, but blending is the best way to produce an excellent wine. Our white Due Uve is a special blend of 50 percent Pinot Grigio and 50 percent Sauvignon blanc. Its rich flavors derive from vineyards with volcanic soils. Two of the three Bertani families have vineyards in Soave. Gaetano Bertani grows the Sauvignon blanc and Giovanni takes responsibility for the Pinot grigio.

We continue to use parts of the winery's facility that date back 150 years, including one ancient cask. Initially, adopting modern technology created some difficulties: We learned stainless steel production wasn't applicable for every wine, but a new fermentation room with conical-shaped stainless steel fermentation tanks makes it easier to move the must and lees during fermentation. Aging wines requires crucial choices. We stopped using oak barrels in the 1960's until we realized it was a mistake. We returned to French barriques for big reds. Each wine rests in different oak barrels of Slovenian, cherry, or acacia wood. Long ago, the winery used chestnut wood and we might use it again because of its tradition.

All the wine types at Bertani amount to 1,600,000 bottles, primarily reds. Italians are our best customers, but the U.S., Japan, and Canada are good markets. Our customers are discovering the Bertani ideal of perfect quality. Amazingly, in 1986 a cache of Recioto della Valpolicella Acinatico from the great 1928 vintage was discovered bricked up behind the walls of a farmhouse on a Bertani estate, forgotten and undisturbed since the end of World War II. It was surprising that the wine's quality was fine. The superb vintage, as exceptional as it is rare, is served exclusively at special tastings and events hosted by Bertani.

# PORTUGAL

TRACES OF VITICULTURE suggest it began around the tenth century B.C., when Phoenician conquerors, famous as wine traders sailing across the Mediterranean Sea, introduced new grape varieties in the Iberian Peninsula. Through the centuries, Greeks, Celts, and Romans planted their local grapes across Europe, including the peninsula, where monks in medieval monasteries took winemaking to a higher level. In the 1600's the country's astringent wines were fortified with brandy to stabilize them for export and make them more palatable. Port wines came to dominate the industry, taking its name from Oporto, a city in the Duoro, the country's highly regarded wine region. The sweet, alcoholic wines found favor with the English, especially after a series of wars ended sales of French wine across the Channel.

Political and economic troubles and phylloxera devastated the country's wine industry in the late nineteenth century. Under the long one-man rule of Antonio de Oliveira Salazar that began in the 1930's, the wine industry was reorganized into cooperatives to help small farmers sell their grapes. Unfortunately, wines deteriorated in quality for a number of reasons. In the halcyon days of the mid-1950's many Americans cut their wine eyeteeth on Mateus and Lancers, two pallid, sweet wines. Lancers hid its contents in small brown ceramic jugs, and Mateus was delivered in pint-sized curvy green bottles. The main attractions of the starter wines were affordability (translation—cheap), recognizable packaging, and relatively low alcohol. The bottle and the jug made cute candleholders. Hopefully, these early wine experiences led to wider wine choices.

Before the 1970's, Portuguese winemakers utilized more than 300 indigenous grapes into wine primarily for domestic consumption. A decrease in Port's popularity encouraged vintners at *quintas*, or wine estates, to develop unfortified wines from a mix of local and international grapes. Production of red wine made from three varieties: Touriga Nacional, Tempranillo, and Touriga Francesa dominate Douro wines. The region also produces smaller amounts of rosés and white wines made from a field blend of grapes.

In some areas, old traditions continue to persist. At some *quintas* fruit is still crushed by foot in shallow stone containers called *lagares*. After Portugal joined the European Union in 1986, young vintners modernized their winemaking techniques with stainless steel fermenting tanks and other modern developments to raise the quality of their wines and compete in the world market.

Portuguese wines, like those throughout Europe, are generally labeled by region rather than by grape varietals. Thirty-one classifications exist for the country's wines. Grape varieties, yields, alcohol levels, and aging for DOC designations must comply with strict regulations. In addition, ten Vinho Verde regions for ordinary table wines do not meet the requirements of the DOC system. A *Selo de Garantia*, or seal of guarantee, ensures that a wine meets quality standards.

# *Duoro*

## CASIMIRO ALVES
### VERCOOPE COOPERATIVE

"Because I had had no background or family history in wine, deciding to become a winemaker was like falling in love. I pursued my passion and studied enology in Lisbon after college," said Casimiro Alves, head enologist at Vercoope. "Today, I work with two other enologists, but I am the chief."

*Vercoope, founded in 1964, is one of several cooperatives dedicated to the production of Vinho Verde. Cooperatives provide strength in numbers and Vercoope does the job by representing the interests of five thousand small to medium-size growers. Vercoope is the second largest cooperative in the country, shouldering the responsibilities for winemaking, marketing, and distribution of the country's most famous wine, Vinho Verde, under a variety of brands. The cooperative and its grape suppliers work together to carefully maintain decades-old wine culture and to control quality of grapes that go into typical Vinho Verde wines made into still and sparkling wines. Vercoope is well equipped with modern techniques to produce ten million bottles of Vinho Verde made from our local grapes—Loureiro, Trajudura, Arinto, and Alvarinho. Our cooperative is large and economically successful.*

*We enologists visit our farmers all year, although in the end, I decide if the grapes meet our quality standards for sugar, fruit, and acid. Some of our growers use organic and biodynamic farming methods, but all of them must meet our principles and regulations. There are ground rules for when and how to till the soil, and there are limitations on production and the use of chemical products to fight insects. The harvest generally pays the farmers an average price per kilo. The same farmers don't always make the cut every year. If the*

## ALVES'S BAKED GOAT

3–5 lb of goat
5 onions cut into wedges
4 cloves garlic, minced
½ tbsp paprika
2 bay leaves
½ bottle of white wine
3 tbsp olive oil
1 cup white wine
2–3 lb peeled potatoes
Juice of half a lemon
Salt and pepper

Cut the goat into pieces and cover with two onions and minced garlic. Season with salt, pepper, paprika, bay leaf and white wine. Marinate about 4 hours. Place the meat and marinade on a tray with the potatoes and additional cup of wine. Add half the olive oil and bake at 400°F for 35–40 minutes. Season with salt, pepper, paprika, and remaining olive oil and continue to bake for 40 minutes or until done. Before serving, sprinkle with lemon juice.

SERVES 8.

*Vinho Verde can stand up to goat's strong flavors.*

fruit is excellent, we pay one price, but if it's not so good, we pay less. Bad grapes are sent back. At the end of the season, the profit is distributed to the farmers based on the amount each one contributed. The cooperative idea works so well for the small farmer that each year the business grows.

Modern technology brought many changes to the industry. We use both new and regional indigenous yeasts and other products during fermentation to help clean the wine. Carbon dioxide is initially trapped naturally in a pressurized container during fermentation, but when it doesn't occur, some extra $CO_2$ is added just before bottling. Sulfur is necessary to prevent oxidation and to keep the color clear.

While I enjoy the year-round aspect of the business, harvest is my favorite time. I hold my breath while the grapes are being picked. Naturally, we are happy when both the quantity and quality of grapes are good. Our climate is mild and very humid, so we have to be watchful for diseases like botrytis that can present some problems. We wait for optimum conditions for picking and hope the rain holds off because the rainy season in the Vinho Verde region starts in September around the time of harvest. Sometimes the results in a year are terrible, as in 1988. Many small producers had problems with disease because of bad weather. Harvesting isn't difficult because vineyards are located on *rolling hills. Our facility has the capacity to handle a million kilos of grapes per day, but complications occur when many farmers ask to bring in fruit on the same day.*

Alves notes the cooperative is large and their blends are different from those of their neighbors.

*Our house style is fruity. Our wines are consumer-driven, easy to drink. We need to sell our wine after bottling. Bordeaux producers can store their wine for long periods before releasing them to the market, but Vinho Verde is meant to be drunk within the first year or two. It's a refreshing, light-acid wine with only 9 to 10 percent alcohol, with apple, pear, and citrus flavors and a slight effervescence. It's great for summer drinking and excellent with seafood. These wines are popular at home, particularly in the Algarve in southern Portugal, where a bottle sells for around 2 Euros. Vercoope sales are aimed at major supermarkets and hypermarkets with an annual billing of over 10 million Euros.*

*Sales are excellent in German, Scandinavian, and French markets, with Brazil and Russia as growing markets. Americans like the wine because it looks like Pinot grigio and also because of its attractive $5 to $8 price range. We sell around a million Bag in the Box filled with Regional Minho, Vercoope's fourth product. It is a very popular item in our region. Fifty percent of this new product is sold to consumers in northern Europe, particularly in Sweden, Norway, and Denmark. The project works really well because it is attractive and hygienic. While most Vinho Verde wines have a slight fizz, Regional Minho in a Bag in a Box wine is a still wine because the malleable plastic bag in the box isn't strong enough to hold the pressure of carbonated wine. The bag would fill up and look like a soccer ball with liquid.*

Alves notes Vercoope maintains Vinho Verde's quality and prestige and is proud of its position as a regional and national landmark.

# DOMINGOS SOARES FRANCO
## JOSÉ MARIA DA FONSECA

Domingos Soares Franco telegraphs he is someone who gives an order and expects it to be followed. Like many winemakers, he sticks to the courage of his convictions with determination and strong opinions. One example is his remark about Portuguese journalists. "They tell me how to vinify, but I don't tell them how to write."

Soares Franco is the younger brother of the family's sixth generation running Fonseca Winery. "Historians went through our winery record book, which dates from 1815. Our family has been making wine since Jose Maria da Fonseca bought the winery in 1850. Perroquita was the first winery we owned. Customers found the winery by following colorful parakeets. Our family kept the name even though the parakeets disappeared a long time ago. The property is south of Lisbon, near the Spanish border. "It's very rough country, with bad roads. It would take two hours to get to the winery with good roads and normal traffic."

The winemaker recalls how Portugal's political revolution in 1974 catapulted the government from the extreme right to the extreme left.

*The Communists discriminated against the wealthy and took over houses and properties. My father was a capitalist who refused to give up our stock of wine. So we finished it all in a month down to the last bottle. I was refused schooling as the son of a capitalist, so my father took me to France. I wasn't up to par for a French school and needed two additional years of education. Fortunately, around that time, Heublein's president visited our home and offered to take me to the States. I applied to U.C. Davis to study enology. The administrators translated my B's into D's and rejected me. I studied chemistry and physics for two years at Menlo Park College.*

*I realized at that point that I couldn't go home. I had run away from the army and if I had been caught, it meant jail. The day after my U.S. visa expired, American immigration agents found me. Eventually, I got a permit to study and was accepted at U. C. Davis, graduating with a degree in fermentation science. I was one of 18,000 students, the first Portuguese to study winemaking at Davis. Imagine 17,000 bicycles and frequent accidents. I learned about different grapes and completely new techniques. I tasted fruity wines, like Gewürztraminer. It's where I learned to think about the future, not the past.*

*I stayed in the U.S. for six years. I bridged the gap between old traditions and new technology when I finally returned home. I brought a lot of new ideas about grapes and technology from California, although it was difficult to translate these ideas to our area because our grapes and technology were so different. I became an outsider in the industry. It was actually enjoyable because I was a young rebel, a pioneer working with ideas I saw as I traveled to wineries around the world. I was more practical and open-minded in a closed-minded culture. I used to get into arguments with other Portuguese vintners. Changes I introduced at Fonseca provoked my friend's father to say I learned to make vinegar in California.*

*I stubbornly took control and pulled up old blocks of Gewürztraminer and Cabernet Franc, leaving 4 acres of Cabernet Sauvignon. Syrah was added to the vineyard because of my fondness for French varietals. In total, 560 mostly Portuguese varietals are planted in Fonseca sites, enough to produce a wide range of white, red, and rosé wines with thirty-four to thirty-five labels a year. I like the wide range of varietals. It's a palette of colors in my hand. I have the opportunity to experiment with various grape combinations from several regions in my country.*

*We anticipated 150,000 liters in my first vintage in 2004 and sold 350,000 bottles in nine months. Most Fonseca wines are classic Portuguese based on local varietals, each delivering specific flavors and showcasing the diversity of native grapes. In 2007, we sold 800,000 liters, even though the vintage was like a mule. In 2008, I changed the blend, always making judgments with my tongue and my brain, until I finally grabbed the style I wanted. Our wines are driven by consumers as well as by what is in my head. When I decide to make a new blend, it takes me a few months to arrive at what I want. I'm in charge of everything from vineyard planting to marketing. I share responsibility with my brother, my nephew, and a team of five winemakers. My brother talks faster than I do and controls the conversation, but I spit out whatever comes*

## SOARES FRANCO'S BACALHAU À GOMES DE SÁ

*Bacalhau à Gomes de Sá is one of the most traditional Portuguese dishes. At J. M. da Fonseca, it is a time-honored Sunday dish served with the refreshing Twin Vines Vinho Verde.*

2 lb dry-weight skinned salted cod, desalted and rehydrated

6 lb boiling potatoes, peeled and cut into 2-inch chunks

2 large onions, thickly sliced

3 garlic cloves

6 hard-boiled and peeled eggs

½ cup extra-virgin olive oil

½ cup finely chopped Italian parsley

½ cup pitted black olives

2 medium, ripe tomatoes, sliced

Simmer the codfish in water until just tender. Drain and cool. Cook the potatoes in boiling water until just tender, but not falling apart. Drain, cool, and reserve. Flake the cooled cod, removing all bones. (Steps 1–4 can be done in advance.)

In a large frying pan, heat the oil and sauté the onions until translucent. Add the garlic and cook until lightly golden. Remove from heat.

Preheat oven to 350°F. In a large ovenproof dish, alternate layers of potatoes, flaked cod fish, eggs, sautéed onions, and garlic. Arrange slices of black olives and tomatoes on top. Bake for approximately 30 minutes, until the top is golden. Remove from oven and drizzle with extra-virgin olive oil. Serve with white rice or green salad.

SERVES 8.

*Pair with Twin Vines Vinho Verde.*

to my mind. I expect each of our five winemakers to have big ideas, but at the end, I'm there for the final blend. If there is a problem, I take the blame.

Portuguese wines are meant to be drunk young, so we generally release them early. Periquita Red, a favorite wine for 160 years, is an important part of our history. It's produced primarily from the Castelão Frances grape, an indigenous variety that thrives in southern Portugal. It used to be aged in barrels, although less so today. It's elegant without being overstructured. We bottle Twin Vines Vinho Verde, Periquita Moscato, and a Moscatel de Setubal dessert wine. Periquita Reserve 2007 is a blend of three local grapes: Castelão, Tourigo Nacional, and Tourigo Franco. Domini is one of the wines at the top of our portfolio. Domini is a joint venture between Jose Maria da Fonseca and

## SOARES FRANCO'S BAKED CLAM RECIPE

6–8 clams per person
2 minced cloves of
    garlic
1 medium-sized sliced
    onion
Bunch of coriander
1 cup of white wine
Olive oil to cover the
    bottom of a pan

Heat the oil and add all the ingredients. Lightly brown. and when softened, add the clams. The dish is ready when they open.

*The wine is the Periquita white 2012. The fatness of the clams and the slight acidity of the blend of Verdelho, Viognier, and Viozinho go well together.*

---

*Cristiano van Zeller, a leading port producer. Our Muscat of Alexander is the father of Muscats around the world. Fermentation is stopped with brandy and the juice is left on the skins for three or four months in old casks for oxidation. The use of old oak reduces the flavor of wood. The wine should be served chilled and is sold in 375-ml bottles. With 18 percent alcohol, it can be recorked and drunk several days later.*

*Domini is my signature wine, even if my brother or our other winemakers don't like it. Domini is what I am, what I like. The rest of our products are for the consumer. My aim is to make a wine like my wife, capturing her elegance, beauty, and finesse in a bottle. My blends are changed by my brain and palate. It might take me a few months to get what I want, since I'm not always quick to find the blends that get me to what I'm searching for. The vintage of 2007 was stubborn as a mule. In 2008, I changed the blend. I knew what I wanted and it is an example of how I grabbed the style.*

*I can't make a Petrus, but I can change my Domini wine so that it's not typically Portuguese. There is no doubt a style of wine can be changed 100 percent at the time of harvest by the way we deal with fermentation, temperature, yeasts, bacteria, and many other factors. I can change Syrah's profile with different yeasts. I believe wine comes down to the winemaker's fingerprint. If a consumer tastes one of the top four Fonseca wines from different areas and different grapes, my fingerprint is present, showcasing my goal for integration and elegance.*

*Too much analysis destroys my creativity. I don't load a wine with descriptions because tasting is so personal. Smell and taste depend on one's environment and mood. I don't want our wine to be too complex, nor do I want our cus-tomers to think too much about the wine. I am against high-alcohol wines, except for dessert wines, like our Muscat of Alexander. Dry wines of 17 percent aren't enjoyable and don't work with food. I like to have more than one glass with dinner, and it's impossible at that high level of alcohol.*

*I don't know much about food or cooking, so I'm not too interested in pair-ing. My preference is to drink different wines according to season. I'll pick a red, white, or bubbly and stick with it for weeks. I tell a sommelier in a restau-rant to pick any wine for me except mine.*

Soares Franco travels continuously, partly to track what consumers want and to learn what's in the market. "I am always on the lookout for innovation. I grow trials of grapes from other wine regions, although as head winemaker, I intentionally maintain the distinctive features of Por-tuguese wines." Asked about the way terroir influences his vineyards, Soares rolled his eyes.

*You don't ask Velasquez about the kind of canvas he used. My concept of ter-roir is a large area where the vines produce consistent variables. I believe tech-nology obviates terroir. Terroir is a term for the market. At the same time, I talk about the term with consumers who equate terroir with specific qualities.*

*In California, wineries generally encourage visits by the public. In Portu-gal, many wineries don't welcome visitors, but it's always possible if you call in advance. That rule applies to my fellow Portuguese winemakers as well. We at Fonseca take a different approach and welcome guests throughout the year. I invite guests to tour our nineteenth-century estate and cellars and stop for a tasting of our wines.*

# SPAIN

S PAIN IS EUROPE'S THIRD LARGEST country and has more acreage under grape cultivation than any country in the world. The country's diverse landscape produces a panoply of whites, reds, sherries and other fortified dessert wines, and Cava—the Spanish sparkling wine. Although many of Spain's wines are sold at home, they are also exported to many countries, including the United Kingdom, Germany, and the United States. Russia and Italy are new, important customers.

Food and wine have been braided into Spanish life for centuries. The history of winemaking across the Iberian Peninsula has much in common with the long, complicated tale of conquest and trade that spread knowledge of viticulture and vinification. Phoenicians in eleventh century B.C. are considered to have started winemaking in Rioja. Many vineyards were founded during the Roman occupation of the peninsula. A Moslem ban against alcohol existed during the Moorish occupation from the eighth century to the fifteenth, although vineyards supplied table grapes and wine for commercial trade with non-Muslim neighbors. After Isabella and Ferdinand expelled the Moslems in 1492, the country reverted to Catholicism and winemaking rebounded. The ships of Christopher Columbus and Magellan carried wine for their sailors on long voyages of exploration.

In the 1860's, French vintners, crushed by a phylloxera outbreak, brought their winemaking skills across the border to Spain. In recent times, the quality of Spanish wines went through its ups and downs, but the country entered the competitive fray of wine production, raising standards with modern techniques in vineyards and cellars in the late twentieth century. As Spain's wines gained international recognition, Frank Gehry, Santiago Calatrava, and Zaha Hadid designed avant-garde wineries that are juxtaposed with medieval palaces, churches, and monasteries.

Rioja in northern Spain has the most name recognition of the country's sixty-eight wine regions. Its reputation outweighs the limitations of its small geographical size. Rioja's population runs to around a quarter of a million people. Around 500 wineries with small production, most comprising around 1 hectare, are handed down in a family for generations. Many small vineyard owners have a long-standing tradition of selling their red and white grapes to large cooperatives, called *bodegas*.

Rioja is divided into three regions: Alta to the north, Baja in the south, and Alexsa, which is sandwiched in the middle. The Ebro River divides the areas from each other. Winemakers have fifty native varieties, along with relatively new varietals like Chardonnay or Cabernet Sauvignon, but Tempranillo is unquestionably the backbone of Spanish wines. Red wines dominate whites in production. Rioja is best known for Tempranillo-based wines, the varietal many Americans associate with Spanish wine. It is Spain's noble grape, the foremost varietal in full-bodied *tintos,* the country's best red wines. Tempranillo, which means "early ripening," is considered to be an adaptation of Pinot noir brought by monks to Spain centuries ago. Rioja reds are blends of 60 percent Tempranillo and up to 20 percent of Garnacha, with smaller proportions of local Mazuelo and Graciano for good aging potential. Garnacha adds body and alcohol, Mazuelo provides additional flavors, and Graciano contributes aromas. White Riojas or Blancos are blends of Viura, Malvasia, and Garnacha blanca. In 1970 the Regulations for Denominación de Origen were approved, and in the early 1990's many Riojas were awarded the valued Calificada (DOCa).

At fine wineries, grapes in Rioja are primarily hand-harvested and go through a double selection to start the winemaking process. Joven, or young, wines are usually drunk early and are often the *muy delicioso* wine for Sangria. Crianza and Reserva wines spend a short time in barrel. Gran Reservas, selected from the best vintages, become more complex after two years in oak.

# *Rioja*

## PEDRO BENITO SAEZ
### BODEGAS URBINA CRIANZA

Pedro Urbino Saez owes his perfect English to the five years he lived in Mendocino, California. The winemaker's graduation from Ukiah High School was followed by a degree in business administration at San Francisco State. He attended viticulture classes and worked part time at the Frie Ranch for a year. He says,

*Frie is a small winery, the first to be certified organic and biodynamic in the States. When I was young, I wasn't interested in making viticulture my career. But once I began, I enjoyed dealing with the world's oldest beverage. Winemaking is all about history and nature. Every new day is an adventure, and the constant contact with nature captivates me. Working with nature is like a religious experience. I tell our workers to pay attention to nature. Horses in a stable lose their instinct and are different from wild horses. Humans, like horses, need to use their instincts and common sense to deal with nature.*

*No one knows where and how humans first drank wine. Perhaps they were encouraged by watching animals get drunk on ripe grapes. We do know that Spanish wines have been famous since Roman times. Phylloxera sapped the vigor of French vines in the late nineteenth century and practically destroyed the industry in France. Many bankrupted French vignerons emigrated to Spain. They settled in Rioja and had a profound influence on Spanish winemaking. Before then, Spanish vintners picked grapes well before ripening and often blended red and white grapes together. Old traditions gave way to new techniques that raised the level of Spanish wines.*

The French chose the terroirs for their new vineyards very well. Mountains in the north and south moderate the climate. Cool nights during August and September are an important factor in ripening grapes. The soil in the area is clay with a mix of limestone and sandstone. A high content of iron and chalk contributes to the reddish color in the soil. Some sources suggest the area is known as Rioja, since rioja is Spanish for "red," although it may be named for the nearby river, the Río Oja.

In the old days, customers came to wineries or bars and transferred wine from barrels to leather bags. It was the way we sold wine at our old winery, which began its life in a mountain cave. A cave was the only way to find cool temperatures needed to control fermentation in large vats. Then the winery moved to a garage, where wine was made in concrete vats. Bodegas Pedro Benito Urbina began bottling and labeling only thirty years ago. Modern equipment improves the standards at our family-owned, single-estate winery. Today we utilize many modern practices to produce a wide spectrum of wine that meets the demands of our customers.

Making wine today is a fashionable industry. Investors in countless regions want to make wine. It's possible for newcomers to read all the viticulture books and do the analysis, but the immense number of variables requires a well-honed instinct. A book can't tell a winemaker when to pick. I can buy new land and use American and Australian toys of technical equipment to test the land for nutrients in the soil. I find it more useful to go to the local bar and listen to the old winemakers. Using intuition and paying attention to our ancestors is key to good wine, but we adapted some new ideas. We farm organically, without pesticides and use natural rather than commercial yeasts. Stainless steel tanks are sanitary and the best technique to control temperature during fermentation.

Our credo is to sell happiness and to achieve that we work together in harmony without any disagreements. It isn't easy to make good wine, but we do it. We believe wine is a liquid expression of a particular place. We take pride in the fact that our style of wine derives from three factors—the vineyard's terroir with fantastic weather, the right choice of grapes, and the winemaker's intentions. Our wines are handcrafted to our particular style from vines that range from thirty-five to forty years of age. Some are merely eighteen to twenty years old, and then there are newer ones added to the mix. Our results can't be imitated.

## PEDRO SAEZ'S CHAR-GRILLED LAMB
## WITH OREGANO

4 large or 8 small
lamb steaks
2 garlic cloves, finely
chopped
2 tbsp olive oil
2 tbsp chopped fresh
oregano
1 cup couscous
1 cup hot vegetable
stock
Handful chopped
fresh herbs:
coriander, parsley,
mint, salt and fresh
ground black
pepper.

*Cooks's tip:* You can vary the flavor of this dish by using different herbs to marinate the lamb, such as rosemary, basil, or mint.

Place the lamb steaks in a shallow, nonmetallic bowl. Mix the garlic, oil, and oregano together and season with salt and pepper. Pour over the lamb steak and turn to coat in the mixture cover and set aside for 20 minutes. Meanwhile, put the couscous in a bowl and pour over the vegetable stock. Let stand for 10 minutes. Heat a griddle pan until hot. Remove the lamb steaks from the marinade and lay them on the griddle pan. Cook for 4–5 minutes each side, until just slightly pink in the centre. Stir the herbs into the couscous and divide between four serving plates. Place the lamb steaks on top. Pour the marinade into the pan and allow to bubble for a few minutes. Pour over the lamb and couscous to serve.

SERVES 4.

*Serve with Urbina Reserva 2001 with a traditional Sunday lunch or with roast lamb, chicken, or duck. A great match with roast turkey and all the trimmings at Christmas.*

We produce several styles of wines: a red Crianza for our classic Rioja blend. A second Urbina Crianza Selección is aged in new oak barrels for twelve months. We produce a 100 percent red Granache made with carbonic maceration, plus an Urbina red Reserva of 100 percent Tempranillo aged in French oak for sixteen months, blended together with a second red Reserva of 100 percent Tempranillo aged in French Allier oak for sixteen months. The red Gran Reserva is again made with the three traditional Rioja red grapes aged for twenty-four months in 100 percent American oak barrels. All of Rioja's terroir shows up in small amounts of white wine made from a neutral grape without complexity, usually used for Cava. The winery's total production is 240,000 bottles. Young, or joven, unoaked wines *and Crianza or oaked wines are both great value. Reservas and Grand Reservas from superior old vines with long aging in bottles are more expensive but priced within reason. The cost of a wine represents the work behind a bottle. The best wine values today come from Spain, as many wine lovers have learned.*

# OSCAR MONTAÑA PORRES
## MARQUÉS DE TOMARES WINERIES

I met Oscar Montaña Porres at a tasting of Spanish wines in New York. Like most winemakers, he is passionately devoted to his profession as the maestro at Marqués de Tomares and Don Roman Wineries in Alta Rioja. Porres began his career with an MBA in business administration in the United States. Afterward, he worked briefly in Bordeaux, where he learned new winemaking technology.

*I returned to Spain with my experiences and shortly became the maestro of the family winery, where I team up with another winemaker trained in great wines. Our winery was started in 1910, which makes me the winery's third-generation vintner. We're always looking for additional land with special terroir, but at the moment, our 52 hectares produces 300,000 bottles sold in forty-one countries. Japan and Brazil are currently our biggest markets. We've been increasing our sales in the U.S. by 25 percent every year. I think the States is moving into first place.*

*It's not necessary to be a prime minister to make wine. It's not as easy as cooking two eggs, but sometimes there are complications that remind me about a restaurant chef who serves a complicated dish with beef from Argentina, lemons from Florida, and exotic ingredients from around the world. Wine isn't a business that makes you rich. It's very difficult to make lots of money in this business, but it gives me a rich life. Wine for me equals love and peace. It makes every occasion special and has the ability to repair relationships. I sit around the table, eating and drinking with family and friends. I watch people after they drink whiskey. They are more aggressive. But with wine, you could be angry with your wife for three days. After the first sip of wine, things look better. After three glasses, it's "Hello, Darling."*

Rioja is an agricultural region. Originally, vegetables and fruit were planted in the best soils. Grain took up the second-best soils. Olive trees and grape vines were relegated to poor alluvial soils. Some of our productive vines were planted in 1920 in poor soil that turned out to be a fortunate choice. Think about a pet dog who is loved and treated like a baby. The dog is fed treats and becomes unhealthy. Like the dog that is better off with less kindheartedness, grapes survive better in poor soil by struggling for nutrients. They send roots down 35 to 50 feet for nourishment and water, and that makes better fruit.

We prune in the winter before flowering. It's necessary to make corrections before winter and the following spring. No irrigation is permitted. It was a problem in 2010, when the summer was exceptionally dry. Yet a plant is more intelligent than a human. The clever plant finds ways to regulate itself. A vine can absorb the morning dew very quickly. It produces tannins in green grapes to defend itself against birds. We use sulfur, but we avoid pesticides because, from our point of view, they can cause problems with fermentation by sending the pH level too high.

All Rioja's wines are blended from four red grapes: Tempranillo, Graciano, Garnacha, and Mazuelo. We having a saying: "One person is wonderful, but everyone needs help." Tempranillo is a wonderful grape, but it needs acidity. Marsuelo provides acidity, but can also give off raisiny flavors. Drinking Mazuelo alone is like drinking lemon juice. Graciano is like Cabernet Sauvignon, but it needs a special terroir to attain good maturity. It is finicky, like Pinot noir.

Rioja's name attracts attention and signals reliability to the consumer. In general, Riojas are feel-good, uncomplicated wines with good, mouth-cleansing acidity. It is a versatile wine that goes well with everything. A two- to three-day-old suckling lamb roasted with potatoes over grape skins is one of my favorite pairings. However, Reservas and Gran Reservas from our house offer both great value and quality. I make these two wines only in a worthy vintage. Our young wines are good for everyday drinking, but they lack the elegance of Reservas and Gran Reservas. Our special wines, like whites from '78 and '87, our Reservas, and Gran Reservas are stored behind the bars of cells in a fourteenth-century cave that once served as a prison.

Harvest is the most important time to me, even more important than fermentation. Picking at harvest starts around 5 P.M. on the first day, and then goes twenty-four hours around the clock. We go to the vineyards and collect seven to ten bunches in plastic bags. We check the pH factors, acids, and tannins in an independent lab with as many as a thousand tests each week. Once the grapes are harvested, our new presses slowly deliver 10 liters of juice an hour under natural pressure. It's a computerized system that works well for red wines. Our tanks are stainless steel, but we make one wine with carbonic maceration. Our harvesting is done mostly by hand, with some machines. We trust our pickers to know when to gather the fruit and which bunches to pick. It's better to pay 10 Euros more per day to get good workers. Some workers have been with the winery for thirty years, together with a Pakistani who hires additional people for his team.

I love the smell of fermenting grapes in the winery. I can tell if the wine is going to be good just by the odor. Oak is important because it creates natural micro-oxygenation. I prefer the best barrel be made with half-French, half-American oak staves with different toasts. One of our red wines is more feminine and elegant from contact with French oak barrels. Good wine also requires time to age in the bottle. One problem is that the market wants the new production in two months to ensure they get the best choice. This has serious financial aspects. It is cheaper to keep my wine at home than to store it in the States.

DOC regulations once restricted Rioja from producing any but red wines. The ban has recently been lifted and we are planting Sauvignon blanc, Chardonnay, White Tempranillo, and Verdejo. Verdejo is Spain's most recognizable white varietal, thought to have been planted by the Moors over a millennium ago. Its best drunk young when its citrus and mineral flavors coupled with good acidity make it an excellent aperitif and a great partner for tapas.

Porres opened a bottle of his Don Román Cava, the Spanish sparkling wine.

We started making Cava twelve years ago, almost as a joke because I love it. I think Cava is perfect before lunch, perfect with lunch, and perfect after lunch. In fact, it is perfect all the time. Our sparkling wine is made in the classic Champagne method from three local Catalan grapes—Xarello, Perellada, and Macabeo. The juice is pressed quickly, put in a tank for one to two days, then bottled for a minimum of nine months for the second fermentation. After the sediment is removed, a traditional dosage is added to the base wine. It's a simple, fruity, and easy-to-drink bubbly. I bought land to make Cava in Brazil, where it's called Spunoma. I predict Brazil will soon be one of the world's top sparkling wine producers.

In Spain, twenty or thirty years ago, wine was generally bought in flasks or in leather bags. Wine was rarely a topic of conversation. When two or three couples went to dinner, they would order any wine or put one person in charge of ordering from the wine list. That has changed. Now choices are more specific and it's not unusual to hear talk about wine go on for an hour. Consumers everywhere are learning to identify wine by varietal and by region. Up to three or four years ago, the global market preferred strong alcohol and oaky wines. It seemed winemakers translated the trend of aggressive politics into aggressive wines. Critics' preference for strong wines made our life difficult. Wines from Rioja don't fit that profile. The terroir of Rioja isn't suited to styles of wine preferred by gurus who evaluate Spanish wines for critics like Robert Parker.

I spend a lot of money on other producers' wines, partly because I love wine and also to know what my competitors are doing. My favorite wines are five to fifteen years old. A person is different when twenty years old, but at forty you should be better and more experienced. The same is true with wine. I love a twelve-year-old Bordeaux or a Contino '94 from Rioja.

Some wineries don't permit guests. I encourage the public to know my wines. If consumers take time to know a winemaker and the team, they will understand how the winemaker's passion goes into the wine. Our approach and philosophy is to make good wine at a good price. Wine should be available to everyone.

Porres has difficulty understanding why some California wines are so expensive. "A bottle should never cost more than $30," he said. "The future is good for us. Consumers are coming back to reality after the financial bubble burst. They will start to buy our very good wine for $20."

# GERMANY

ROMANS PLANTED VINEYARDS IN TRIER, Germany, as early as the second century B.C. Winemaking flourished in Germany from the Middle Ages, when monastic communities and feudal lords controlled huge swaths of vineyards and food crops. According to legend the origin of sweet Riesling is the result of poor timing. The abbot of a monastery was absent during harvest and sent a messenger to the monks to bring in the grapes. The messenger was delayed and the grapes rotted. In a simple case of waste not, want not the monks vinified the grapes. The resulting wine was amazing.

## *Mosel*

Although Germany produces a small amount of red wine, Riesling maintains its position as the country's dominant grape. The hardy, frost-resistant varietal does extremely well in a climate with the short hours of sunlight and cool nights of Germany and Alsace. In the prestigious wine region of Mosel, the eponymous river is a critical component of the microclimate. Its waters reflect the sun's warmth onto the vines, adds humidity, and sends fog into the vineyards at night to protect grapes from frosts.

Riesling is susceptible to soil and geology. Small berries derive aromas and flavors from vineyard soils. Slate absorbs heat during the day and helps the grapes ripen. Minerality picked up from slate is one of the defining characteristics of Riesling. Rieslings are produced in a wide variety of styles from bone dry to oily to very sweet. Knowledgeable wine lovers appreciate all the grape's permutations and consistently rank it as one the world's finest white wines.

The Mosel, one of thirteen Riesling regions, with wines from its best vineyards is considered the Riesling benchmark. There are vines in the Mosel that date back 150 years, producing tiny berries noted for their concentrated flavors and aromas. Scenic vineyards, some planted at a 70° angle, make harvest a precipitous event.

It is hard to sort out the difference between inexpensive, mass-produced, mass-marketed German wines and high-quality Rieslings. Once shunned in the United States, Riesling is reportedly surging ahead in sales as wine buyers break through the mysteries of its styles and rankings. Even as its popularity is rising, Rieslings present daunting problems to Americans. Start with complicated words like *Trockenbeerenauslese.* Some winemakers are updating their labels, cropping hard-to-read fonts that list wine region, producer, vintage, varietal, ripeness and alcohol levels, village, and quality classifications. Descriptions of four basic, sometimes overlapping classifications are *trocken,* or dry; *halbtrocken,* or half-dry; medium-sweet; or sweet. Sweet by itself stops short of classifying the sweetest wines. Wines grow sweeter, more distinct, and extraordinary as they reach the top level. *Trockebeerenauslese* and *Eiswein* are the sweetest.

Quality is also classified. Tafelwein is basic table wine, and rankings go to a fifth level—*Qualitätsweine mit Prädikat* (QmP), or quality wine with attributes. An important clue to quality is a small eagle printed on a label, a cluster of grapes, and the number one that signifies the highest quality for first growth vineyards, similar to France's Premier Cru.

# RAIMUND PRÜM

## S.A. PRÜM

Raimund Prüm comes from a renowned family of Riesling producers and heads one of the Mosel's top wineries.

*Our company's history stretches back 200 years. In the old days, sales were driven by loyalty to our winery's name. Generations of consumers, from father to son, bought our wine, and what they bought was noted in our heritage book. Around the time of World War I, family factions split the company. In 1964, three of my grandfather's children stepped out of the business. I came into the business in 1970, after I finished studying winemaking and barrel production in California for one year. I had only my studies and enthusiasm to bring to my first vintage in August of '71. It was an incredible start for a beginner because it was a phenomenal vintage. That vintage produced 3,400 cases. Now we produce 45,000 cases, making us one of the largest wineries in Germany.*

*Our industry needed to meet the demands of the market. The bewildering, fanciful Gothic calligraphy on our old-fashioned labels was almost indecipherable, even to young Germans. I came up with a new marketing program. After checking critter labels from California and Australia, I traveled to Norway to create a new stylish label. Simplifying our label worked and attracted new buyers. We didn't change the wine, but found a better way to reach the consumer. I found a niche where we can survive. Today we sell worldwide and the U.S. is our biggest market. I do what is good for S.A. Prüm, although I don't swim too much against the stream. I maintain my relationships in Germany and organize events for our industry.*

*Our winery lies in the middle of one of Germany's most beautiful valleys. The soil and terroir of hills rising from the south-facing steep slopes of the Mosel River profoundly influence our wines. The vineyard land is limited to steep slopes 300 to 900 feet high, planted with 60- to 120-year-old ungrafted* rootstock. We think Riesling reaches its pinnacle in the Mosel region. Different slates deposited in the soil by ocean sediments play a part in the special characteristics of our wines. Slates establish a climate in our vineyards that determines the special taste of minerality. Red slate holds in the warmth of the sun. Gray slate adds elegance and blue slate enhances racy qualities. Our Rieslings have distinct benchmarks from these slates, marked by concentrated fruitiness with exquisite flowery, honey, and mineral aromas. Ultra-long ripening in our northerly location extracts flavor, vibrancy, and concentration with generally low alcohol levels, ranging from 5 to 10 percent.

It's exciting to produce wines. Each season presents a different scenario. We start to prepare each vineyard in the summer, working to educate our grape producers about better growing practices. Grapes for our wines must be handpicked even though machines are now able to harvest on our steep slopes. At harvest, we collect what we judge will make good wine. Each harvest has fantastic potential, but 1980, 1984, and 1987 were disasters because of cool summers, late bud break, little sunshine during the summer, and cold weather at harvest. We recently served the '87. It was still young. The acidity wasn't harmonious, but it was interesting and will change during another thirty years in the bottle. Unlike many other white wines, Rieslings can age from ten to fifty years, developing different characteristics in the bottle that are a joy to discover.

I say Riesling requires a warm foot and a cool head. Making wine depends on whether you listen to your experience to make great wine or follow the demands of consumers and the market. Following the market is tricky because it changes faster than the ripeness of the grapes.

The start of harvest is one of the most important events of each vintage. The quality of grapes is dramatically affected by weather, especially in our climate. We check sugar content, acidity, pH levels, and other factors, but it is difficult to wait for perfect ripeness. It is imperative that our wines maintain their style. I believe ripeness is a more valid way to describe Rieslings. For us, ripeness develops great concentration of sugars, acidity, and balance.

It is the winemaker who is the main influence on which course to take in vinification. Versatile Riesling has the capacity to be vinified in an extraordinary range of styles that have a very wide range of sweetness that defines different styles. A winemaker decides when to harvest and what proportion of Riesling grapes to harvest each season, making determinations based on the crucial balance between acidity and sugars, and then electing to chapitalize,

~ℓℓ~

## PRÜM'S ROAST DUCK BREAST

| | |
|---|---|
| 1 duck breast per person | Lightly sear duck breasts in a pan until the skin is crisp. Put the breast into the oven for 20 minutes until the meat is pink. Add wine and orange juice to the pan juices. Add raisins to add sweetness. The acidity of red cabbage matches the Riesling perfectly. Roast new potatoes or prepare in any style. |
| ¼ cup orange juice | |
| ¼ cup white wine | |
| ½ cup raisins | |
| 2 sliced red cabbage | |
| 1 lb new potatoes | |

Serve wine as an aperitif together with a starter like a paté, then with the main course and later with a variation of soft, creamy cheeses. A perfect dessert with the Auslese is a not-too-sweet apple tart or fresh strawberries.

*Drinking wine while cooking inspires the chef. The duck is paired perfectly with Wehlener Sonnenuhr Riesling Auslese 2006.*

or add sugar. Great Rieslings are marked by finesse, vinified from bone-dry to unctuously sweet and ambrosial.

Basic easy-to-drink Kabinett is the most common and least sweet, but with fruitiness coming from green grapes. Spätlese refers to wine made from grapes with more concentrations of sugar and acidity. Flavors intensify with longer hang-time at harvest. As the structure of the grapes changes with ripeness in the vineyard, they begin to lose water, shrink, and turn yellow. S.A. Prüm's wide range of styles includes semi-sweet and sweet wines, along with a sparkling Sekt, Germany's sparkling wine. Essence, our dry Grand Cru Riesling wine, rests on lees in old oak barrels for one year. I think of our Kabinett Spätlese as Mozart and our Trockenbeerenauslese as Beethoven.

Climate conditions have changed with global warming, ripening grapes earlier. We pick in September rather than in mid-October. Some grapes are hand-selected and picked when the juice runs like syrup. I look for healthy grapes for dry wines. Our rich, sweetest, and highest-quality wines like Trockenbeerenauslese, or TBA for short, are produced with choice, hand-selected, overripe, shriveled grapes affected by botrytis, or Noble Rot. Botrytis is one of *nature's accidents and doesn't happen every year. When it does, we only pick grapes with good, clean botrytis; otherwise the wine tastes moldy. The conditions for Eiswein, one of the sweetest wines, are erratic and require a fortuitous combination of events. The berries for Eiswein hang long on the vine until mid-winter, when they are frozen and unappetizing in appearance. The frozen juice from shriveled raisins is very concentrated and honeyed. Some winemakers wait until the middle of the night to pick to avoid fermentation before the berries get to the winery. If botrytis doesn't appear, the grapes left on the vine could have been vinified into other wines. It's why the project is very risky and potentially expensive.*

*It's hard for Americans to give up the traditional white-with-fish, red-with-meat concept. Germans drink a small amount of red wine, but enjoy a range of Rieslings in different styles from aperitifs to dessert. Fruity Rieslings are excellent with Asian dishes, while both fruity and dry ones are very well matched with smoked foods. Rieslings cut the fat in goose and duck and are excellent partners to rich, red beef dishes. Coupling sweet wines with certain cheeses and foie gras is fabulous, but dry white wines are better with savory foods. Our Essence wine has body and weight plus a distinct taste of its vineyard. It's a lovely aperitif and a great partner for fish and sushi. It's best decanted because it needs hours to open. It should be served in large Bordeaux glasses to free its fabulous aromas.*

*Americans are experimenting with different wines to expand their knowledge and experience. They are coming around from their long resistance to the charms of Rieslings. Sales are picking up in the States because of Riesling's favorable prices and wide variety of attractive flavors and aromas. We historically followed the policies of our domestic competitors. Until as recently as a decade or so ago, a German system of regulations blocked sales around the world. We had no presence in the global market until I realized sticking to old-fashioned principles was wrong for the international market and for the winery. The winery changed to screw-top caps because corks can have problems. Yet German clients are hooked on corks. A German math professor declared his love for S.A. Prüm Rieslings but objected to the new closures. Other consumers think they are often associated with cheap wine. But screw-tops are here to stay, even with their own problems. Every change has its benefits and downsides.*

Prüm relishes life and exudes happiness.

*When I'm not occupied with winemaking, I enjoy walking and experiencing wildlife. I like to taste wines from other parts of the world and take time out at my second home in Finland, where I cook for my Finnish wife Pirjo. We dance the Tango, the country's popular dance. I also enjoy spending time with my family. Meeting with close friends and slowing down from hectic business give me energy for continuing my winemaking activities.*

# GREECE

WALL PAINTINGS DATING from 3500 B.C. are ample proof of the historical significance of wine and food in Greece. Beyond that indisputable pictorial truth, archeologists uncovered ancient wine presses, carbonized grape seeds, and other relics that indicate the importance of alcoholic beverages in ancient times. Amphorae filled with wine and olive oil in the remains of Greek ships are strewn across the seabed of the Mediterranean and prove the importance of the wine trade. In those ancient times, pine resin sealed the clay vessels and infused the liquids with sharp turpentine tastes and aromas. By the time other storage containers replaced clay, Greek winemakers continued to replicate the taste for an audience that appreciates wines with distinctive resin qualities. The appeal of Retsina was lost on wine drinkers beyond the country's borders, who turned up their collective noses at the wine.

By the 1980's, changes in Greek vineyards and wineries across the country were in the wind. Younger, adventuresome Greek winemakers, anxious to raise their wine standards, went to other viticultural regions to learn about modern technology. They brought home new ideas and often butted heads with winemakers reluctant to abandon their traditional grapes and winemaking styles. Although Greece has a number of indigenous grapes, vineyards were planted with Sauvignon blanc, Cabernet Sauvignon, and other international varietals, ridding some newer wines of the unpalatable Retsina reputation.

# Santorini

Santorini, in the distant past, was called Thera. It is one of the Cycladic Islands strung along the Aegean Sea off the coast of Greece. Homer poetically called the Aegean "the wine-dark sea." Santorini is one of the most spectacular of its islands. Its fascinating history and unforgettable presence rising sharply out of the blue water make it a mecca for tourists. A dramatic half-moon caldera was the result of a devastating volcanic explosion 3,600 years ago that tore away half the island. Desperation for wine must have been the driving force that led generations of ingenious vintners to take up the challenge posed by the catastrophe. Local winemakers, perched hundreds of feet above the sea, developed an inventive technique to overcome the harsh conditions. Santorini's vineyards are among the world's oldest, with the majority of its vines averaging fifty to a hundred years old.

Grapes did more than grow. They flourish in deep layers of volcanic ash, chalk, slate, lava, and pumice that cover the island. The peculiarities of soil and terroir provide desirable qualities of taste and aromas to the grapes. Grapes get their only source of water from morning fog and dew. The hostile environment of saltwater spray, aridity, and extreme heat is overcome with a unique, inventive planting system. Vines are trained into a low-lying basket to protect the berries from harsh winds and intense summer heat.

White wines dominate production on Santorini and are produced in a number of wineries from phylloxera-resistant Asyrtiko, Athiri, and Aidani grapes. Asyrtiko, indigenous to the island, is the mainstay of the island's charming wines, with their taste of minerals, an occasional touch of iodine, and the sea. Asyrtiko vines, some sixty years old, are cultivated in areas called *stefani*. The grape represents about 80 percent of the island's vines. Aidani adds floral aromas and Athiri adds creaminess to the blend of dry or sweet wines. An unctuous, sweet Vin Santo, a traditional Santorini version of the wine, is made from the very best ripe grapes laid out to dry in the sun for ten to fifteen days, then fermented and aged in oak barrels.

# YIANNIS PARASKEVOPOULOS
## GAIA WINES

Yiannis Paraskevopoulos exhibits the exuberant Greek love of life. I met him shortly after he arrived in New York to lead a seminar on wines from Santorini. The long flight did nothing to dampen his charm and enthusiasm for championing local wines he produces at two wineries—whites on Santorini and reds on the Peloponnesus. The Athenian-born winemaker says,

*Winemakers like me went to Europe to study. Although I have a Ph.D. in enology from the University of Bordeaux, I didn't want to become a Bordeaux clone. The world didn't need another French Chardonnay. When I came home to Greece I realized I wanted to produce a wine with attributes from Santorini. After my training in Bordeaux, I lucked out and got a job at home with the well-known Boutari Winery. They sacked me because I couldn't keep my mouth shut. I figured I should start my own business and that's when my partner, Leon Karatsalos, and I founded Gaia Wines. Gaia celebrated its first vintage of Santorini wines in 1994. We are committed to the potential of producing quality wine from the unique indigenous grapes of Greece.*

*Our boutique winery is located on Santorini's east coast in Monolithos. It was constructed from the remains of an old tomato-processing plant, proof of Santorini's former agricultural history.*

Although some aspects of Santorini's agricultural history have disappeared, Paraskevopoulos built his distinctive vineyard and helped revitalize the island's wine industry.

*I am a scholar and I bring my experiences from tasting wines to my job. I teach eager young students who in turn expose me to new techniques. I adopt*

some and leave out others. I am constantly innovating and seeking improvement. There about 300 indigenous wine grapes in Greece and eighteen different strains of wild yeast on Santorini. Each varietal has its own limitations and strengths. I want to go into depth with good varieties. It comes down to a question of character. I like extremes. I prefer high peaks and valleys. For me, Belgium is too flat. In terms of wine, I want to get everything a berry can give, mainly pigments, ethanols, and aromas.

Santorini is most known for its popular, dry white wines made from Assyritko, the island's finest white grape variety. It is a bone-dry wine with acidity similar to Riesling with a combination of citrus aromas and characteristic earthy, mineral flavors, a remarkable sense of terroir and ability to age. It owes its unique character to the island's volcanic soil and other aspects of terroir. Interestingly, some Assyrtiko vines are being grown in Australia. Other varietals include Agiorgitiko for rosé wines. Malagousia is a lush variety filled with lovely aromas like a great Viognier.

Thalassitis was the first Gaia wine we produced in 1994. It is one of our signature wines made from Assyrtiko. Our first vintage yielded less than 10,000 bottles, but our production now exceeds 100,000 bottles yearly. Every year we see changes brought about by new information. So far we haven't repeated a vintage, but at Gaia we are aiming for consistency. For a while we tried big blockbuster wines. Our soils can't support that over-the-top style. What we have equals the old European style of elegant, food-friendly wines.

We totally changed from the procedures of old winemakers who dealt with what they had in hand. In some places, the knowledge of cultivation is still quite medieval. Some vineyards are experimenting with different kinds of trellising to see what will work in the heavy winds. There are also questions about oak. The international market likes unoaked wines, but the home market likes oak flavors. It makes working with oak hard to resist. While some of the old guys use old oak, we adopted a different oak program. We fill different barriques with wine from separate vineyards. Four of us at the winery continually taste and test, taste and test, then do a statistical analysis of the barriques to see which are appropriate for our wines because it's not only what I think is best. Most of us winemakers have strong egos, so it took me time to learn to delegate.

A new era began when Greek wineries made a great leap to obtain twenty-first-century equipment and more modern practices. We put our recently acquired knowledge of new technologies into advancing our local grapes. It was similar to what happened when Italians rediscovered and recultivated

Sangiovese. We are working more intensely with vines, channeling our efforts in the vineyards by choosing better clonal selections. The 1998 wines we produced are poles apart from the wines of 2010 because since then we replanted densely, developing different, bigger berries. We throw away somewhere between 15 and 20 percent of unsuitable wine.

Santorini's small parcels of vines are affected by a daunting mix of intense sun, high summer temperatures, and meltemia, or strong winds. Many of our 100-year-old vines are still productive, although with a very low yield. We winemakers inherited an age-old, labor-intensive, ingenuous ecological system that protects vines from the harsh environment. At the end of each season after harvest, the vines are cut back to stumps. In the following season, the best new canes are pruned into wreaths (kouloures) or baskets (kalathia) set close to the gray-white soil to protect the grapes from the scouring winds. The vineyards appear to be covered with large birds' nests. The system protects local white wine grapes like Assyrtiko, Aidani, Athiri, and Nychteri from the island's harsh environment.

Our soils are rich in inorganic ingredients and very poor in organic ingredients, making it one of the few phylloxera-free viticultural areas in the world. The system is essentially organic farming, as the soil's pH level and the winds create an inhospitable environment for insect pests and fungi. The porous, chalky, volcanic soil forces vines to go deep to find water. Rains are rare, so morning mists, nocturnal fogs, and sea spray hydrate the vines and are a source of natural irrigation in the vineyards, helping grapes mature during the intense heat and drought of summer months.

Our wines are so terroir-driven, it's crazy. The volcanic soil imparts distinct minerality in the wine. The Aegean's salinity level is higher than that of any other body of water on earth, so the amount of sodium from sea spray on the berries can be tasted in the wines. On the island, white grape vines draw up mineral and fruity flavors from the soil and salinity from the sea, which results in well-balanced acids and low alcohol levels. When you smell our wines, you know where they are from, and that is nowhere but Santorini. The challenge requires educating the public about its flavorful profile and the fact that it is the world's most vin de terroir.

The characteristics of crisp acidity and intense minerality in our dry, full-bodied white wines are excellent for pairing with a variety of cuisines. Earthy, citrus and elegant aromas with vibrant acidity, great structure, and minerality are their main attributes. We vinify them like reds without color. They have great lasting power.

*A good, courageous winemaker will be extra-cautious and focus on handling the skin and lees from fermentation. We treat the yeast lees well because if we don't, they can give us trouble. Some winemakers on the island get rid of sediments quickly because they see wine as merely a combination of sugar and acid. Their wines are thin enough to read a newspaper through. All five Gaia wines—three whites, one between a red and rosé that resembles a Pinot noir and Vin Santo—are handcrafted from the beginning through harvest. At harvest, we squeeze the berries to see how resistant the skins are. We pick at 24 brix for dry wines and a higher level for Vin Santo. There are some technicians who only get their input from the lab, but we rely on our ability to discern flavors and aromas. Nevertheless, our lab is the heart of the winery, giving us helpful chemical analysis at crucial times when information from our senses loses the ability to determine precursors of aromas.*

*Gaia Wines is the name of my wine-producing company. Thalassitis, Thalassitis oak fermented, and Assyrtiko by Gaia–Wild Ferment are three labels we produce in our Santorini winery. Gaia also produces noteworthy naturally sweet Vinsanto, as we spell it. The original Vin Santo was already famous in ancient times, and Venetians who occupied and traded with the islands called it Vini di Santorini, shortened to Vin Santo. Our Vinsanto is made from at least 75 percent Assyrtiko blended with the aromatic Aidani grape. Aidani is dried in the traditional method of setting grapes in the sun for ten days to develop thick juice. Afterward, the wine is stored in barrels for several years to develop wonderful color and bouquet. Gaia Vinsanto utilizes every last droplet of the must for its flavor. We press and press again, sometimes for over four hours to get crucial aromas. Occasionally, because of our climate, fermentation gets stuck, so it can be an adventure to get wine in the end. New oak would destroy the delicacy of Vinsanto, so the wines rest in eighty-year-old neutral Russian oak barrels for twenty-four months, where they attain aromas of spices and raisins. We visit the wines in the barrels once a year to adjust for sulfur, but there is no addition of alcohol, sugar, or other wines.*

According to Paraskevopoulos, many issues need resolution, including a more economically sustainable system for the Santorini's thirty wineries.

*A cooperative was formed in 1947 that includes all the growers on the island who bring in their grapes for vinification. A board of directors determines vinification, production, and marketing. We have a system of quality control* to sort grapes destined for either quality or bulk wines as well as for Vin Santo. The cooperative must buy all the Assyrtiko, Ageri, and Vinsanto grapes. Nykteri is a varietal picked at night until the early morning and sent to cold caves, a technique historically used to control fermentation before the adaptation of stainless steel tanks with temperature controls. The cooperative encourages growers to continue production rather than to give up grape cultivation in favor of better-paying tourist activities.

Wines from Agiorgitiko vines at my other winery on the Peloponnesus are easy-going reds meant for consumption in the first or second year.

At the time of our interview, vines on the mainland were infected with a virus.

The disaster gives me a chance to develop new ideas. My wish is that in twenty years, most vineyards on the mainland will grow virus-free clones with more flavorful berries. I want this speculation to come true.

Until a couple of years ago, Greek wines seemed alien to foreign consumers. It was another case of difficulty with strange labels and grape varieties. If Americans drank Greek wine, they were probably in a Greek restaurant and the wine was often of poor quality with the taste of resin. On the other hand, the Greek public hasn't been exposed to different grapes other than their own familiar ones. We are consistently behind many other wine-drinking populations around the world, but as Greeks travel they are slowly experimenting with international wines. We are becoming more adventuresome. More and better wines are available, with credit going to our producers who are involved in an exploration of wines made from obscure grapes with personality from a specific terroir. Some of those wines have already gained a good reputation, particularly from Santorini. I think today Greek wines are being promoted from alcoholic oddities to reliable wines with a specific style of their own. Because of modern techniques that raised the quality of many of our wines, if you're in a restaurant without a Greek wine on the list, you know that the owners just don't get it. Our whites can have character and are worth having on the table.

My personal choices are different. I am adventuresome and rarely drink my own wines. I will ask a sommelier to suggest a wine I haven't tasted before, Greek or non-Greek. I discovered Verdejo, and a tasting of Albarino blew me away. It's my new role model.

# SLOVENIA

A N INVITATION to a tasting of Croatian and Slovenian wines in New York was irresistible. Croatian wines were more familiar, but I wasn't quite sure where Slovenia was. The Balkans? Yugoslavia? The country, its general history, and wine production were indefinable to me. So, curiosity aroused, I joined a small group of winemakers, the Croatian consul, and a few fellow journalists who were invited to help wineries break into the American wine market. Expanding their market was going to be tough sledding for wines made from unfamiliar varietals with unpronounceable names and winery names on their labels. Slovenia's geographic position abuts the southern slopes of the Alps and the Adriatic. Stajerska is in the northeast corner of the country and is one of its largest grape-growing areas in the country. The region is affected by hot summers and cool, dry winters, with steep mountainsides and gravelly, clay soil—perfect conditions for Pinot noir, Chardonnay, Welch Reisling, Tramminer, and Pinot gris.

The area was a natural crossroad from every direction going well back into history. The small country was buffeted by constant invasion because of its strategic position. Celts and other barbarian tribes occupied Slovenia until the Romans displaced them. Then it was a succession of invaders: Charlemagne, Napoleon, Germans, Austrians, and Hungarians. Italy and Austria were the most dominant cultural influences in the last two centuries. Invasions left distinct marks on the country's language, culture, viticulture, and winemaking traditions. A national language exists in Slovenia, but many Slovenes living in the western part of the country speak Italian.

After World War I, Slovenia declared its independence from Austrian domination. It joined Montenegro, Serbia, and Croatia in 1918 to form the Kingdom of the Serbs, Croats, and Slovenes. It became Kingdom of Yugoslavia in 1929. Germans and Italians carved up the area during World War II, and Communists, led by Marshal Tito, fought a guerilla war against the Fascists. Slovenia became a republic in 1945, after the defeat of the Axis powers. After centuries of domination, it finally achieved independence from Yugoslavia in 1992. Agricultural and manufacturing industries brought economic growth, which led to membership in the EU and an alliance with NATO in 2004. Winemaking, which had declined during the succession of wars, was revitalized. Slovenia maintains it has the highest number of indigenous wine grape varieties in the world. Vineyards cover the hills in several small regions, and the industry is slowly adopting new technology. Its early winemaking techniques were highly influenced by Austria,

At the tasting, I was given a book on Slovenia. Its colorful pages showed picturesque wine regions barely touched by the twenty-first century. Folk music and dancing play a significant role, especially when Lent marks the end of winter. A celebration takes place in the city of Moribor around a 400-year-old local red Zametovka grapevine that claims to be the world's oldest. The vine is pruned every March and grafts from the ancient vine are sent to selected towns across the country. Zametovka wine is bottled as gifts for visiting celebrities from the vine's annual yield.

# JURIJ BRUMEC
## SANCTUM

Jurij Brumec is winemaker at Sanctum Winery located in Loce in the region of Stajerska, an area contiguous to Austria. *Sanctum* is a Latin word for "inner peace" or the place where one would find inner peace. Brumec says his father and grandfather were winemakers and winemaking is in his blood.

*I make wine with Marko Podkubovsek, who started in the tourism business but found that wine was his passion. He focuses on importing wine through his company, Vinum, U.S.A. His grandfather and father were also winemakers who owned a Pinot noir vineyard originally planted in 1374 by local Carthusian monks at their huge monastery. About ten years ago, on a trip back to Slovenia from his home in the States, Podkubovsek met a local monk who possessed archives from a local order. Records show monks had sustained the art of winemaking during turbulent periods. In the seventeenth century, the Austrians expelled the monks. Peasants took over the land, tore out French varietals. and planted local grapes.*

*It took some time, but then we tore out local varieties and replanted the vineyard with Pinot noir, Chardonnay, and Welsh Riesling, a grape of mysterious origin that isn't a Riesling or from Wales. We're on the same parallel as Burgundy and our cool climate and rocky soil are perfect for these varieties, leading to wonderful aromas in our wines. Sanctum now produces 12,000 bottles of Pinot noir and 15,000 bottles of Chardonnay. Sanctum's red table wines contain a general alcohol level of 10 to 12 percent and are sold to the international market.*

*Pinot noir is always the most challenging wine to make. Our Pinot noir is different because of our terroir, coupled with my winemaking decisions. The vineyard's soil is sand, clay, and limestone set on a 30–40° pitch, with a southern*

## BRUMEC'S ROAST DUCK WITH APPLES AND CABBAGE

*This excellent aromatic and tasty combination of a traditional dish is served on November 11 during the festivities of St. Martin, the patron saint of wine.*

1 duck
Small amount of goose fat or vegetable oil
Several thin slices of smoked bacon
½ bottle of red wine
1 large red cabbage, chopped
1 chopped onion
2 grated apples
1 tbsp flour
Salt to taste

Rinse the duck inside and outside. Dry it well. Rub with salt. Cover the duck breasts with the bacon and roast at 350°F, until the meat is soft. Continually baste the duck with wine, water, and duck fat and juices. While the duck is roasting, fry the cabbage and onions in a small amount of goose fat or oil. Lower the flame and simmer it. Stir several times, adding the apples with wine and water. Add the flour to the cabbage mixture, salt to taste, and continue to cook until the flavors are blended.

*Brumec recommends Sanctum's Pinot noir as the perfect match to enhance the duck, apple, onion, cabbage, and bacon.*

exposure. Small, porous limestone rocks retain moisture and heat. Evening breezes promote a beautiful merger between acid and sugar in the grapes that leave us with wonderful aromas from the skins.

Our wines are totally natural. We use no machinery, no fertilizer, and dry-farm the vineyard. We crop grape clusters so there is only one cluster left on each cordon. This intensifies the flavor in the remaining bunches. During seasons of little sun, vines are pruned twice to expose the berries to whatever sunlight they can absorb. At harvest, rather than hire hourly workers who work haphazardly, our willing friends agree to pick. Marko and I meet the pickers at seven in the morning for breakfast and schnapps. We give them instructions on how to pick grapes from clusters by hand. Ripe berries with good acid, sugar, and pH levels go into a special bin. Any that fail to meet our requirements are dropped on the ground. That way we end up with 99 percent perfect grapes.

Grapes are sent to the cellar, where leaves and stems are removed. Red berries are macerated in open oak and plastic barrels for two days to aerate the juice. Selective yeasts are used for different wines to help promote fermentation.

The must is stirred manually every six hours and stays in the barrels for about two to three weeks. Then it goes back in the press and the secondary juice goes into French and Slavonian barrels. Slavonian oak breaks the sugar and acid beautifully. I constantly taste, looking for the correct aromas and flavors at the first inclination of oak in wine. The wines rest on oak as long as necessary, usually between twelve and eighteen months to become gentle and elegant. Then I blend the best barrels from different blocks together. White wines go through a separate process. The time between picking, pressing, and fermentation in tanks is as short as possible, to avoid oxidation and preserve freshness. Cold fermentation at 15°C keeps aromas intact. The fermented juice rests sur-lie in a mix of new and old oak, inoculated with yeast, because natural yeast from the vineyard produces unpredictable results. Certain yeasts add to the aromas and fruitiness of the wine.

Sanctum makes an Eiswein from thirty-year-old Welsh Riesling vines, the oldest at our winery. The conditions for Eiswein happen only in years with very cold temperatures, like 2010, when the temperature fell to −7°C. When the sugars and acids are high, the grapes are pressed frozen. Then the wine is vinified in a dry style.

We've had tough years when heavy rain at harvest destroyed a lot of grapes. Because it's normal for each vintage to have something that you don't think measures up, we sell a poor blend at a lower price or throw it away. My goal is to produce the best wines in our region.

# ISRAEL

L ANDS ONCE LUMPED together on the eastern shore of the Mediterranean Sea are likely the ancient cradle of wine production. It is recorded that ships sailed from there exporting wine to Egypt as payment for taxes. Two-handled clay amphora found in sunken ships, some inscribed with vintage date and names of Jewish winemakers, sailed with cargoes of wine to Greece and Rome. In ancient times a Jewish family probably consumed an average of 350 liters of wine a year. Wine was safer and more delicious to drink than water.

The history of wine in the region is also tied to religion. Moses sent twelve scouts in different directions to check the fertility of surrounding lands. Only Caleb and Joshua came back with evidence of the land's fecundity. So it is apt that the symbol of Israel's tourism logo portrays Caleb and Joshua carrying their bountiful burden of grapes. Archeological excavations in ancient Palestine are proof of wine's crucial role in Jewish life. Digs uncover ancient wine presses and coins with motifs of grapes and grapevines. The Old Testament and the Talmud make 141 references to wine, or *yayin* in Hebrew. Modern Jews continue the ancient tradition of reciting the first of three Sabbath blessings, one offering thanks for the fruit of the vine. At wedding ceremonies, a bride and groom share a cup of wine, and four cups of wine are drunk at the Passover Seder.

The New Testament has fewer references to wine. Perhaps the most telling is the story of a wedding at Cana in Galilee attended by Jesus, his mother, and his disciples. When the guests ran out of wine, Jesus turned the water in six large stone jars into wine. It was the first of his miracles.

Islamic conquest in the seventh century A.D. ended alcohol production and consumption in the region except during the time Moslems permitted Christians to make wine for the Eucharist. Viticulture rebounded when Christian Crusaders occupied the Holy Land from 1100 to 1300 A.D. When Jews reestablished their historical presence in Palestine at the end of the nineteenth century, Baron Edmond de Rothschild, owner of the celebrated Château Lafite-Rothschild in Bordeaux, sent French viticulturists to test the area's terroir for wine production. Rothschild's gift of 60 million gold francs and grape rootstock buoyed a fledging industry. After the establishment of the modern state of Israel, 90 percent of the country's vineyards were in the hot southern regions where grapes had been cultivated since biblical times. The higher elevations, critical fluctuations in day and night temperatures, and well-drained volcanic soils of the Golan Heights, annexed to Israel after the war in 1967, proved excellent for viticulture.

More than 300 wineries, from boutique enterprises to large corporate entities, flourish in four wine-growing regions in a country the size of New Jersey. Ten major wineries play the most significant role. Local vintners often train abroad, and some wineries hire consultants from the United States, South Africa, and Canada to raise the standards of Israeli wines. Wineries are investing in new equipment for crushing, pressing, fermentation, and barrel aging. They are experimenting with a variety of grapes and clones to develop new wine styles.

Israeli winemakers face special challenges. While their peers around the world worry about the weather and insect infestations, Israeli vineyards are often bombarded by rocket attacks from hostile neighbors. Day-to-day work goes on in spite of continuing regional hostilities. In addition, Syria presses for the return of the land it lost during the war. Israeli winemakers agree to deal with any changes in the political and territorial situations, if and when they occur.

Orthodox Jews present another challenge to winemakers. Kashruth are a series of religious laws designed to ensure purity of food and beverages. Kashruth dictates wine production follow strict regulations and careful controls in order to be certified kosher. Orthodox rabbis are on hand in the wineries to supervise from the moment harvest begins. Since separation of meat and dairy products is commanded in the Bible, ingredients like casein and gelatin from dairy or animal products are prohibited. Wines that pass the requirements receive kosher certification. However, the Ultraorthodox insist that wines be boiled to guarantee absolute purity. The substitution of flash pasteurization to maintain wine's integrity is an acceptable alternative for many religious Jews.

Once kosher wines dominated the Israeli industry, but the production of nonkosher wines in Israel has increased in the last few decades. Continual improvements in the country's wines have been made possible using modern techniques in viticulture and vineyard management. The standards of Israeli wines continue to overshadow their once-poor reputation. Wine is increasingly popular in all segments of Israeli society and plays an important role in the nation's domestic and export economy. The United States, France, United Kingdom, Germany, and Canada are the country's largest markets.

## MICHA VAADIA
### GALIL MOUNTAIN WINERY

Micha Vaadia, winemaker at Galil Mountain Winery in the Golan region of Israel, is fascinated by the 5,000-year-old history of the Jewish connection to winemaking. He says, "Archeological sites throughout Israel unearthed numerous grape presses and images of grape-growing, testimony to the significant role wine played in the religion and mercantile life of those early days. Wine, grain, and olives, three products that can be stored, sustained our forefathers in ancient times. I believe wine had valuable health benefits to ward off pathogens because of its combination of high acid and alcohol."

Vaadia is an ex-paratrooper who came to winemaking by chance. After he served the required three years in the Israeli Defense Force, he started a degree in electrical engineering. "I ultimately rejected the course as uninspiring, although I admit engineering comes in handy when I rehabilitate machinery at the winery. It helped me develop a system for cleaning stainless steel fermentation tanks with less water consumption."

Early in his career, and in search of adventure, Vaadia signed up to work on a boat sailing the Caribbean. Each evening the skipper uncorked a bottle of wine and speculated about life with the deckhand. The wine he drank planted a seed for a career that combined his love for agriculture, nature, technology, and art. "My plan to create something tangible crystallized slowly. I registered at the University of Jerusalem, completing a degree in horticulture. I found my life's path." A master's degree in enology at U.C. Davis in California set him on his peripatetic quest to discover various methods of winemaking. "New World viticultural regions drew me like a magnet. I worked at Navarro, La Crema, and Jordan wineries in California. I headed for Catena in Argentina and Cloudy Bay in New Zealand."

Vaadia returned to Israel when the wine industry was seven years old. His global experience boosted his credentials. He landed a job at Galil Mountain Winery in the Golan. In less than a decade Vaadia became head winemaker. "The region's mountain vistas, the highest in Israel, stoke my unquenchable love of nature. A quick drive or hike near the vineyards is inspirational and elevates my mood," he says.

*Before the 1980's, the emphasis was on production of sacramental and sweet wines. Golan Heights Winery revolutionized Israel's wine production with modern technology and joined with Galil Mountain Winery. Serious winemaking took root in the 1990's, when finding compatible locations for each varietal became a priority as the industry evolved to high-quality wines. The two wineries balance tradition and technology that remains true to its roots. Galil Mountain's 200-million-year-old soil is volcanic, with evidence of a shallow sea that produced limestone and fertile soils, some brown and others red from evidence of iron.*

Vaadia experiments with different grape varieties as substitutes for the old Israeli standby Carignan. "It takes time to see what works where. Our vineyards at Galil Mountain Winery are planted with Cabernet Sauvignon, Merlot, Shiraz, Sauvignon blanc, Chardonnay, Barbera, Pinot noir, and an experimental lot of Viognier. We look to define the difference between what should work and what actually works."

Expertise from around the world coupled with Israel's advanced technology helps wineries like Galil Mountain raise standards.

*I manage the managers and our mainly Israeli Druze pickers. I decide when to irrigate, prune, harvest, and bottle. When you work alone, there's no one to check if you're in line. That's why I'm happy to have Boaz Mizrachi, who is in charge of production, to act as my safety net. Two egos help each other without colliding when we taste and make decisions together. I play the dominant role and must climb a mountain every day to catch all the nuances in the process of making good wine. My job requires an open mind, an ability to deal with*

# VAADIA'S ROAST LEG OF LAMB
## WITH GALILEE FLAVORS

*The Galilee is well known in Israel for its high-quality and tender meat. The area has many local herbs that compliment the great taste of the lamb: rosemary, coriander seeds, and za'atar (a local herb also known as marjoram). All these aromatic herbs are mixed with olive oil from the Galilee and give the lamb wonderful flavors.*

1 whole leg of lamb
8 cloves of garlic
Juice and zest of one
  big lemon
5 tbsp of (Galilee)
  olive oil
3 tbsp of mustard
1 tbsp of whole grain
  mustard
2 tbsp of chopped
  (Galilee) fresh sage
2 tbsp of chopped
  (Galilee) fresh
  za'atar or fresh
  oregano
2 tbsp of chopped
  fresh rosemary
2 tbsp of chopped
  fresh parsley
1 tbsp of crushed
  dried paprika
1 tsp honey
1 tsp crushed
  coriander seeds
Sea salt and fresh
  ground pepper

Cut each garlic clove into small pieces. Make small incisions into the lamb and insert the garlic into the meat. Mix the rest of the ingredients except the zest into a paste and massage it all over the lamb. Sprinkle salt and pepper and allow to rest at least four hours. Roast the lamb in a preheated oven at 450°F for 25 minutes, reduce the heat to 350°F and roast for an hour. Take the leg out of the oven; sprinkle the lemon zest. Let the leg rest for 15 minutes at room temperature and then slice thinly.

*Pair with Galil Mountain Meron, which is deep purple, full-bodied, and rich with berry, plum, crème de cassis, and a hint of chocolate. The silky texture and long finish are great with the lamb.*

what comes, and adaptability to new situations when nature presents a lot of options. We have lots of sunshine, so we do fruit thinning to control yield. Proper exposure through canopy management ensures berries get equal amounts of exposure to the sun to obtain the right balance of sugar and acid.

*Ultimately, I have a lot of faith in what the vineyard yields. I love all my wines unconditionally, the good and the bad.*

Vaadia's first vintage included a Pinot noir.

*Pinot is a difficult grape, more difficult than any other. It teaches you a lot even when it's a failure. You learn to control variables. It's a cross-dresser that could be red or white, but I treat it as a fragile white wine. I let the fruit lead and am always looking for good aromas and mouth textures. After harvest, Pinot noir can start fermentation by itself, so it requires fast pressing. Dealing with cap management is a difficult but necessary step to control color and to prevent an overdose of overwhelming tannins. It is barreled with lots of grape solids to soften the wine for ten months. My goal is a Pinot with a velvety finish. I invest my soul in this wine. Pinot will always be my baby. Galil Mountain produces between 2,000 and 3,000 cases of Pinot noir, depending on the season.*

*Galil Mountain Winery's modest production of Barbera presented itself well from day 1, although occasionally it's a problem. It's easy to make when the crop is good. Three hectares of volcanic soil in the vineyard creates a wine aged in older oak. We didn't produce the disappointing 2009 vintage. The quality wasn't there and didn't meet the benchmark of 2006, our first vintage with this grape, although our 2008 is really lovely. Our Shiraz, Cabernet, and Merlot are produced without oak, tasting young, fresh, and unpretentious— easy and fun to drink. These are wines that represent here and now, wines that make no excuses, wines that don't require five years to mature. They are wines with a yummy factor. I've learned to make accessible wines with good tannins and good fruit without too much astringency. Everything must be in balance. If there is too much tannin, there had better be a reason.*

*Wines labeled Meron and Yiron are blended for great concentration of flavors, which I get with varying concentrations of Shiraz. Each varietal can be only fair, but when blended, creates a lovable wine because blending makes the sum greater than its individual parts. Blending detaches the winemaker from specific varietal characteristics and preconceptions. It reminds me of the birth of something new.*

*I'm not committed to change as an ideology. I'm open to possibilities and don't have to stay with what happened yesterday.*

To prove his point, Vaadia welcomed the expertise of two highly respected consultants. Winemaker Zelma Long and Vineyard Manager

Phil Freeze brought their well-defined aims and expertise from California and from their winery in South Africa. "Consultants push you away from what you know and from the comfort of what you always do. This attitude helps us reach our ultimate strategy to produce accessible wines in terms of taste and price."

Israel plays a growing role in the competitive world of wine, although Israelis buy much of the homegrown product. Galil Mountain Winery produces 1 million bottles, or 72,000 cases of several varietals contributing to Israel's annual wine exports. The country sees a jump in worldwide distribution of its high-quality wines, many priced under twenty dollars. The United States, Canada, and Europe are major consumers of Israeli wines, many certified as kosher. The country's wines receive increasingly important accolades in ratings and commendations by leading wine authorities. Vaadia admits ratings are an evil necessity.

"It's a human trait to compare and gauge since the invention of the watch and other measuring devices. The rating system may give a lot of power to people who create it, but it can also be a helpful marketing tool." Daniel Rogov was a leading Israeli wine critic. He said, 'Galil Mountain's Meron from 2006 is an unusual but highly successful blend of Syrah, Cabernet Sauvignon, and Petit Verdot that most assuredly represent the terroir of the Upper Galilee. It's aromatic, long, and generous, reflecting sixteen months in French oak.' As Vaadia says,

*An old wine region with a young wine culture presents an exciting challenge to a vintner. What's cool about winemaking is the fascinating challenge of each new season, each new year. Winemaking takes patience and nerves of steel. It is a career that teaches humility. You need a lot of self-confidence to keep your balance throughout the season's various days and changing moods. I want to make wine without pushing for a certain result. My goal is to always aim to make the average better. Man strives to navigate around and influence the end result, but it is the sun, soil, and forces of nature that dictate the outcome. It's how the dance goes.*

*L'Chaim* means "to life," the Jewish version of "Cheers." Let's drink to that!

# CONCLUSION

**M**YRIAD WINE BOOKS fill bookstore and library shelves. Most are clones of each other. *The Winemaker's Hand* takes the extra step to present the voices of vintners, and in so doing, to peer into their hearts and souls. Heart and soul are probably not our first thoughts when we sip a glass of red, white, or sparkling wine, but in truth, reading about the joys and tribulations that go into getting grapes to ferment and grace our lives enhances the experience.

I chose to write about winemakers because few groups are so accessible and articulate about their jobs. Conversations with the forty-odd vintners in *The Winemaker's Hand* revealed the similarities and differences among them that became counterpoints to the wines they craft. The conversations brought to the fore their daily battles with nature and how they often win and sometimes lose. Too often, nature and war set back production, but determined winemakers and enterprising entrepreneurs stayed the course.

In turn, each vintner spoke about the slow, steady, incremental steps that incorporate tradition with exponential developments in technology. Wine has always been and will continue to be an important ingredient in human life, leading those involved with its production on a constant quest for improvement. Adventuresome winemakers are experimenting with new clones, creative technology, and inventive blends. Witness the expansion of wine regions around the world and an endless supply of new labels. Few winemakers are rich, but they tenaciously agree they have a rich life. If they devoted as much time and energy to another task, and if money were their main goal, they might well be wealthy.

The range and depth of wine varietals and styles will always be in flux. Consumers' changing preferences and critics' subjective opinions created fads in wine. In the future, there will be many changes as one varietal or region fades from popularity, allowing others to move up.

It's easy to make contact with winemakers. Travelers can locate wineries in every state between California and New York. Throw a rock in almost any region in Europe to find a nearby winery. Look for vineyards in far-flung countries like Morocco and China. Language barriers melt away when wandering through vines, past fermentation tanks and barrels.

It's possible to order a glass or bottle of wine without delving into its history. The study of wine's origins or the manifold steps required to change grape juice into wine isn't as profound as a lifesaving medical breakthrough. But the study of any subject enriches its understanding. Getting to know the winemaker who stands behind a wine adds an extra dimension to the experience. Learning in depth about any new subject is one of life's greatest joys. In the end, hoist a glass of your favorite wine and give three cheers for the red, white, and rosé.

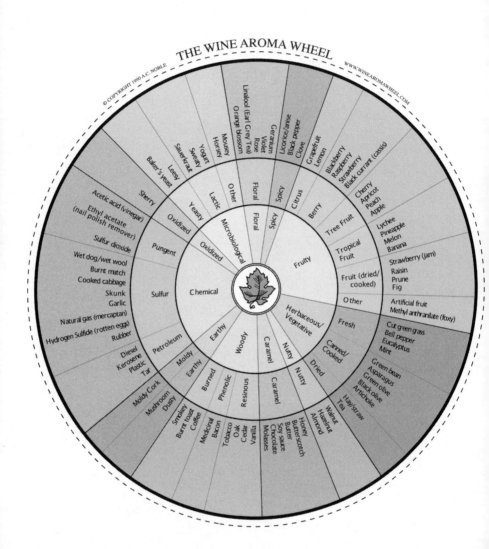

THE WINE AROMA WHEEL

© COPYRIGHT 1990 A.C. NOBLE

WWW.WINEAROMAWHEEL.COM

# THE AROMA WHEEL

"Novice wine drinkers, in particular, often complain that they can't smell anything or think of ways to describe the aroma of wine because they don't have the words," says Ann C. Noble, sensory chemist and retired professor at the Department of Viticulture and Enology, University of California, Davis. Noble's development of the creative Aroma Wheel boosts understanding of descriptive terms for good and unpleasant aromas in still and sparkling red and white wines. It broadens awareness of the complexity of individual wines. What we taste actually begins with a sensitivity and perception to detect and discern aromas. Taste buds are limited to sweet, sour, salty, bitter, and umami, a relatively new term that describes yummy flavors. The Wheel's amazing classification of aromas is a tool to help attach words to hundreds of aromas. The center of the wheel describes the most general terms for aromas, like fruity or spicy. Descriptors become more specific as they fan out into tiers of increasingly descriptive terms.

Add to the pleasure of wine by applying the four S's. Swirl wine in the glass. Sniff its aromas. Savor its flavors. Swallow.

For more information about purchasing The Aroma Wheel go to www.winearomawheel.com.

# GLOSSARY OF WINE TERMS

AC OR AOC. *Appellation controlée* is a French term for appellation. It states strict adherence to quality controls establishing type of varietals, density of vines, and minimum alcohol yields. It is designed to reflect a wine's place of origin.

ACIDITY. Citric, malic, and tartaric acids are basic components in grapes. Acids determine wine's fresh, lively character, particularly that of white wine, as well as helping its aging potential.

AGING. The length of time it takes for a wine to mature, either in a stainless steel tank, barrel, or bottle, from a few days to decades.

ALCOHOL. The percent of alcohol found in the wine, usually printed on a bottle's label.

ALCOHOL CONTENT. The percentage of alcohol in a bottle of wine.

AMPELOGRAPHY. The science of classification, description, and identification of the vine *Vitis vinifera* and its cultivated vine varieties.

AMPHORA. Clay vessels with curved lips and two handles used to store and ship wine, olive oil, and grain, particularly in ancient times.

APERITIF. Wine enjoyed alone or before a meal with hors d'oeuvres.

APPELLATIONS. Rules that differ from country to country, including restrictions about geographical locations where grapes are grown, varieties of grapes allowed to be grown, maximum grape yields, alcohol level, and other factors. They delineate wines that come from a particular place. Chianti has the distinction of being designated the first legal appellation, in 1716, followed by Tokaj-Hegyalja, Hungary, in 1730.

AVA. An abbreviation for American Viticultural Areas, indicating rules regarding the federal recognition of a winery's regional pedigree based on geography and terroir.

BARREL. A storage container, usually oak from various forests. Winemakers convey their preferences to the cooper for levels of light, medium, or heavily toasted wood to add taste and aroma to wine.

BARRIQUE. A 225-liter, or 59-gallon, French wooden barrel used to hold wine, yielding twenty-four cases containing twelve bottles. Burgundian barriques hold 228 liters, or 60 gallons. The size of a barrel determines the effects of oak on wine. The flavor of oak increases with the time wine ages in oak. Barrel size and diverse woods have different impacts on wine.

BIODYNAMICS. A philosophy of agriculture based on Rudolph Steiner, who advocated a holistic approach, balancing the relationships of soil, plants, animal manures, and composts. It eliminates pesticides and artificial fertilizers. Some winemakers believe it crucial to developing excellent wine. Others think it is a hoax.

BORDEAUX BLEND. The various combinations of red wine grapes blended from Cabernet Sauvignon, Merlot, Cabernet Franc, Petit Verdot, and Malbec.

BOUQUET. The aromas in wine.

BOUTIQUE WINERY. A small-run, artisanal, limited-production winery.

BRUT. A term associated with Champagne or sparkling wine, indicating a lesser amount of sugar and level of dryness.

CLASSICO. A designation for traditionally produced regional wines.

CORKED. The taste an unclean or moldy cork imparts to wine.

CRU. A French term meaning "growth," used to classify French wines or a particular place where grapes are grown. Two levels in France are Premier Cru (First Growth) or Grand Cru (Great Growth).

CUVÉE. Wine of a specific blend or batch stored in a vat or tank. It is often intentionally misused to indicate a high standard, but cuvée-labeled wines are usually special blends or higher-quality bottles than a winemaker's standard wine.

DECANTING. The transfer of wine from the bottle to another container, generally a glass decanter, to improve aroma and to separate sediment from the wine.

DÉGUSTATION. A French term for wine tasting.

DOCG. *Denominazione di origine controllata* (Controlled denomination of origin). A classification of Italy's most prestigious wine. It signifies quality assurance for food and wines from a specific appellation. DOCG wine bottles are sealed with a numbered governmental seal across the cap or cork. DO or *Denominazione di Origine* and DOC or *Denominazione di Origine Controllata* are lesser levels.

ÉLEVAGE. A designation of the numerous nurturing steps winemakers take to bring wine to full maturity, including storing and aging.

ENOLOGY. The science of wine and winemaking.

ENOPHILE. Someone who has a deep appreciation of wine. Sometimes used as a synonym for *connoisseur*. (Can also be spelled *œnophile*.)

FERMENTATION. The process in which sugar from grapes combines with yeast to convert into alcohol in stainless steel tanks, wooden vats, wooden barrels, or wine bottles.

FLASH PASTEURIZATION. A modern system of heating wine to 194°F (90°C). It substitutes for the Jewish religious requirement that makes wine kosher by boiling or cooking it to ensure its purity and maintains better flavors and aromas.

FRENCH PARADOX. The paradox denoted by a relatively low rate of heart disease among the French, even though their classic diet is high in saturated fats, because they regularly drink wine high in resveratrol. (They also eat smaller portions than Americans.)

GRAND CRU. The highest possible classification for a French wine, referring to a winery or the land from which the wine comes. Premier Cru is a step down and is used two ways, denoting the highest tier within an existing Grand Cru classification, called the Premier Grand Cru Classé, and land of superior quality, but below that of Grand Cru.

HARVEST. The gathering of a crop. Harvesting is done by hand or with mechanical pickers. It is one of the most labor-intensive and crucial steps in winemaking. The time of harvest is determined by the ripeness of grapes as measured by levels of sugar, acid, and tannin. The style of wine winemakers want also impacts on the decision of when to pick.

HECTARE. A unit of 10,000 square meters equal to 2.47 acres.

HOCK BOTTLE. A distinctive tall, slender bottle in varying shades of amber, olive green, and blue, typically used for Rieslings, Gewurtztraminer, and other German grape varietals. *Hock* is an English term for German or Rhine wine, an abbreviation for Hockheim, a German vineyard village.

MACERATION. The part of the winemaking process that gives red wine its color and tannins when it comes into contact with grape skins.

MADERIZED. Exposure to too much oxygen or poor storage conditions. Oxidation most often occurs in white wines, resulting in a brown or amber color and stale odor.

MILLESÎME. French term for a wine's vintage.

MUST. The freshly pressed grape juice that contains the skins, seeds, and stems.

NÉGOTIANT. French term for a merchant who buys grapes, juice, or wine from growers and sells the wine under his private label, or buys and sells the wines of a Bordeaux chateau.

PALATE. A term that describes the flavors and sensation of wine in the mouth.

PHENOLICS. One of the chemical compounds that contribute to the taste, color, and mouth-feel of wine.

PHYLLOXERA. A general term for a species of aphids that devastate grapevines.

PUNCHING DOWN. An action performed throughout the fermentation process (either by equipment or by stomping) to keep grape skins in continual contact with the must to extract flavors, aromas, and color.

RESERVE/RISERVA. A winery's best wine, set aside by the winemaker as higher quality in a vintage, often aged longer.

RESIDUAL SUGAR. The sugar remaining in wine after fermentation stops. Even dry wines can have some level of residual sugar. Many great sweet wines, like Sauternes, Riesling, and Tokaji, have extremely high levels of sugar.

ROSÉ WINES. Wines with a color ranging from pale to more intense tones of pink, depending on the grape varietals and winemaking techniques, including pressing and blending.

SOMMELIER (OR WINE STEWARD). A knowledgeable wine professional who advises restaurant clientele about wine.

SPLITS. Half-bottles of wine, 375 ml, or approximately 12 ounces.

Sur-lie. A French term meaning "on lees." Wine rests on lees—the deposits of residual yeast that settle to the bottom of the wine vat after fermentation—before filtering and bottling. This step increases the intensity and flavors in wine.

Tannins. The bitter or mouth-puckering tastes in red wine that occur naturally when grape juice is in contact with grape skins, seeds, and stems, becoming more pronounced with the amount of time wine ages in oak barrels.

Tastevin. A small, shallow silver cup or saucer that hangs from a chain around the neck of sommeliers traditionally used to taste and judge a wine's quality.

Terroir. The sum of the specific regional characteristics of a place (geography, climate, weather, geology, soil, etc.) that together contribute to unique qualities of grapes and wine.

Vendage. A French term that signifies harvest.

Vendage tardive. A French term meaning "late harvest."

Véraison. A French term for the time that signals the oncoming of harvest, when red wine grapes begin to ripen, changing color from green to red. Seeds turn brown, sugars increase, the acid and water balance changes, and the skins soften.

Vignoble. A French term for vineyard.

Vinification. The process of making wine, starting with selection of the grapes and ending with finished wine in the bottle.

Vintage. The year wine is made from grapes that were all, or primarily, grown and harvested, rather than the year the wine was bottled.

Viticulture. The science of making wine, incorporating all the tasks that are the basis of wine production in the vineyard, including fertilization, trellising, cropping, pest control, pruning, and harvesting.

Vitis vinifera. The common grape vine cultivated since Neolithic times that became the basis for the majority of modern wines around the world. Its fruit is called grape or berry. The extremely adaptable vine often mutates to adapt to new environments. It is found everywhere around the world except for the Arctic regions.

# GLOSSARY OF WINE VARIETALS

## White Wine

ALBARINO. The Spanish name of a distinctive, thick-skinned grape. Fruity with peach and apricot aromas.

CHARDONNAY. Many wine regions produce this grape. Currently the most popular cool-climate white wine grape vinified in a variety of styles.

CHENIN BLANC. A versatile, warm-climate grape, the backbone of whites from the Loire Valley, where it is called Pineau. It can be produced as either sweet or dry, in still or sparkling wine. Has excellent aging potential in better wines.

GEWURTZTRAMINER. One of the most aromatic, spicy wines with rose petal, litchi, and grapefruit aromas, rich and unctuous. It is often shortened to *Gewurtz* because it is difficult to pronounce.

GRUNER VELTLINER. The most widely planted varietal in Austria. The wine is best drunk young. Suddenly appearing on wine lists.

MALVASLIA BIANCA. Grown for 2,000 years around the Aegean Sea. The wines are golden-hued, highly perfumed, and flavorful with hints of apricots and almonds. Produced both in dry and sweet styles, occasionally with a light sparkle.

MARSANNE. Grown mainly in the northern Rhone, usually blended with Roussanne. California's Rhone Rangers and Australians also produce wines from this grape.

PINOT BLANC. Known also as Pinot bianco and Weissburgunder. Not particularly aromatic, it shows good flavors of green apple and some spice.

PINOT GRIS. Known also as Pinot grigio. It is often bland, but in the hands of a good winemaker is more full-bodied, with good, spicy flavors and charming aromas.

RIESLING. Considered one of the great wine varietals. Vinified in an amazing range of styles from dry to very sweet, generally with lower alcohol levels and great aging potential. Often has floral or petrol aromas.

ROUSSANNE. Produces delicate, aromatic, refined wines often blended with Marsanne in the northern Rhone.

SAUVIGNON BLANC. Many wine regions produce this grape in a wide variety of styles, generally crisp and with aromas and flavors ranging from grassy to tropical fruit flavors.

SEMILLON. The major partner for Sauvignon blanc in the Sauternes region of Bordeaux and elsewhere.

VIOGNIER. An intense dry white wine with delicious aromas of honeysuckle, apricots, and pears.

VIURA. The most important workhorse grape of the Rioja region in Spain. Generally light, high in acid, slightly floral, and fruity.

# Red Wines

BARBERA. Most popular of the many productive grapes in northern Italy and currently being planted in some areas of the New World. A dark, fruity wine.

CABERNET FRANC. Less distinguished cousin to Cabernet Sauvignon. Cab Franc is less full bodied, has fewer tannins, has less acid, and is more aromatic and herbaceous.

CABERNET SAUVIGNON. Indisputably the king of the red grapes.

CARIGNANE. The most commonly grown bulk grape in France and once the most widely grown in California. Known for blending.

CHARBONO. An uncommon grape varietal found almost exclusively in northern California.

CINSAULT. Highly productive grape in France and crossed with Pinot noir in South Africa to make Pinotage. Light in body and neutral in flavor, Cinsault is most often found blended with Grenache and/or Carignane.

GAMAY. The wonderful grape of Beaujolais. These light purple, fragrant, and fruity wines often suggest peaches, berries, and bananas. Perhaps not meaty or complex enough for some, these wines usually offer plenty of joyous charm.

GRENACHE. The most widely grown red grape in Spain, where it is called Grenacha, often blended with Tempranillo.

MERLOT. Popular, plummy red wine used both as a blending partner to Cabernet Sauvignon and as a stand-alone varietal. Merlot is the primary grape of Saint-Émilion and Pomerol and one of two primaries in Bordeaux. Merlot tends to be more supple and rounder than Cabernet Sauvignon and can usually be enjoyed much younger.

NEBBIOLO. Wines made from Nebbiolo grapes are known by a number of names, including Barolo and Barbaresco. The fog (*nebbia* in Italian) that rolls over the hills of northern Piedmont helps ripen the grapes into rich, full-bodied, and chewy wines with hefty fruit flavors of chocolate, truffles, licorice, and flowers.

PETIT VERDOT. A high-quality grape grown mainly in France's Bordeaux region, where it produces full-bodied, extremely deep-colored wines with high tannins and alcohol. It's traditionally been used to add flavor, color, and tannins to the Bordeaux blend. Smaller amounts are now planted in Chile and California.

PETITE SIRAH. Grown mainly in California and not to be confused with Syrah, this grape produces a deep-colored, robust, and peppery wine that packs plenty of tannins.

PINOT MEUNIER. The most widely grown grape in France's Champagne region, though overshadowed by Pinot noir and Chardonnay grapes. Usually blended into the region's sparkling wines, Pinot Meunier is known for its fruitiness and brisk acidity.

PINOT NOIR. The famous red grape of France's Burgundy region, Pinot noir at its best can produce ethereal and sublime wines quite unlike any others. Unfortunately, it is often disappointing and inconsistent.

PRIMITIVO. Thought by many to be the original Zinfandel, grown first in Italy's Puglia region. A hearty, robust wine often with briary, berryish flavors, plenty of tannins, body, and alcohol.

SYRAH. Grown in France's Rhone Valley at least since the Roman times, this important red grape serves as the backbone for the esteemed wines of the northern Rhone today. In the New World the potential for this grape may be boundless.

TEMPRANILLO. An important red grape of northern Spain and a principal component in the famous Rioja wines. Because of its lower acid and alcohol levels, Tempranillo is usually blended with other varietals.

# ACKNOWLEDGMENT

Thanks to the team at Columbia University Press, especially Jennifer Crewe, Ron Harris, and Kathryn Schell, whose talents contributed significantly to the successful completion of *The Winemaker's Hand*.